COMMUNICATION IN MECHANISM DESIGN

Mechanism design is the field of economics that treats institutions and procedures as variables that can be selected in order to achieve desired objectives. An important aspect of a mechanism is the communication among its participants that it requires, which complements other design features such as incentives and complexity. A calculus-based theory of communication in mechanisms is developed in this book. The value of a calculus-based approach lies in its familiarity as well as the insight into mechanisms that it provides. Results are developed concerning (i) a first-order approach to the construction of mechanisms, (ii) the range of mechanisms that can be used to achieve a given objective, as well as (iii) lower bounds on the required communication.

Steven R. Williams is Professor of Economics at the University of Illinois in Urbana-Champaign, where he has also served as head of the economics department. He earned a B.A. from Kenyon College in 1976 and M.S. and Ph.D. degrees from Northwestern University in the field of mathematics in 1977 and 1982, respectively. After postdoctoral appointments at the Institute for Mathematics and Its Applications at the University of Minnesota and at Bell Laboratories, he served as a faculty member at Northwestern University before moving to the University of Illinois. Professor Williams has published articles in the top journals in his field of microeconomic theory, including *Econometrica*, the *Review of Economic Studies*, and the *Journal of Economic Theory*.

ii

Communication in Mechanism Design

A Differential Approach

STEVEN R. WILLIAMS

University of Illinois, Urbana-Champaign

CAMBRIDGE UNIVERSITY PRESS
Cambridge, New York, Melbourne, Madrid, Cape Town,
Singapore, São Paulo, Delhi, Mexico City

Cambridge University Press
The Edinburgh Building, Cambridge CB2 8RU, UK

Published in the United States of America by
Cambridge University Press, New York

www.cambridge.org
Information on this title: www.cambridge.org/9781107407398

First published 2008
First paperback edition 2012

A catalogue record for this publication is available from the British Library

Library of Congress Cataloguing in Publication data
Williams, Steven R., 1954–
Communication in mechanism design : a differential approach / Steven R. Williams.
p.   cm.
Includes bibliographical references and index.
ISBN 978-0-521-85131-2 (hbk.)
1. Econometric models.   2. Information theory in economics.
3. Mathematical economics. I. Title.
HB141.W557   2008
330.01′ 5195–dc22   2007051003

ISBN 978-0-521-85131-2 Hardback
ISBN 978-1-107-40739-8 Paperback

To Christine

Contents

Preface

This text develops a calculus-based, first-order approach to the construction of economic mechanisms. A mechanism here is *informationally decentralized* in the sense that it operates in an environment in which relevant information is dispersed among the participating agents. A mechanism thus requires a "language," or *message space*, that defines how the agents may communicate with one another. This text focuses on the task of constructing the alternative message spaces that a group of agents may use as languages for communicating with one another and thereby achieve a common objective. The relationship between the language that a group of agents may use and the ends that they may accomplish was identified in Hurwicz (1960); the model of a mechanism that is the main object of study in this text originated in this paper and in the long-term collaboration of Leonid Hurwicz with Stanley Reiter. Whereas constructing the message space is but one aspect of the design of a mechanism, it is fundamental in the sense that other aspects (such as dynamic stability and incentives) revolve around the choice of messages with which agents may communicate.

It is assumed here that the sets in the model of a mechanism are subsets of Euclidean space. Appropriate regularity assumptions are imposed on mappings and correspondences so that it is possible to identify necessary and sufficient differential conditions for the design of an economic mechanism. The technique of assuming that all sets in a model are Euclidean and all mappings and correspondences are differentiable is a standard method for making progress and gaining intuition into a scientific problem. Progress is facilitated because the techniques and concepts of a rich field of mathematics in this way become applicable to the problem. Intuition is gained because calculus is nearly universal in science. Although such a continuum model may not capture all aspects of the problem that may be of interest, and though it may in some cases seem to inadequately fit a particular instance of the problem, the successful development of a calculus-based approach is in general a significant step forward in the theoretical study of a problem.

This text complements Hurwicz and Reiter (2006), which develops a set theoretic approach to the construction of mechanisms. Because of the regularity assumptions imposed here, this text elaborates a branch of the theory of mechanism construction, with the set theoretic approach serving as the trunk. Insight and results are produced using the calculus approach; however, that may not be derived purely with set theory. It is worth noting that the calculus approach preceded and inspired much of the set theoretic approach of Hurwicz and Reiter (2006).

The target audience of this text is anyone interested in the field of economic theory known as mechanism design. Because some methods and concepts of differential geometry are not widely known among economic theorists, the second chapter presents the relevant mathematical theory in a style that is intended to be accessible to this community. The difficulty of a journey through differential geometry has deterred most economic theorists from learning about this approach to mechanism design; the second chapter thus provides a shortcut directly to the needed material. The third chapter then develops the first-order approach to the construction of an economic mechanism in a manner that parallels the mathematical theory of Chapter 2. This theory is then applied in the fourth chapter to explore the relationship between the ends that a group of agents can accomplish and the languages that they may use for communicating among themselves.

Acknowledgment

I was introduced to this topic when I was a graduate student at Northwestern University, working under the supervision of Donald Saari. In the summer of 1979, I was hired to proofread Hurwicz et al. (1978), which remains an incomplete manuscript that is full of promising ideas. The main purpose of this text is to assist in the completion of the research program that is outlined in Hurwicz and colleagues' manuscript. Over the years 1979–1982, Leonid Hurwicz and I discussed several results and proofs in the manuscript by phone, by mail, and with an occasional visit. As part of our dialogue and with Leo's encouragement, I wrote proofs of several results. The relevance of the Frobenius Theorem to the objective of developing a calculus-based approach to mechanism design had been identified in Hurwicz et al. (1978). I formulated and proved a version of the Frobenius Theorem (Theorem 6 in Chapter 3) that addresses aspects of the model of a mechanism. This theorem has proven useful in formalizing the Hurwicz, Reiter, and Saari research program. I profited from numerous conversations with Donald Saari while working on these results, and I also benefited from discussions with Stanley Reiter and Kenneth Mount concerning the broader research program. I therefore acknowledge the many contributions of Leo, Ken, Stan, and Don to this text.

A difference between my approach in this text and the approach of Hurwicz et al. (1978) is that I develop the theory of message processes as a separate topic from the theory of the relationship between an objective and a mechanism that realizes it. A message process is the component of a mechanism that captures the communication among the agents. Chapter 3 develops the calculus of message processes, and Chapter 4 applies this methodology to the relationship between objectives and mechanisms. Most of the results of Chapter 3 on message processes would only be complicated by including the objective to be realized; I thus separate the calculus of message processes from the topic of realization of objectives for the sake of clarity. I mention this point at the beginning of this text to avoid confusing the reader who compares results of Chapter 3 of this text with cited results of Hurwicz et al. (1978), which mostly concern aspects of a mechanism that realize a given objective.

There is an alternative to the analytical approach followed in this text that is more algebraic in flavor. This approach formalizes the first-order conditions for the design of a mechanism using the theory of differential ideals. It was first presented in Part IV of Hurwicz et al. (1978). It has been extensively developed in a series of papers by Saari,[1] and so it is discussed in this text only in Section 3.7 and Subsections 4.1.2, 4.6.5, and 4.6.6. The differential ideal approach is mathematically equivalent to the approach described in this text; all results obtainable with one approach can be obtained with the other. The differential ideal approach is an alternative way of formulating and expressing ideas, however, which can provide intuition and facilitate proofs. Much of mathematics involves finding the right way to formally express complex ideas in order to facilitate further proof and understanding. This is especially true in the field of differential geometry, which underlies the first-order approach to the construction of mechanisms. This text therefore complements and does not perfectly substitute for the differential ideal approach to the construction of mechanisms.

Many of the results in this field of research have been presented at the Decentralization Conference, which is supported by the National Science Foundation. Attending this conference has greatly enhanced my understanding of the topic of decentralization and the field of mechanism design. I thank the many organizers and attendees of this conference over the more than twenty years that I have attended, especially Roy Radner, Ted Groves, and Matt Jackson, who managed the conference during this period. Among the attendees, I have particularly benefited from my conversations with Jim Jordan, John Ledyard, and Stefan Reichelstein. I also thank Tom Marschak for his encouragement and support of this project. The broad research program of which this text represents just one thread was furthered by a year of emphasis in 1983–1984 at the Institute for Mathematics and Its Applications at the University of Minnesota. This institute is also supported by the National Science Foundation.

I acknowledge my debt to Michael Spivak's excellent texts, *A Comprehensive Introduction to Differential Geometry*, vol. I (1979) and *Calculus on*

---

[1] Saari (1995) is perhaps the most accessible source on this approach (1984, 1985, 1988, 1990).

Manifolds (1965), from which most of the material in Chapter 2 is drawn. My debt goes beyond the results and the arguments from these texts that I have cited here: I learned most of what I know about the mathematics that I use here from reading these texts, and Spivak's distinctive style and geometric perspective have greatly influenced my presentation of this material. I encourage readers who wish to delve more deeply into the mathematics presented here to consult these texts.

Finally, I thank Naoko Miki for her assistance in preparing this manuscript for publication.

1

Introduction

1.1 The Model of a Mechanism

A fundamental problem in economic theory is to explain how acceptable choices can be made by a group despite the fact that only a small portion of the information that may a priori seem relevant can be taken into account. This problem arises in many settings, ranging from the largest scale problems of macroeconomic systems to the smallest problems of coordination among individuals in an organization. A market economy, for instance, coordinates production by firms and purchases by consumers through prices and quantities. The enormous amount of information held by each firm concerning its production processes and the knowledge of each consumer concerning his own tastes are not communicated among the participants in a market. General equilibrium theory, however, explains a sense in which the production plan selected by each firm and the purchases of each consumer in a market equilibrium are optimal despite the fact that a vast amount of the information known by firms and consumers remains private. A similar phenomenon arises within organizations. Employees cannot communicate all that they know to their manager, and if they could, then the manager could not possibly absorb all of this information. Communication is instead typically limited to conversations and memos. Determining exactly what information should be transmitted to a manager in order to allow him to make good decisions is a fundamental problem in the design of organizations and in the theory of accounting. Firms successfully function, however, despite this limited communication among its layers of management.

The root of the problem is *informational decentralization*, i.e., the information relevant to a group's collective decision may be dispersed among the group members and communication among members is costly or limited. In the two examples cited above, for instance, a consumer cannot possibly

1

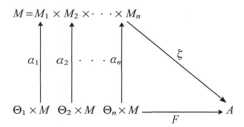

Figure 1.1. The Mount–Reiter diagram.

communicate his comparative ranking of all the different bundles of goods that he can afford, and an employee who communicates more and more about his job to his manager takes an increasing amount of his and his manager's time away from other tasks. Communication by necessity is limited to a reduced set of signals, or *messages*: consumers and firms communicate in a market by means of prices and proposed trades, and an employee may communicate particular statistics (e.g., the profit of a division, costs, or return on equity) to his manager.

An essential issue in the selection of the *mechanism* (or protocol) for group decision making is thus the choice of the set of messages with which group members communicate with each other. In his seminal 1960 paper, Hurwicz initiated a model of communication among agents that encompasses both macro- and microeconomic problems.[1] The problem that motivated Hurwicz was to precisely define the term "mechanism"; prior to Hurwicz's work, it was common to discuss the comparative properties of different mechanisms in various economic situations, and even to claim that a particular mechanism was "optimal," without specifying the alternative mechanisms with which the given mechanism was being compared. The accomplishment of Hurwicz's paper was thus not only the development of a model that has since been widely used to investigate the comparative properties of mechanisms, but more fundamentally to push economists toward a higher level of rigor in evaluating mechanisms.

The model of mechanisms that is considered in this text is depicted in the Mount–Reiter diagram (Mount and Reiter, 1974) of Figure 1.1. Consider first the left side of this diagram. There are n agents. Associated with each agent is a set of parameters Θ_i and a set of messages M_i. An element $\theta_i \in \Theta_i$ represents the *information* known by agent i but not by the other agents.

---

[1] See Reiter (1977) for an introduction to the economic purposes of this model and Hurwicz (1986) for a survey of the literature on informational decentralization in economic mechanisms.

The elements of M_i represent the range of *messages* that the ith agent may select in order to communicate his information. Let

$$\Theta \equiv \prod_{i=1}^{n} \Theta_i$$

and

$$M \equiv \prod_{i=1}^{n} M_i. \tag{1.1}$$

An element $\theta \in \Theta$ is the *state of the world* or *state*. An element $m \in M$ is a vector of publicly observable messages

$$m = (m_1, m_2, \ldots, m_n).$$

The model considered in this text originated as the equilibrium state of a myopic, dynamic adjustment process. Let $m(t) = (m_i(t))_{1 \leq i \leq n}$ denote the messages at time t. Agent i's message $m_i(t+1)$ at time $t+1$ is determined by a *message adjustment rule*

$$m_i(t+1) - m_i(t) = \alpha_i(\theta_i, m(t)), \tag{1.2}$$

which is a function of his private information θ_i and the messages $m(t)$ that he observes from all the agents at time t. The ith agent's *message correspondence* μ_i specifies for each θ_i the set of messages m at which the agent would not alter his message m_i:

$$\mu_i(\theta_i) \equiv \{m \,|\, 0 = \alpha_i(\theta_i, m)\}. \tag{1.3}$$

Agent i's message correspondence μ_i is *privacy preserving* in the sense that it depends only on his information θ_i and not on the information θ_{-i} of the other agents.[2] Equilibrium is given by the *equilibrium correspondence*

$$\mu(\theta) \equiv \bigcap_{i=1}^{n} \mu_i(\theta_i). \tag{1.4}$$

A correspondence $\mu : \Theta \to M$ is *privacy preserving* if it can be expressed as an intersection of form (1.4).[3]

---

[2] The use of "privacy" in this sense originates in Hurwicz (1972).

[3] A correspondence μ of the form (1.4) is also referred to as a *coordinate correspondence*. Mount and Reiter (1974) identified this property of correspondences and its central role in modeling informational decentralization.

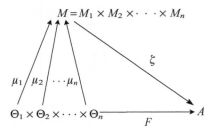

Figure 1.2. A mechanism $\mathcal{M} = (\Theta, M, (\mu_i)_{1 \le i \le n}, \zeta)$ that realizes the objective F.

The equilibrium state is depicted in Figure 1.2. Notice that in equilibrium, it is not necessary to assume that M is a Cartesian product of the form (1.1). In the general formulation considered in this text, an arbitrary set M can serve as the set of equilibrium messages and equilibrium is addressed without reference to the process by which it may be achieved.[4]

The triple

$$\mathcal{M}P = \left(\Theta, M, (\mu_i)_{1 \le i \le n}\right) \tag{1.5}$$

is a *message process*. On the right side of Figure 1.2 is the set A, the *set of alternatives* for the group. Selecting an element of this set represents a collective decision. The mapping $\zeta : M \to A$ is the *outcome mapping*, which represents the selection of an alternative based on the messages of the agents. Together,

$$\mathcal{M} = \left(\Theta, M, (\mu_i)_{1 \le i \le n}, \zeta\right) \tag{1.6}$$

is a *mechanism*. The mechanism is *informationally decentralized* in the sense that each agent i's message correspondence μ_i depends only on his parameter vector θ_i and not on those of the other agents. It thus respects the constraint of information decentralization on the group's decision problem that is the focus of this text.

The correspondence $F : \Theta \to A$ is the *objective*. The objective may be specified by a welfare criterion such as Pareto optimality; in communication among divisions of a firm, the objective may be maximizing the firm's profit. In the central problem of mechanism design, the objective F is given

---

[4] Resource allocation mechanisms are formulated in Hurwicz (1960) as dynamic processes in the sense described above. Mount and Reiter (1974) focus on the equilibrium state, which generalizes mechanisms by allowing M to be an arbitrary set. This text builds most directly on the equilibrium approach of Mount and Reiter.

and the task is to compare mechanisms $\mathcal{M}$ that *realize F* in the sense that[5]

$$\zeta \circ \mu(\theta) = F(\theta) \tag{1.7}$$

for all $\theta \in \Theta$. This means that the mechanism collects a sufficient amount of information about θ from the agents in its equilibrium state to calculate the alternative $F(\theta)$. Equality (1.7) is sometimes weakened to the requirement that

$$\zeta \circ \mu(\theta) \subset F(\theta) \tag{1.8}$$

for all $\theta \in \Theta$. In this case, the mechanism *weakly realizes F*. Alternatively, particular message spaces M and outcome mappings ζ are sometimes of interest because they model aspects of real mechanisms. In this case, the problem is to determine the equilibrium correspondence μ that is appropriate for the model. The goal is then to evaluate the welfare properties of the objective F that is defined by the mechanism through formula (1.7).

The Revelation and Parameter Transfer Mechanisms

There are two types of mechanisms that realize any objective F. In the *revelation mechanism*, each agent i's message m_i is his information θ_i and the outcome mapping ζ is the objective F. Formally, the revelation mechanism is defined as follows:[6]

$$\text{for all } i, \quad M_i = \Theta_i \text{ and } \mu_i(\theta_i) = \{m \mid m_i = \theta_i\};$$

$$\zeta(m) = F(m).$$

The second mechanism is actually a family of n mechanisms, indexed by the selection of one of the n agents. Select agent j. In the *parameter transfer mechanism*, all agents except agent j transfer their parameters to the message space M, which then permits agent j to compute the objective. The mechanism is defined formally as follows:

$$\text{for } i \neq j, \, M_i = \Theta_i \text{ and } \mu_i(\theta_i) = \{m \mid m_i = \theta_i\};$$

$$M_j = A \text{ and } \mu_j(\theta_j) = \{m \mid m_j = F(\theta_j, m_{-j})\};$$

$$\zeta(m) = m_j.$$

[5] The use of the term "realize" in this sense originated in Mount and Reiter (1974).
[6] Despite its simplicity, the revelation mechanism is fundamental in game theory because of the revelation principle. See Myerson (1991), for instance, for a discussion of this topic.

Agent j has special status in this mechanism as a "head" who receives information from the other agents and then realizes the objective. Parameter transfer is in this sense an elementary model of hierarchical decision making.[7]

The revelation and the parameter transfer mechanisms demonstrate that mechanisms exist that realize any given objective. The realization problem is thus never vacuous. These mechanisms share the flaw, however, of requiring all but at most one of the agents to communicate all his information. They are therefore implausible in many real settings, and they fail to address the fundamental problem posed at the beginning of this chapter.

1.1.1 Example: The Competitive Mechanism

Modeling the mechanism of perfect competition is one of the problems that inspired the development of mechanism design. The competitive mechanism is a special case of the equilibrium model depicted in Figure 1.2; notably, this model also provides a framework for designing and evaluating alternatives to the competitive mechanism for achieving gains from trade among agents. This subsection presents a model of the competitive mechanism in the case of an exchange economy. The goal is to familiarize the reader with the general model through examining this central mechanism of microeconomic theory. The competitive mechanism is addressed further in this text in Subsections 3.1.2, 4.3.1, and 4.3.3 and in Sections 4.5 and 4.6.

There are n agents and l goods that may be traded. Each agent i's information consists of a pair $\theta_i = (U_i, w_i)$, where $U_i : \mathbb{R}_+^l \to \mathbb{R}$ is his utility function over his consumption space $\mathbb{R}_+^l$ and $w_i \in \mathbb{R}_+^l$ is his initial endowment of the goods. The set of possible utility–endowment pairs is

$$\Theta_i = \mathcal{U} \times \mathbb{R}_+^l,$$

where $\mathcal{U}$ is the set of all increasing, continuous, and concave functions on $\mathbb{R}_+^l$. A state

$$\theta = ((U_i, w_i))_{1 \le i \le n}$$

in this context is commonly referred to as an *economy*.

The objective of trading is the assignment of a net trade vector $\triangle x_i \in \mathbb{R}^l$ to each of the agents in each economy θ. Trader i then receives $w_i + \triangle x_i$ as his final allocation. Let $\triangle x = (\triangle x_i)_{1 \le i \le n}$ denote a vector of net trades for

---

[7] This interpretation is pursued in Section 4.9.

the agents. The set of alternatives A consists of all balanced net trades for the n agents,

$$A = \left\{ \Delta x = (\Delta x_i)_{1 \leq i \leq n} \in \mathbb{R}^{nl} \;\middle|\; \sum_{i=1}^{n} \Delta x_i = 0 \right\}.$$

It is desirable that the allocation should be feasible, Pareto efficient, and individually rational. A net trade vector Δx is *feasible* for the economy $((U_i, w_i))_{1 \leq i \leq n}$ if

$$w_i + \Delta x_i \in \mathbb{R}_+^l,$$

i.e., no trader is assigned a negative amount of some good in his final allocation. *Pareto efficiency of Δx for the economy $((U_i, w_i))_{1 \leq i \leq n}$* is the requirement that no feasible net trade $\Delta x'$ exists for this economy such that

$$U_i(w_i + \Delta x_i') \geq U_i(w_i + \Delta x_i), \tag{1.9}$$

with strict inequality in (1.9) for at least one agent i. It is thus not possible to select a feasible net trade $\Delta x'$ that is as good for every agent as Δx and strictly better for at least one agent i. *Individual rationality* is the requirement that no trader is made worse off by trading, i.e.,

$$U_i(w_i + \Delta x_i) \geq U_i(w_i)$$

for each agent i. This insures that each agent will voluntarily participate in trading. Let $F^* : \Theta \to A$ denote the correspondence that assigns to each economy $((U_i, w_i))_{1 \leq i \leq n}$ the set of all possible, feasible, balanced, individually rational, and Pareto efficient net trade vectors Δx for that economy.

Let $p \in \mathbb{R}_+^l$ denote a vector of prices for the l goods.[8] The message space for the competitive mechanism is $A \times \mathbb{R}_+^l$ with a message denoted as $(\Delta x, p)$. Agent i's message correspondence $\mu_i(U_i, w_i)$ specifies those net trade vectors Δx^* and price vectors p^* such that his final allocation $w_i + \Delta x_i^*$ maximizes his utility U_i subject to his budget constraint:

$$\mu_i(U_i, w_i)$$

$$= \left\{ (\Delta x^*, p^*) \;\middle|\; \Delta x_i^* \in \arg\max_{\Delta x_i \in \mathbb{R}_+^l} U_i(w_i + \Delta x_i) \text{ s.t. } p \cdot \Delta x_i = 0 \right\}.$$

---

[8] While prices can normalized in a number of different ways, normalization is not needed for this introductory discussion of the competitive mechanism.

The equilibrium correspondence μ specifies for the economy $((U_i, w_i))_{1 \le i \le n}$ all pairs $(\triangle x^*, p^*)$ such that $w_i + \triangle x_i^*$ maximizes each trader i's utility U_i subject to his budget constraint. Because $\triangle x^*$ satisfies the balance condition, such a pair $(\triangle x^*, p^*)$ is a *Walrasian equilibrium*[9] for the economy $((U_i, w_i))_{1 \le i \le n}$.

The outcome mapping of the competitive mechanism is the projection mapping $\zeta (\triangle x, p) = \triangle x$. Classic results in general equilibrium theory imply that (i) an equilibrium message $(\triangle x^*, p^*)$ exists for each economy $((U_i, w_i))_{1 \le i \le n}$; (ii) if $(\triangle x^*, p^*)$ is an equilibrium message for $((U_i, w_i))_{1 \le i \le n}$, then $\triangle x^*$ is Pareto optimal and feasible for $((U_i, w_i))_{1 \le i \le n}$. The competitive mechanism thus weakly realizes the objective F^* in the sense of (1.8).

1.1.2 Example: Mechanisms and Noncooperative Solution Concepts

The equilibrium model depicted in Figure 1.2 is sufficiently general to include most noncooperative games as special cases. In this interpretation, M_i is agent i's strategy set and ζ is the outcome mapping of the game. Agent i's message correspondence $\mu_i : \Theta_i \rightarrow M$ reflects his strategic choice. The definition of a game is completed by specifying a function $U_i(a, \theta)$ for each of the agents that computes his payoff based on the alternative $a \in A$ and the state θ. A *solution concept* is a theory that explains each agent i's strategic choice of a message in terms of his information and his self-interest. Examples that fit this model include the dominant, ex-post Nash, and Bayesian Nash solution concepts.[10]

These three solution concepts are now reviewed in order to illustrate the relationship between this text and noncooperative game theory. The Nash correspondence is then discussed at the end of this subsection. It fits the model of this text if the agents' preferences are *private* in a sense that is discussed below.

In all four of these cases, existence of equilibrium (i.e., nonemptiness of the equilibrium correspondence) is a significant issue that depends on

---

[9] This is also referred to as a *competitive* equilibrium in the literature. In order to distinguish clearly between an objective and a particular mechanism that may be used to realize it, "Walrasian" in this text refers to the allocation and prices in the standard equilibrium of an exchange economy (i.e., an objective of trading), while "competitive" refers to a particular mechanism that realizes a Walrasian objective.

[10] In game theory, the problem of devising a mechanism $\mathcal{M}$ that realizes a given objective F is modified by the addition of the constraint that the message correspondences must be consistent with a particular solution concept. *Implementation* is the special case of the realization problem defined in this way by adding an incentive constraint.

the problem under consideration. Each of these four solution concepts has been used to model incentives in situations in which agents have private information. Noncooperative game theory typically focuses on the rationale for the selection of particular message correspondences (or strategies) by the agents. The emphasis in this text is instead on the different ways in which each agent i can encode his private information through the choice of the message set M and his message correspondence μ_i. The point of this section is that this can be a more general topic that includes noncooperative game theory as a special case in the sense that a solution of a game may define such a communication structure. A particular issue of interest in this text is that different solution concepts may present different opportunities for encoding of information. This issue is addressed in Sections 1.2 and 4.8.

Dominant, Ex-Post Nash, and Bayesian Nash Equilibrium

These three solution concepts can be motivated by interpreting information as revealed over time: agent i chooses his message m_i after learning θ_i but without knowing θ_{-i}. An equilibrium in each case therefore posits a *strategy* $\sigma_i : \Theta_i \to M_i$ for agent i's selection of a message m_i based on his information. The strategy σ_i is *privacy preserving* in the case of these three solution concepts in the sense that it depends only on agent i's information θ_i. In each of these three cases, the message correspondence $\mu_i : \Theta_i \to M$ is defined from the strategy σ_i by the formula

$$\mu_i(\theta_i) \equiv \{\sigma_i(\theta_i)\} \times M_{-i}, \qquad (1.10)$$

and the equilibrium correspondence is the function

$$\mu(\theta) \equiv (\sigma_i(\theta_i))_{1 \leq i \leq n}. \qquad (1.11)$$

Privacy preserving strategies thus define a privacy preserving equilibrium correspondence.

Dominance is the strongest notion of incentive compatibility in the sense that an agent's choice is optimal given his information regardless of the information and messages of the other agents. A strategy σ_i^d for agent i is *dominant* if the message $\sigma_i^d(\theta_i)$ that it specifies for each $\theta_i \in \Theta_i$ maximizes his payoff regardless of the messages m_{-i} chosen by the other agents or their information $\theta_{-i} \in \Theta_{-i}$: for each $\theta_i \in \Theta_i$,

$$\sigma_i^d(\theta_i) \in \arg \max_{m_i \in M_i} U_i(\zeta(m_i, m_{-i}), (\theta_i, \theta_{-i})) \qquad (1.12)$$

for all $\theta_{-i} \in \Theta_{-i}$ and $m_{-i} \in M_{-i}$. An n-tuple of strategies $(\sigma_i^d)_{1 \leq i \leq n}$ is a *dominant equilibrium* if σ_i^d is a dominant strategy for each agent i.

Optimality of an agent's choice in each of the next two solution concepts is weaker than in dominance in that it depends on the strategies chosen by the other agents. An n-tuple of strategies $(\sigma_i^x)_{1\leq i\leq n}$ is an *ex-post Nash equilibrium* if, for each agent i and each $\theta_i \in \Theta_i$, the message $\sigma_i^x(\theta_i)$ maximizes agent i's payoff given the choice of $\sigma_{-i}^b(\theta_{-i})$ by the other agents for every value $\theta_{-i} \in \Theta_{-i}$ of their information: for each agent i and each $\theta_i \in \Theta_i$,

$$\sigma_i^x(\theta_i) \in \arg\max_{m_i \in M_i} \ U_i\left(\zeta\left(m_i, \sigma_{-i}^b(\theta_{-i})\right), (\theta_i, \theta_{-i})\right) \tag{1.13}$$

for all $\theta_{-i} \in \Theta_{-i}$.

An n-tuple of strategies $(\sigma_i^b)_{1\leq i\leq n}$ defines a *Bayesian Nash equilibrium* if, for each agent i and each $\theta_i \in \Theta_i$, the message $\sigma_i^b(\theta_i) = m_i$ maximizes agent i's conditional expected payoff assuming that each other agent j uses the strategy σ_j: for each agent i and each $\theta_i \in \Theta_i$,

$$\sigma_i^x(\theta_i) \in \arg\max_{m_i \in M_i} E_{\theta_{-i}}\left[U_i(\zeta(m_i, \sigma_{-i}^b(\theta_{-i})), (\theta_i, \theta_{-i})) \,\middle|\, \theta_i, \sigma_{-i}^b\right]. \tag{1.14}$$

The expected payoff in (1.14) is calculated with respect to a probability distribution on Θ that is postulated as part of the Bayesian approach. It is typically assumed with both the ex-post Nash and Bayesian Nash solution concepts that agent i knows the strategies of the other agents so that he may verify the optimality of his message.[11]

Nash Correspondence

The *Nash correspondence* $\mu^{ne} : \Theta \to M$ specifies all Nash equilibria in each state θ.[12] An n-tuple $m' = (m_i')_{1\leq i\leq n}$ lies in $\mu^{ne}(\theta)$ if each m_i' maximizes agent i's utility given θ and the choice of m_{-i}' by the other agents:

$$\mu^{ne}(\theta) \equiv \left\{ m' \,\middle|\, m_i' \in \arg\max_{m_i \in M_i} \ U_i(\zeta(m_i, m_{-i}'), \theta), 1 \leq i \leq n \right\}.$$

[11] There is now a large literature in game theory concerning how players learn to play equilibria. Much of this literature studies the dynamic stability of message adjustment rules of the form (1.2) in a variety of special cases. A special case is typically defined by assumptions concerning the incentives of the players, their information, and how they learn. A more abstract approach that focuses on the informational requirements for the local stability of message adjustment rules was initiated by Reiter in 1979, with subsequent contributions by Jordan (1987), Mount and Reiter (1987), Saari and Williams (1986), and Williams (1985).

[12] A similar analysis can also be made for the *dominant correspondence*, which specifies all dominant strategy equilibria in each state θ. Ex-post Nash and Bayesian Nash equilibria, however, are not defined by a single state θ; the condition for the optimality of agent i's choice in each case depends on the other agents' strategies over for all $\theta_{-i} \in \Theta_{-i}$. Equilibrium correspondences are therefore not defined for these solution concepts in the same sense as they are for the dominant and Nash solution concepts.

This correspondence has been extensively studied in the implementation literature. Of particular interest here is whether it is privacy preserving in the sense of (1.4), i.e., whether or not it is expressible in the form

$$\mu^{ne}(\theta) \equiv \bigcap_{i=1}^{n} \mu_i^{ne}(\theta_i)$$

for some choice of privacy preserving correspondences $(\mu_i^{ne})_{1 \leq i \leq n}$ for the agents. This property is necessary for application of the model of this text to the Nash correspondence.

The assumption that preferences are privately known to each agent as he selects his message is crucial in addressing this issue. Agent i *privately knows his preferences* over the alternatives A once he observes θ_i if his payoff U_i depends on $\theta_i \in \Theta_i$ and $a \in A$ but not on the parameters $\theta_{-i} \in \Theta_{-i}$ of the other agents. The more general case allows *informational externalities*, i.e., agent i's payoff U_i can depend on the parameters θ_{-i} observed by the other agents. While informational externalities complicate the study of incentives, they occur in many real problems and therefore must be addressed by our theories.

Consider first the case of private preferences. It is reasonable to try agent i's *best response correspondence* as a candidate for his message correspondence. This correspondence specifies for each θ_i all messages m' such that m'_i maximizes agent i's payoff given the choice of m'_{-i} by the other agents:

$$\mu_i^{br}(\theta_i) \equiv \left\{ m' \,\middle|\, m'_i \in \arg \max_{m_i \in M_i} U_i(\zeta(m_i, m'_{-i}), \theta_i) \right\}.$$

In words, m'_i is a *best response* to m'_{-i} given θ_i. With the assumption of private preferences, the Nash correspondence in this case satisfies

$$\mu^{ne}(\theta) = \bigcap_{i=1}^{n} \mu_i^{br}(\theta_i),$$

and so it is privacy preserving.

The case of informational externalities is more complicated. One definition of agent i's best response correspondence requires that m'_i maximizes agent i's payoff given the use of m'_{-i} by the other agents for all $\theta_{-i} \in \Theta_{-i}$:

$$\mu_i^{br}(\theta_i) \equiv \left\{ m' \,\middle|\, m'_i \in \arg \max_{m_i \in M_i} U_i(\zeta(m_i, m'_{-i}), \theta), \forall \theta_{-i} \in \Theta_{-i} \right\},$$

The condition that m_i' must be a best response to m_{-i}' for all $\theta_{-i} \in \Theta_{-i}$ severely restricts the set of Nash equilibria; while it is clear that

$$\mu^{ne}(\theta) \supset \bigcap_{i=1}^{n} \mu_i^{br}(\theta_i),$$

the containment may be proper because $\mu^{ne}(\theta)$ does not require that the best response property hold for agent i in states $(\theta_i, \theta_{-i}') \neq \theta$, as required by $\mu_i^{br}(\theta_i)$.

Alternatively, agent i's best response correspondence can be redefined to specify for each state θ all m' for which m_i' is a best response to m_{-i}':

$$\mu_i^{brx}(\theta) \equiv \left\{ m' \,\middle|\, m_i' \in \arg\max_{m_i \in M_i} U_i(\zeta(m_i, m_{-i}'), \theta) \right\}.$$

The equation

$$\mu^{ne}(\theta) = \bigcap_{i=1}^{n} \mu_i^{brx}(\theta)$$

holds for this definition of the best response correspondences. It does not verify that the Nash correspondence μ^{ne} is privacy preserving, however, because each correspondence μ_i^{brx} is not necessarily privacy preserving.

Example: The Nash Correspondence Need Not Be Privacy Preserving
It may not be possible to show that the Nash correspondence is privacy preserving using the best response correspondences when informational externalities are present. The following example demonstrates that the Nash correspondence in fact may not be privacy preserving in the presence of informational externalities.

The example is illustrated in Figure 1.3. For $i = 1, 2$, let

$$\Theta_i = \{\theta_i', \theta_i''\} \quad \text{and} \quad M_i = \{m_i'', m_i''\}.$$

The agents play one of four 2×2 games depending on the state θ. Each of the four games is a prisoner's dilemma game with the strategies permuted so that the games have the following properties: (i) in state (θ_1', θ_2') and in state (θ_1'', θ_2''), the message pair (m_1', m_2') is a Nash equilibrium; (ii) in state (θ_1', θ_2''), the pair (m_1', m_2') is not a Nash equilibrium. Informational externalities are present because the payoff to agent i depends not only on his message m_i and his opponent's message m_{-i}, but also on his opponent's information θ_{-i}.

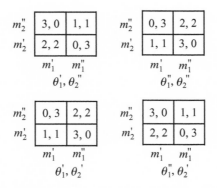

Figure 1.3. The pair (m_1', m_2') is the unique Nash equilibrium in states (θ_1', θ_2') and (θ_1'', θ_2''), and the pair (m_1'', m_2'') is the unique Nash equilibrium in states (θ_1', θ_2'') and (θ_1'', θ_2'). The correspondence μ^{ne} that specifies the Nash equilibria in each state is therefore not privacy preserving.

Suppose $\mu^{ne} = \mu_1 \cap \mu_2$ for privacy preserving correspondences μ_1 and μ_2. It follows from (i) that

$$(m_1', m_2') \in \big(\mu_1(\theta_1') \cap \mu_2(\theta_2')\big) \cap \big(\mu_1(\theta_1') \cap \mu_2(\theta_2'')\big).$$

It follows that $(m_1', m_2') \in \mu_1(\theta_1') \cap \mu_2(\theta_2'')$, which contradicts (ii). The Nash correspondence is therefore not privacy preserving in this example.

Because the Nash equilibrium in each state is in fact a dominant equilibrium, this example shows that the correspondence that specifies all dominant equilibria in each state need not be privacy preserving when informational externalities are present. This is distinct from the analysis at the beginning of this subsection, which posits a dominant strategy $\sigma_i^d : \Theta_i \to M_i$ for each agent i. In this example, agent 1 (for instance) does not have a choice m_i given θ_1' that is best for him regardless of agent 2's choice and the value of θ_2. Agent 1 therefore does not have a dominant strategy σ_i^d in the sense of (1.12), even though he has a dominant strategy in each state θ.

1.2 Encoding and Product Structure

Agents may encode their private information by using a set of messages M that is smaller than Θ. This focuses attention on the left side of Figure 1.2. Encoding of information requires that distinct states are represented using the same equilibrium messages. Formally, this means that for $\theta' \neq \theta''$ the intersection $\mu(\theta') \cap \mu(\theta'')$ is nonempty; equivalently, $\mu^{-1}(m)$ contains more than one state θ for some $m \in M$. Economizing on the set of signals is in this way reduced to the structure of the level sets of the equilibrium correspondence μ, and intuitively, larger level sets reflect successful encoding.

The level sets of a privacy preserving equilibrium correspondence μ have a property that distinguishes it from an arbitrary correspondence: for any $m \in M$, the level set $\mu^{-1}(m)$ is a Cartesian product of n subsets of the parameter spaces $\Theta_1, \ldots, \Theta_n$,

$$\mu^{-1}(m) = \prod_{i=1}^{n} \mu_i^{-1}(m), \tag{1.15}$$

where

$$\mu_i^{-1}(m) \subset \Theta_i \tag{1.16}$$

for all $1 \leq i \leq n$. This property of a correspondence is known as *product structure*, and it was first identified by Stanley Reiter. It fundamentally reflects the fact that μ models communication when information is dispersed among the agents. Any mechanism $\mathcal{M}$ determines a correspondence μ that exhibits product structure, and constructing a mechanism to realize a given objective requires the construction of a correspondence μ with this property. Understanding product structure is thus an essential component in building a theory of mechanism design that takes language (i.e., the choice of M) and communication (the choice of $(\mu_i)_{1 \leq i \leq n}$) into account.

Referring back to Figure 1.2, suppose that the mechanism $\mathcal{M}$ realizes the objective F. Let $m^* \in \mu(\theta^*)$ and $\zeta(m^*) = a^*$. The realization equality $\zeta \circ \mu = F$ together with (1.15) imply that

$$\mu^{-1}(m^*) = \prod_{i=1}^{n} \mu_i^{-1}(m^*) \subset F^{-1}(a^*). \tag{1.17}$$

Encoding of information in realizing F thus requires covering each level set $F^{-1}(a^*)$ of this objective with Cartesian products of the form (1.15). It is clear from (1.17) that

$$\bigcup_{m \in \zeta^{-1}(a^*)} \left(\prod_{i=1}^{n} \mu_i^{-1}(m) \right) = F^{-1}(a^*), \tag{1.18}$$

because realization requires that there exists for each $\theta \in F^{-1}(a^*)$ an $m \in \zeta^{-1}(a^*)$ such that $m \in \mu(\theta)$. If the equilibrium correspondence μ is a function so that a unique equilibrium message is assigned to each $\theta \in \Theta$, then the sets of the form

$$\left\{ \mu^{-1}(m) \,\middle|\, m \in \zeta^{-1}(a^*) \right\}$$

partition $F^{-1}(a^*)$. This partitioning property will prove particularly useful in this text.

Product structure to this point has been *message indexed* in the sense that the sets in (1.17) are labeled with the equilibrium message m. Starting with an objective $F : \Theta \to A$ and faced with the problem of designing a mechanism $\mathcal{M}$ to realize F, one does not have the mechanism $\mathcal{M}$ at hand to index the product structure. It is thus desirable to derive conditions directly on Θ and on F for the construction of the mechanism that realizes F. This is now accomplished in the case in which the equilibrium correspondence $\mu : \Theta \to M$ is a mapping.

Consider any $\theta^* \in \Theta$ and suppose that $\mathcal{M} = (\Theta, M, (\mu_i)_{1 \le i \le n}, \zeta)$ realizes F. The goal is to eliminate M, $(\mu_i)_{1 \le i \le n}$, and ζ from the realization equality (1.7). Let $\mu(\theta^*) = m^*$ and $\zeta(m^*) = a^*$. Define $S_i^*(\theta^*) \subset \Theta_i$ as

$$S_i^*(\theta^*) = \mu_i^{-1}(m^*) = \mu_i^{-1}(\mu(\theta^*)) \tag{1.19}$$

and let $S(\theta^*)$ denote

$$S(\theta^*) = \mu^{-1}(m^*) = \mu^{-1}(\mu(\theta^*)). \tag{1.20}$$

The second equality in each of (1.19) and (1.20) uses the assumption that $\mu(\theta^*) = m^*$ to eliminate the message m^* and thereby express $\mu_i^{-1}(m^*)$ and $\mu^{-1}(m^*)$ in terms of the state θ^*. Substitution into (1.15) implies

$$S(\theta^*) = \prod_{i=1}^{n} S_i^*(\theta^*). \tag{1.21}$$

This is *state-indexed product structure;*[13] throughout most of this text, "product structure" refers to this formulation. The realization of F implies

$$S(\theta^*) \subset F^{-1}(a^*). \tag{1.22}$$

Notice that

$$\{ S(\theta) \mid \theta \in \Theta \} \tag{1.23}$$

is a partition of Θ because of the assumption that μ is a mapping. The design of a mechanism that realizes F with a unique equilibrium message for each state thus requires devising a partition (1.23) of Θ, indexed by the states $\theta \in \Theta$, such that each set $S(\theta^*)$ in the partition lies inside the level set of F determined by θ^* and exhibits product structure as in (1.21). This completes a set theoretic statement of the design problem.

---

[13] It is also commonly called "parameter-indexed product structure."

This formulation of the design problem is investigated in this text using calculus. Differential and regularity conditions are imposed on the components of a mechanism so that a first-order approach to constructing product stuctures and message correspondences in relation to the level set of an objective can be developed. The focus is thus on the choice of language in a mechanism and communication among agents. Other issues in mechanism design (such as incentives or dynamic stability of message adjustment) are of secondary importance here; while such issues are surely essential in the evaluation and design of mechanisms, language and communication are also essential in this task, and they have for the most part been neglected in the field of mechanism design.[14, 15] This text is part of an effort to address this deficiency.

1.2.1 Product Structure and Noncooperative Solution Concepts

As part of introducing the topic of product structure, the less restrictive form that the Nash correspondence permits in comparison to the dominant, ex-post Nash, and Bayesian Nash correspondences is now discussed. This less restrictive form provides the mechanism designer with more freedom in constructing message correspondences to implement a given objective, which suggests that Nash implementation may permit savings in communication beyond what can be attained with either of these other three solution concepts. This discussion starts from the discussion of solution concepts in Subsection 1.1.2, and the above conjecture is then illustrated in Subsections 1.2.2 and 4.8. Consistent with most of this text, it is assumed throughout this subsection that the equilibrium correspondence μ is a

---

[14] The literature on implementation has typically focused on incentive constraints without regard to constraints on communication, while the literature on realization has typically focused on communication without regard to incentives. Reichelstein (1984) is an early attempt to consider both kinds of constraints in the study of mechanisms. See also Reichelstein and Reiter (1988) and Williams (1986), which study the relationship between realization and Nash implementation.

[15] There is a rich literature in mechanism design concerning the Bayesian approach in which agents share a common prior concerning the distribution of types $(\theta_i)_{1 \leq i \leq n}$. For tractability, this literature has for the most part been restricted to the special case in which each agent i's type space Θ_i is 1-dimensional. The possibility that agents might communicate with less than complete revelation grows in importance as this subfield of mechanism design begins to address the special problems and results that arise when the private information of agents may be more complex (e.g., an agent's type may be multidimensional). A common example arises in combinatorial auctions, which studies the sale of multiple heterogeneous items. The preferences of a bidder become more and more complex to the extent that they depend on (i) which subset of items the bidder receives and (ii) which items are assigned to each of the other agents.

function, i.e., a unique equilibrium is determined for each state. This may reflect refinement or selection among the equilibria that are determined by the solution concept in question.

The key point is that any message process defined by strategies defines a particularly simple and restrictive form of product structure. Examples include the dominant, ex-post Nash, and Bayesian Nash solution concepts. Recall from Subsection 1.1.2 that if agent i uses the strategy $\sigma_i : \Theta_i \to M_i$, then his message correspondence is $\mu_i(\theta_i) = \sigma_i(\theta_i) \times M_{-i}$ and the equilibrium correspondence is the function $\sigma(\theta) = (\sigma_i(\theta_i))_{1 \leq i \leq n}$. Let $\mu(\theta^*) = m^* = (m_i^*)_{1 \leq i \leq n}$. It follows that

$$S_i^*(\theta^*) = \mu_i^{-1}\left(m^*\right) = \sigma_i^{-1}\left(\sigma_i(\theta_i^*)\right)$$

and

$$S(\theta^*) = \mu^{-1}(m^*) = \prod_{i=1}^{n} \sigma_i^{-1}\left(\sigma_i(\theta_i^*)\right).$$

Notice that each set $S_i^*(\theta^*)$ depends only on i's information θ_i^* and not on the information θ_{-i}^* of the other agents. The set $S_i^*(\theta^*)$ can thus be represented as $S_i^*(\theta_i^*)$.

This restricts the product structure; in the general case in (1.19), the set $S_i^*(\theta^*)$ may depend on the entire state θ^*. The level sets of an objective that is realized using strategies for the agents are thus partitioned by sets of the form

$$S(\theta^*) = \prod_{i=1}^{n} S_i^*(\theta_i^*) \tag{1.24}$$

rather than the more general form of (1.21). This is an added constraint on the partitioning problem that must be solved in designing the mechanism that realizes the given objective.

In contrast, the Nash solution concept does not necessarily impose this added constraint on product structure. The difference arises because the optimality of agent i's message m_i^* in a Nash equilibrium depends on both his information θ_i and the messages m_{-i}^* chosen by the other agents for their information θ_{-i}; through m_{-i}^*, the set

$$S_i^*(\theta^*) = \mu_i^{-1}(m^*)$$

may depend on θ_{-i}^*. This is illustrated by the "alternative mechanism" in the example that follows below.

1.2.2 Example: The Efficient Level of a Public Good

Encoding and product structure are now illustrated in a simple public good model. There are $n = 2$ agents, each of whom receives utility from the selection of a real-valued level of a public good together with a monetary transfer. Agent i's utility U_i has the form

$$U_i(x, t_i) = V_i(x) + t_i,$$

where $x \in \mathbb{R}_+$ is the total dollar amount that is spent on the public good and $t_i \in \mathbb{R}$ is a monetary transfer. Agent i's *valuation function* $V_i(x)$ lies in some set Θ_i. A choice x^* is *efficient* for the pair (V_1, V_2) if and only if

$$x^* \in \arg\max V_1(x) + V_2(x) - x, \tag{1.25}$$

i.e., x^* maximizes the total value it provides to the two agents minus the cost of provision. For simplicity, it is assumed that $\Theta = \Theta_1 \times \Theta_2$ is restricted so that

(i) the valuation functions V_1 and V_2 are differentiable, increasing, and concave;
(ii) a unique efficient choice exists for each $(V_1, V_2) \in \Theta$ and it is strictly positive.

Define $f : \Theta \to \mathbb{R}_{++}$ as the mapping that selects the efficient choice for each (V_1, V_2). Monetary transfers are also assigned to the agents, and so the set of alternatives A is

$$A = \mathbb{R}_+ \times \mathbb{R}^2,$$

with generic element (x, t_1, t_2). Of interest in this example is any objective $F : \Theta \to A$ that agrees with f in its selection of the efficient level of the public good. The transfers are thus variables in the design problem that can be selected to influence the incentives of the agents.

The Clarke–Groves–Vickrey Transfers

Efficient choice depends on the agents' valuation functions V_1 and V_2. Because each agent privately knows his own valuation function, efficient choice requires communication. The valuation functions may simply be announced through a revelation mechanism. For reported valuation functions (V_1^*, V_2^*), the *Clarke–Groves–Vickrey* outcome mapping $\zeta = (f, t_1, t_2)$ selects the efficient choice $f(V_1^*, V_2^*)$ based on the reports and awards transfers to the agents according to the formula

$$t_i(V_1^*, V_2^*) = V_{-i}^*(f(V_1^*, V_2^*)) - f(V_1^*, V_2^*) + \tau_i\left(V_{-i}^*\right),$$

where $\tau_i(V_{-i}^*)$ can be any function.[16] The key incentive property of these transfers is that they sustain honest reporting as each agent's dominant strategy, i.e., each agent i's utility is maximized by reporting $V_i^* = V_i$ when V_i is his valuation function, regardless of the report V_{-i}^* of the other agent. This is clear from the formula for agent i's utility when he reports V_i^* and the other agent reports V_{-i}^*:

$$\left[V_i(f(V_1^*, V_2^*)) + V_{-i}^*(f(V_1^*, V_2^*)) - f(V_1^*, V_2^*) \right] + \tau_i\left(V_{-i}^*\right).$$

The last term $\tau_i\left(V_{-i}^*\right)$ is independent of agent i's report. Reporting $V_i^* = V_i$ insures that the level of the public good $f(V_1^*, V_2^*)$ maximizes the term in brackets, as in the efficiency criterion (1.25).

As a revelation mechanism, information is not successfully encoded by the agents in the Clarke–Groves–Vickrey mechanism in their reported messages. The corresponding product structure is trivial,

$$S_i^*(\theta_i) = \{\theta_i\} \text{ and } S(\theta) = \{\theta\} \text{ for all } \theta \in \Theta.$$

It is difficult to imagine that reporting a function $V_i(x)$ is feasible. This motivates the following mechanism.

An Alternative Mechanism

Suppose now that each agent i announces $m_i \in \mathbb{R}_{++}$.[17] Recall that m denotes the pair (m_1, m_2). The outcome mapping $\zeta^* = (f^*, t_1^*, t_2^*)$ of an alternative mechanism selects a level of the public good and awards transfers according to the formulas

$$f^*(m) = m_1 + m_2$$

and

$$t_i^*(m) = -m_i + m_{-i} \log(m_1 + m_2). \tag{1.26}$$

It is shown below that (i) there exists for each $(V_1, V_2) \in \Theta$ a unique Nash equilibrium pair of messages and (ii) the level of the public good determined by this equilibrium pair is efficient. The mechanism with $\mathbb{R}_{++}^2$ as its message space, ζ^* as its outcome mapping, and the Nash equilibrium correspondence as its equilibrium correspondence μ is discussed in greater detail below once these properties are established. A special case is then analyzed in Subsection 1.4.1.

---

[16] This well-studied outcome mapping originated in Clarke (1971), Groves (1973), and Vickery (1961).

[17] This mechanism originates in Sanghavi (2006) and Sanghavi and Hajek (in press).

The first-step is to derive the first-order conditions for Nash equilibrium and for efficiency. Fixing (V_1, V_2) and m_{-i}, the derivative of agent i's utility with respect to his message m_i is

$$\frac{\partial}{\partial m_i} U_i \left(f^* (m), t_i^* (m) \right) = \frac{\partial}{\partial m_i} U_i \left(m_1 + m_2, t_i^* (m) \right)$$

$$= V_i'(m_1 + m_2) - \frac{m_i}{m_1 + m_2}. \qquad (1.27)$$

This implies the following first-order condition for m_i to be a best response to m_{-i}:

$$V_i'(m_1 + m_2) (m_1 + m_2) - m_i = 0. \qquad (1.28)$$

Condition (1.28) holding at $m^* = (m_1^*, m_2^*)$ for each agent i is necessary and sufficient for m^* to be a Nash equilibrium because each $U_i(m_1 + m_2, t_i^*(m))$ is concave in m_i. Turning next to efficiency, the efficient level $f(V_1, V_2) = x > 0$ satisfies the first-order condition

$$V_1'(x) + V_2'(x) = 1. \qquad (1.29)$$

Condition (1.29) is necessary and sufficient for efficiency by virtue of the concavity of V_1 and V_2.

Existence, uniqueness, and efficiency of Nash equilibrium for each $(V_1, V_2) \in \Theta$ are shown by establishing the following: (i) the efficient level $f(V_1, V_2)$ determines a unique Nash equilibrium m^* that implements it; (ii) conversely, an arbitrary Nash equilibrium m^* necessarily implements the efficient level $f(V_1, V_2)$. Starting with (i), substitute $f(V_1, V_2)$ for $m_1 + m_2$ in the first-order condition (1.28) for a Nash equilibrium and solve for m^*. It follows that

$$m_1^* + m_2^* = V_1'(f(V_1, V_2))f(V_1, V_2) + V_2'(f(V_1, V_2))f(V_1, V_2)$$

$$= \left[V_1'(f(V_1, V_2)) + V_2'(f(V_1, V_2)) \right] f(V_1, V_2) = f(V_1, V_2).$$

The first line follows from the definition of m_1^* and m_2^* using (1.28) and the second line follows from the efficiency of $f(V_1, V_2)$ together with (1.29). The message vector m^* therefore implements the efficient level $f(V_1, V_2)$. By virtue of satisfying the first-order conditions given by (1.28), m^* is also a Nash equilibrium. Turning to (ii), the efficiency of any Nash equilibrium m^* is demonstrated by applying (1.28) to establish

$$m_1^* + m_2^* = V_1'(m_1^* + m_2^*) \left(m_1^* + m_2^* \right) + V_2'(m_1^* + m_2^*) \left(m_1^* + m_2^* \right)$$

$$= \left(V_1'(m_1^* + m_2^*) + V_2'(m_1^* + m_2^*) \right) \left(m_1^* + m_2^* \right).$$

The assumption that each $M_i = \mathbb{R}_{++}$ allows cancellation of $m_1^* + m_2^*$. The sufficient condition (1.29) for efficiency therefore holds at $m_1^* + m_2^*$.

Relationship to This Text
This mechanism can be formalized in the notation of this text as follows:

Message spaces:

$$M_1 = M_2 = \mathbb{R}_{++}, \tag{1.30}$$

$$M = M_1 \times M_2 = \mathbb{R}_{++}^2.$$

Agent i's message adjustment rule:

$$\alpha_i(V_i, m) = V_i'(m_1 + m_2) - \frac{m_i}{m_1 + m_2}. \tag{1.31}$$

Agent i's message correspondence:

$$\mu_i(V_i) = \left\{ m \in \mathbb{R}_{++}^2 \mid \alpha_i(V_i, m) = 0 \right\}. \tag{1.32}$$

Equilibrium correspondence:

$$\mu(V_1, V_2) = \left\{ m \in \mathbb{R}_{++}^2 \mid \alpha_1(V_1, m) = \alpha_2(V_2, m) = 0 \right\}. \tag{1.33}$$

Outcome mapping:

$$\zeta^*(m) = (m_1 + m_2, t_1^*(m), t_2^*(m)). \tag{1.34}$$

Agent i's message adjustment rule $\alpha_i(V_i, m)$ is formula (1.27) for his marginal utility in m_i given V_i and m_{-i}. Because the main interest here is the solution set to $\alpha_i(V_i, m) = 0$ in M, other formulas could be used instead of (1.31). Agent i's message correspondence $\mu_i(V_i)$ specifies all pairs (m_1, m_2) for which m_i is a best response to m_{-i} when V_i defines agent i's utility function. The equilibrium correspondence $\mu \equiv \mu_1 \cap \mu_2$ specifies all pairs (m_1, m_2) such that each m_i is a best response to m_{-i}. It is therefore the Nash equilibrium correspondence. The equilibrium correspondence μ is in this case a mapping because there is a unique Nash equilibrium for each (V_1, V_2).

Turning next to product structure and encoding, fix $m^* = (m_1^*, m_2^*)$ and consider the set $\mu^{-1}(m^*)$ consisting of all pairs $(V_1, V_2) \in \Theta$ for which m^* is a Nash equilibrium. A pair (V_1, V_2) belongs to this set if, for each i, m_i^* is a best response to m_{-i}^* for the utility function defined by V_i. With m^* specified, $\mu^{-1}(m^*)$ is thus characterized by two conditions, one on Θ_1 (m_1^* is a best response to m_2^* given V_1) and one on Θ_2 (m_2^* is a best response to m_1^* given V_2). Applying the first-order conditions for Nash equilibrium, $\mu^{-1}(m^*)$ is given formally by

$$\mu^{-1}(m^*) = \left\{ (V_1, V_2) \in \Theta \,\middle|\, \alpha_1(V_i, m^*) = \alpha_2(V_i, m^*) = 0 \right\}$$
$$= \left\{ V_1 \in \Theta_1 \,\middle|\, \alpha_1(V_i, m^*) = 0 \right\} \times \left\{ V_2 \in \Theta_2 \,\middle|\, \alpha_2(V_i, m^*) = 0 \right\}$$
$$= \mu_1^{-1}(m^*) \times \mu_2^{-1}(m^*),$$

which illustrates product structure. Encoding occurs in this mechanism in the sense that distinct pairs (V_1, V_2), (V_1', V_2') can share the same Nash equilibrium m^*. Notice that the sets

$$\left\{ \mu^{-1}(m^*) \,\middle|\, m^* \in \mathbb{R}^2_{++} \right\}$$

partition Θ because there is a unique Nash equilibrium m^* associated with each $(V_1, V_2) \in \Theta$.

Product structure in this example does not have the restricted form of (1.24) that holds for the dominant, ex-post Nash, and Bayesian Nash solution concepts. The equilibrium correspondence here is the function

$$\mu(V_1, V_2) = f(V_1, V_2) \cdot \left(V_1'(f(V_1, V_2)), V_2'(f(V_1, V_2)) \right).$$

For given $(V_1^*, V_2^*) \in \Theta$ and $m^* = \mu(V_1^*, V_2^*)$, the set $S_i^*(V_1^*, V_2^*)$ is therefore

$$S_i^*(V_1^*, V_2^*) = \left\{ V_i \,\middle|\, \alpha_i(V_i, m^*) = 0 \right\}$$
$$= \left\{ V_i \,\middle|\, \alpha_i(V_i, \mu(V_1^*, V_2^*)) = 0 \right\}.$$

The set $S_i^*(V_1^*, V_2^*)$ clearly depends on both V_i^* and V_{-i}^*, with the dependence on V_{-i}^* occurring through its effect on the equilibrium message $m^* = \mu(V_1^*, V_2^*)$.

Discussion

Much of the research on the Clarke–Groves–Vickrey transfers has focused on the monetary deficit that they may entail and the possibilities for addressing this shortfall. This budgetary issue is sidestepped here to focus instead on another flaw of the Clarke–Groves–Vickrey transfers, which is that they require complete revelation by the agents. The alternative mechanism above demonstrates that complete revelation is not necessary to realize the efficient level of the public good, at least in this simple example; in fact, reporting of a real number instead of a function may be sufficient for each agent, even while the alternative mechanism retains a form of incentive compatibility (Nash instead of dominant strategy).

The purpose of including this example at this stage of the text is not, however, to propose a new solution to the public good problem. Besides simply illustrating the model of a mechanism, this example raises a number of questions that motivate this text. Here are a few of these questions, listed in order of increasing generality:

(i) What are the distinguishing properties of the efficiency mapping $f : \Theta \to \mathbb{R}$ in this example that allow it to be realized with a mechanism whose message space is small in its dimension?

(ii) Given an arbitrary objective $F : \Theta \to \mathbb{R}$, or given the efficiency mapping in a model that is not as restrictive as the one above, how would one recognize that F can be realized with mechanisms whose message spaces are much smaller in dimension than those required by parameter transfer or revelation mechanisms?

(iii) Can one construct all the alternative mechanisms that realize a given objective F, so that they might then be compared using a variety of criteria?

This last question is the main motivation of this text, with the objective here to develop a first-order approach to mechanism construction.

Finally, an economic theorist might ask the following sets of questions concerning this example:

(iv) Does the savings in communication in moving from the revelation mechanism to the alternative mechanism reflect the relaxation of the solution concept from dominant strategy to Nash? Is this a general phenomenon with these solution concepts? This conjecture was suggested in Section 1.2.

(v) Does the alternative mechanism have practical value in public choice problems? Is it significant for the theory of public goods? In particular, do the messages have some economic interpretation?

The questions in (iv) are addressed as an application of the first-order approach to mechanisms in Subsection 4.8, which concerns the especially large amount of communication that is typically required for dominant strategy or Bayesian Nash implementation. The second set of questions is not addressed in this text, which is instead focused on presenting the array of possible mechanisms that achieve a given goal as opposed to weighing the merits of particular mechanisms. It is left to the mechanism designer to assess the virtues and viability of the candidate mechanisms in the problem that he addresses. It may be worthwhile to add, however, that the now familiar Clarke–Groves–Vickrey transfers were seen as unintuitive and

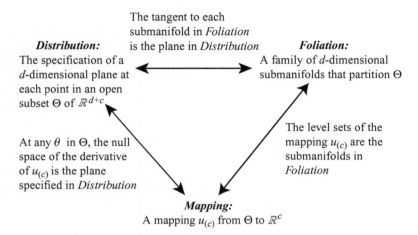

Figure 1.4. *Distribution* specifies first-order conditions, while *Foliation* and *Mapping*, respectively, specify geometric and analytic solutions to these conditions.

impractical in the early years of their development. The lesson is that alternatives to familiar mechanisms should not be dismissed out of hand.

1.3 A Theme in Differential Equations

This section presents some basic features of the theory of differential equations followed by the parallel features concerning the construction of message processes. These parallel features are the main subject of this text.

There are both geometric and analytic senses in which a system of differential equations can be solved. A *geometric* solution means proving the existence of a solution surface whose tangent at any point is defined by the equations. An *analytic* solution means proving the existence of a mapping that satisfies the equations and possibly even solving for it explicitly (i.e., in *closed form*). The two approaches are depicted in Figure 1.4, which concerns a system of c differential equations in $d + c$ real variables.[18] *Distribution* is the statement of the problem (i.e., the system of differential equations), while *Foliation* and *Mapping* are, respectively, the geometric and the analytic solutions. The relationship between the three corners of this diagram is central in the theory of differential equations and is well understood: the Frobenius Theorem states smoothness and integrability conditions on

[18] Throughout this text "c" denotes codimension (i.e., the number of independent equations) and "d" denotes the dimension of the solution set.

the d-dimensional planes for the equivalence of *Distribution, Foliation,* and *Mapping* locally.[19]

1.3.1 Example: Does a Given Mapping Represent Inverse Demand?

The usefulness in economic theory of the equivalence in Figure 1.4 is illustrated by its role in a classic problem from the theory of consumer behavior. Stated in its most general form, the problem is to identify properties that distinguish purchases of goods by an individual in a market that are consistent with the theory of preference maximization from arbitrary purchases of goods. Such properties provide a basis for testing the theory of consumer behavior. One aspect of this problem is captured by the following question: Given a mapping that specifies a bundle of goods for each vector of prices, do there exist preferences for which the given mapping represents a consumer's *inverse demand*? In other words, what properties must such a mapping satisfy in order to be *rationalized* as a consumer's inverse demand mapping? The purpose of this subsection is to formalize this problem and then relate it to the equivalence of *Distribution, Foliation,* and *Mapping.* The problem is then addressed more thoroughly in Subsection 2.7.1 after the Frobenius Theorem has been presented. In addition to illustrating the equivalence, a goal of these two subsections is to demonstrate the significance of the integrability condition of the Frobenius Theorem within a cornerstone theory of microeconomics.

Posing the problem first in its most elementary form, suppose that for time periods $t = 1, \ldots, m$ a consumer is observed purchasing the bundle $\theta^{(t)} \in \Theta = \mathbb{R}^n_{++}$ when prices for the $n \geq 2$ goods are given by $p^{(t)} \in \mathbb{R}^n_{++}$. Do continuous, convex, and increasing preferences for a consumer exist on Θ that are maximized for each t by the choice of $\theta^{(t)}$ among bundles $\theta \in \Theta$ that satisfy his budget constraint $p^{(t)} \cdot \theta \leq p^{(t)} \cdot \theta^{(t)}$? This states the problem in the form that is appropriate for analyzing a finite data set.

This problem is now abstracted to a continuum model in which the data set is the entire space Θ. For each $\theta^* \in \Theta$, a price vector $p(\theta^*)$ is specified such that the consumer purchases θ^* when prices are given by $p(\theta^*)$. A C^∞ mapping $p : \Theta \to \mathbb{R}^n_{++}$ is thus now postulated. At issue is whether or not there exist continuous, convex, and increasing preferences for the consumer on Θ relative to which each $\theta^* \in \Theta$ is optimal among all θ

---

[19] A statement holds *locally* if it is true in a neighborhood $O(\theta)$ of each $\theta \in \Theta$ and a statement holds *globally* if it is true throughout Θ. Precise statements of differentiability, integrability, and locality conditions are bypassed in this Introduction to focus attention on the relationship among *Distribution, Foliation,* and *Mapping* in Figure 1.4.

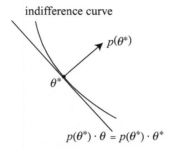

Figure 1.5. The commodity bundle θ^* is optimal for the consumer given the price vector $p(\theta^*)$ and his budget constraint $p(\theta^*) \cdot \theta \leq p(\theta^*) \cdot \theta^*$.

that satisfy the budget constraint $p(\theta^*) \cdot \theta \leq p(\theta^*) \cdot \theta^*$. This is depicted in Figure 1.5. In the terminology of consumer theory, is the given mapping p an *inverse demand mapping* for some selection of preferences, i.e., is $p(\theta^*)$ a price vector at which θ^* is the consumer's demand when $p(\theta^*) \cdot \theta^*$ is his income? The goal is now to determine necessary and sufficient conditions that distinguish inverse demand mappings from arbitrary mappings with domain Θ and range $\mathbb{R}^n_{++}$.

The problem can now be expressed in terms of the equivalence of Figure 1.4, with the given mapping p reformulated as *Distribution* and the step from *Distribution* to *Foliation* the key to solving for the desired preferences. As depicted in Figure 1.5, an $(n-1)$-dimensional plane (the consumer's budget hyperplane) is defined at each $\theta^* \in \Theta$ as the orthogonal set to $p(\theta^*)$,

$$p(\theta^*) \cdot (\theta - \theta^*) = 0. \tag{1.35}$$

The mapping p is in this sense expressed as *Distribution* with $c = 1$ and $d = n - 1$. Solving for the appropriate preferences is largely accomplished by the step in Figure 1.4 from *Distribution* to *Foliation*. As depicted in Figure 1.5, the $(n-1)$-dimensional submanifold of Θ that is tangent to the hyperplane (1.35) at each θ^* in the submanifold is an indifference surface of the preferences that are sought. The smoothness of p insures continuity of the preferences and $p(\theta) \in \mathbb{R}^n_{++}$ for all $\theta \in \Theta$ insures monotonicity. An additional condition on p is required to insure that the preferences are convex so that tangency between the indifference surface through θ^* and the budget hyperplane (1.35) implies the optimality of θ^*. This condition is discussed below and in Subsection 2.7.1. Notice that the requirement in *Foliation* that the submanifolds partition Θ means that distinct indifference surfaces do not intersect. This is standard in the theory of consumer behavior.

Passing from either *Distribution* or *Foliation* to *Mapping* is a step toward the construction of a utility function that represents the preferences. Some care is required in this step to insure that the resulting function $u_{(c)}$ of *Mapping* is increasing in each of its variables so that it can be interpreted as a utility function.

The Frobenius Theorem states an *integrability* condition on the hyper-planes of the form (1.35) or equivalently on the mapping p for the existence of an indifference surface through each θ^* that is tangent to the budget hyperplane (1.35) at θ^*. The integrability condition is necessary for a mapping p to represent inverse demand for a consumer. The integrability condition is well known within the theory of consumer behavior as symmetry of the Slutsky or Antonelli matrices. A set of sufficient conditions for rationalizing p as inverse demand consists of this integrability condition together with negative semidefiniteness of the Slutsky or Antonelli matrices, where the latter is a sufficient condition for convexity of the resulting preferences. These necessary and sufficient conditions constitute a local solution to the problem posed above. The integrability condition and the sufficient condition for convexity are developed in greater detail in Subsection 2.7.1.

1.4 Investigating Mechanisms Using Calculus

Aspects of the equivalence in Figure 1.4 that arise in the model of a mechanism are surveyed in this section. Establishing this equivalence and then applying it to examples are the main objectives of this text.

The Model
The first step is to restrict the model to a Euclidean form suitable for the use of calculus. Each agent i's parameter space Θ_i is now assumed to be an open subset of $\mathbb{R}^{d_i+c_i}$ for some $d_i, c_i \geq 0$, with

$$\theta_i \equiv (\theta_{i,t})_{1 \leq t \leq d_i+c_i}$$

denoting a generic element of Θ_i. Agent i's message space M_i is $\mathbb{R}^{c_i}$ with generic element m_i. Letting

$$d \equiv \sum_{i=1}^{n} d_i \text{ and } c \equiv \sum_{i=1}^{n} c_i,$$

$M \equiv \mathbb{R}^c$ is the message space with generic element

$$m \equiv (m_1, \ldots, m_n).$$

For a C^∞ mapping $\alpha_i : \Theta_i \times M \to \mathbb{R}^{c_i}$, the message correspondence $\mu_i(\theta)$ of agent i is the solution set in M of the system of c_i equations $\alpha_i(\theta_i, m) = 0$,

$$\mu_i(\theta) = \{m \,|\, \alpha_i(\theta_i, m) = 0\}.$$

As suggested in Section 1.1, $\alpha_i(\theta_i, m) = 0$ can be interpreted as the equilibrium state of a smooth or a discrete adjustment rule for agent i's message (i.e., $\alpha_i(\theta_i, m)$ is $\dot{m}(t)$ or $m(t+1) - m(t)$). Other interpretations are also possible. The equilibrium correspondence $\mu(\theta)$ of the message process consists of all solutions in M of the system of c equations,

$$\mu(\theta) = \{m \,|\, \alpha_i(\theta_i, m) = 0, 1 \le i \le n\}. \tag{1.36}$$

The components *Mapping*, *Distribution*, and *Foliation* of Figure 1.4 are now modified to reflect informational decentralization. Starting with *Mapping*, $\mu(\theta)$ is the solution set in $\mathbb{R}^c$ of c equations. With appropriate regularity assumptions on the model, the Implicit Function Theorem implies that this solution set is given locally by a C^∞ mapping $u_{(c)} : \Theta \to \mathbb{R}^c$, i.e.,

$$\mu(\theta) = \{u_{(c)}(\theta)\},$$

which will commonly be written as $\mu(\theta) = u_{(c)}(\theta)$. The subscript "$(c)$" serves as a reminder of the number of equations in the formula $u_{(c)}(\theta) = m$. Unlike *Mapping*, however, $u_{(c)}$ cannot be picked arbitrarily: reflecting the informational decentralization, $u_{(c)}(\theta) = m$ solves a system of the particular form in (1.36). As shown in this text, this is a substantial constraint on $u_{(c)}$. It is added below to *Mapping* of Figure 1.4 in order to investigate the consequences of informational decentralization.

Turning next to *Foliation* and *Distribution*, each m in the range of μ determines a level set $\mu^{-1}(m)$ in $\Theta \subset \mathbb{R}^{d+c}$, which (again with appropriate regularity assumptions) is a d-dimensional submanifold of Θ. With the assumption that μ is given by a mapping $u_{(c)} : \Theta \to \mathbb{R}^c$, these submanifolds partition Θ. A particular θ^* is in the submanifold $\mu^{-1}(m)$ if and only if each agent i's parameter θ_i^* satisfies the system of c_i equations $\alpha_i(\theta_i^*, m) = 0$. This system defines $\mu_i^{-1}(m)$ as a d_i-dimensional submanifold of Θ_i. The submanifold $\mu^{-1}(m)$ thus also reflects the information decentralization in that it is a Cartesian product of n submanifolds, each of which lies entirely within a single agent's parameter space:

$$\mu^{-1}(m) = \prod_{i=1}^{n} \{\theta_i \,|\, \alpha_i(\theta_i, m) = 0\} = \prod_{i=1}^{n} \mu_i^{-1}(m).$$

The tangent space to $\mu_i^{-1}(m)$ at each of its elements θ_i is a d_i-dimensional plane in $T_{\theta_i}\Theta_i$. The tangent space to $\mu^{-1}(m)$ thus also reflects the informational decentralization in that it is a *direct sum* of n tangent spaces, the ith of which lies entirely within the tangent space $T_\theta(\Theta_i \times \{\theta_{-i}\})$ to agent i's parameter space $\Theta_i \times \{\theta_{-i}\}$ through θ.

To summarize, informational decentralization alters *Distribution*, *Foliation*, and *Mapping* as follows:

>*Direct Sum:* A d-dimensional tangent plane is given at each point $\theta \in \Theta$, each of which is a direct sum of n tangent planes, the ith of which is d_i-dimensional and lies within $T_\theta(\Theta_i \times \{\theta_{-i}\})$.
>
>*Product Structure:* The space Θ is partitioned with d-dimensional submanifolds, each of which is a Cartesian product of n submanifolds, the ith of which is d_i-dimensional and lies within Θ_i.
>
>*Message Process:* A mapping $u_{(c)} : \Theta \to M$ is given that specifies for each $\theta \in \Theta$ the solution m to a system of equations $\alpha_i(\theta_i, m) = 0, 1 \le i \le n$, where for each i, $\alpha_i : \Theta_i \times M \to \mathbb{R}^{c_i}$.

The names of the three components of Figure 1.4 have been altered in each case to capture the effect of informational decentralization on the standard problem. They will be presented more formally in Chapter 3.

Discussion

The source of the mathematical difficulty of this text is the separation of parameters among the agents. This separation of parameters models informational decentralization, i.e., the dispersal of information among agents. In capturing the fundamental topic of interest in this model and in this text, this separation of parameters is inviolable in the analysis, which precludes arbitrary changes of coordinates in Θ. Such coordinate changes are commonly used in modern geometry to simplify functional forms, identify canonical structure, etc. Modern geometry is mainly "coordinate-free" in the sense that results should be independent of the local numbering of points so that they identify intrinsic properties of the geometric objects themselves and not the coordinates. While changes of coordinates within each agent i's parameter space Θ_i are permissible in this text, the coordinates of distinct Θ_i and Θ_j generally cannot be intermixed without undermining the purpose of the model. The separation of parameters among the agents is thus the constraint that distinguishes this text from most of modern geometry. It is this constraint that necessitates the development of the mathematical theory in Chapter 3.

The primary mathematical problem of this text is to establish the equivalence among *Direct Sum, Product Structure,* and *Message Process.* The value of establishing this equivalence lies in the significance of the model of decentralized communication that is depicted in Figure 1.1: just as the equivalence of *Distribution, Foliation,* and *Mapping* is fundamental to the study of differential equations, the equivalence of *Direct Sum, Product Structure,* and *Message Process* is fundamental to investigating the model of decentralized communication using calculus.

The value of this equivalence is illustrated by its use in constructing a mechanism that realizes a given objective, which is now summarized. Consistent with the calculus-based approach of this text, assume that the objective is a C^∞ mapping $F : \Theta \to \mathbb{R}^k$. Suppose that the mechanism $\mathcal{M} = (\Theta, M, (\mu_i)_{1 \le i \le n}, \zeta)$ realizes F. The realization equality $\zeta \circ \mu = F$ implies that

$$\mu^{-1}(\mu(\theta)) \subset F^{-1}(F(\theta))$$

for every $\theta \in \Theta$. This means that each submanifold $\mu^{-1}(m)$ in the *Product Structure* defined by $\mathcal{M}$ is contained within a level set of F. Constructing a mechanism that realizes F thus requires that one partition its level sets in the particular way described in *Product Structure.* *Direct Sum* "linearizes" this partitioning problem by expressing it in terms of derivatives, which ultimately allows this set-theoretic problem to be reformulated as a system of algebraic equations whose coefficients are determined by the derivatives of F. The partitioning problem is in this way made more tractable by following the first-order approach of calculus.

The realization problem will be discussed in more detail in Chapter 4. It should be clear at this point that *Direct Sum, Product Structure,* and *Message Process* are the mathematical language for the first-order approach to the problem of realization, in the same sense that matrices are the language of multivariable calculus. The equivalence of *Direct Sum, Product Structure,* and *Message Process* is therefore fundamental in applying calculus to mechanism construction.

1.4.1 Example: Selecting the Efficient Level of a Public Good for Restricted Valuation Functions

This example concerns a special case of the alternative mechanism of Subsection 1.2.2 within the Euclidean model of this text. The purpose of this example is to provide the reader with a better understanding of *Direct Sum, Product Structure,* and *Message Process* by expressing them in terms of a specific problem with explicit functional forms. This example is also intended to familiarize the reader with the notation for the Euclidean model.

The Model

Recall from Subsection 1.2.2 that each agent i's utility has the form

$$U_i(x, t_i) = V_i(x) + t_i,$$

where $x \in \mathbb{R}_+$ is a level of the public good, V_i is agent i's valuation function, and t_i is a monetary transfer to agent i. In a general analysis, the set of possible valuation functions for agent i need not be a subset of a finite dimensional Euclidean space. To place this example within the Euclidean model outlined above, restrict V_i to the form

$$V_i(x) = \theta_{i1} x + \theta_{i2} \log x, \tag{1.37}$$

where

$$0 < \theta_{i1} < 0.5 \text{ and } 0 < \theta_{i2}. \tag{1.38}$$

The upper bound on θ_{i1} is explained below. The set Θ_i in this example is therefore

$$\Theta_i = \left\{ \theta_i = (\theta_{i1}, \theta_{i2}) \in \mathbb{R}^2_{++} \mid \theta_{i1} < 0.5 \right\}. \tag{1.39}$$

The functional form (1.37) is selected purely to simplify the analysis that follows. As is commonly observed in mechanism design, however, there is no reason a priori to exclude valuation functions of the form (1.37). Such special cases can therefore provide insight into what may be required in addressing a more general case.

Formulas from Subsection 1.2.2 are next reduced to this special case. Given the restrictions in (1.38), functions of the form (1.37) are differentiable, increasing, and concave, as required in Subsection 1.2.2. Recall that the first-order condition (1.29) is necessary and sufficient for efficiency of the public good level x. Equation (1.29) can be solved in this setting for the efficient choice $f(\theta)$ in terms of $\theta = (\theta_1, \theta_2)$:

$$f(\theta) = \frac{\theta_{12} + \theta_{22}}{1 - (\theta_{11} + \theta_{21})}. \tag{1.40}$$

The condition $\theta_{i1} < 0.5$ for $i = 1, 2$ insures that $f(\theta) > 0$ as required in Subsection 1.2.2.

Consider now the alternative mechanism of Subsection 1.2.2 as defined in (1.30)–(1.34). Recall that $M_1 = M_2 = \mathbb{R}_{++}$. From (1.27), the necessary and sufficient first-order condition (1.28) for m_i to be the best response of agent i to m_{-i} is

$$\alpha_i(V_i, m) = \left(\theta_{i1} + \frac{\theta_{i2}}{m_1 + m_2} \right) - \frac{m_i}{m_1 + m_2} = 0$$

$$\Leftrightarrow \theta_{i1}(m_1 + m_2) + \theta_{i2} - m_i = 0. \tag{1.41}$$

Agent i's message correspondence μ_i is therefore

$$\mu_i(\theta_i) = \left\{ m \in \mathbb{R}^2_{++} \,|\, \theta_{i1}(m_1 + m_2) + \theta_{i2} - m_i = 0 \right\}. \tag{1.42}$$

As before, μ_i specifies the pairs (m_1, m_2) for which m_i is a best response to m_{-i} when θ_i determines agent i's valuation function V_i. The equilibrium correspondence of the mechanism is

$$\mu(\theta) = \mu_1(\theta_1) \cap \mu_2(\theta_2)$$

$$= \left\{ m \in \mathbb{R}^2_{++} \,|\, \theta_{i1}(m_1 + m_2) + \theta_{i2} - m_i = 0,\, i = 1, 2 \right\}. \tag{1.43}$$

This is the Nash equilibrium correspondence. Finally, recall that a Nash equilibrium necessarily produces an efficient level of the public good, i.e.,

$$m \in \mu(\theta) \Rightarrow m_1 + m_2 = f(\theta). \tag{1.44}$$

Direct Sum, Product Structure, and Message Process. Starting first with *Message Process*, substitution of $f(\theta)$ for $m_1 + m_2$ in Equation (1.41) that defines μ and solving for m_1 and m_2 produces

$$m_i = \theta_{i2} + \theta_{i1} f(\theta) \tag{1.45}$$

for $i = 1, 2$. The mapping $u_{(c)} : \Theta \rightarrow \mathbb{R}^2_{++}$ in *Message Process* is therefore

$$u_{(c)}(\theta) = (\theta_{12} + \theta_{11} f(\theta), \theta_{22} + \theta_{21} f(\theta)). \tag{1.46}$$

The "c" in $u_{(c)}$ is the dimension of this mapping's range and therefore equals 2 in this case.

Product Structure is considered next. For $m \in \mu(\Theta)$, $\mu_i^{-1}(m)$ is the line in Θ_i given by Equation (1.41). For $u_{(c)}(\theta^*) = m^*$, the d-dimensional submanifold through θ^* is the level set

$$u_{(c)}^{-1}(m^*) = \mu^{-1}(m^*)$$

$$= \mu_1^{-1}(m^*) \times \mu_2^{-1}(m^*)$$

$$= \left\{ \theta_1 \,|\, \theta_{11}(m_1^* + m_2^*) + \theta_{12} - m_1^* = 0 \right\}$$

$$\times \left\{ \theta_2 \,|\, \theta_{21}(m_1^* + m_2^*) + \theta_{22} - m_2^* = 0 \right\}. \tag{1.47}$$

It is thus a $d = 2$-dimensional plane. Each line lies within an agent's parameter space, as required in *Product Structure*.

The set

$$\left\{\mu_1^{-1}(m) \times \mu_2^{-1}(m) \,|\, m \in \mu(\Theta)\right\} = \left\{\mu^{-1}(m) | m \in \mu(\Theta)\right\}$$

partitions Θ because each $\mu(\theta)$ is a singleton. This is the partition described in *Product Structure*.

Notice that the set

$$\left\{\mu_i^{-1}(m) \,|\, m \in \mu_i(\Theta)\right\}$$

does not partition Θ_i because there are a multitude of different lines of the form (1.41) for $m \in \mu_i(\Theta)$ that pass through a given θ_i. As a general fact in this text, the set

$$\left\{\mu_i^{-1}(m) \,|\, m \in \mu_i(\Theta)\right\}$$

need not partition Θ_i because each $\mu_i(\theta_i)$ may contain multiple values of m. This observation suggests the richness and potential complexity of *Product Structure*: while *Product Structure* posits a partition of Θ using Cartesian product subsets, it does not stipulate a unique partition of each individual's parameter space Θ_i. *Product Structure* is thus not as simple as it may first appear.

Product Structure to this point in the example has been message indexed. It can be expressed in terms of the state by substituting $u_{(c)}(\theta^*) = m^*$. In the notation of Section 1.2,

$$S_i^*(\theta^*) = \mu_i^{-1}(u_{(c)}(\theta^*))$$
$$= \left\{\theta_i \,\left|\, (\theta_{i1} - \theta_{i1}^*) f(\theta^*) + \theta_{i2} - \theta_{i2}^* = 0\right.\right\}$$

and $S(\theta^*) = S_1^*(\theta^*) \times S_2^*(\theta^*)$. The set $S_i^*(\theta^*)$ depends on θ_{-i}^* through the value of $f(\theta^*)$, which again indicates the potential richness of *Product Structure*.

Finally, *Direct Sum* is particularly simple in this example because the manifolds of *Product Structure* are planes. Consider θ^* in the plane (1.47) determined by m^*. The direction of the line

$$\theta_{i1}\left(m_1^* + m_2^*\right) + \theta_{i2} - m_i^* = 0$$

in Θ_i through θ_i^* is given by the vector $(-1, m_1^* + m_2^*)$. The distribution D at θ^* is therefore $D_1 \oplus D_2$, where $D_1(\theta_1^*)$ is the line in $\mathbb{R}^4$ spanned by $(-1, m_1^* + m_2^*, 0, 0)$ and $D_2(\theta_2^*)$ is the line spanned by $(0, 0, -1, m_1^* + m_2^*)$.

Again, this can be expressed directly in terms of the state θ^* by replacing $m^* = (m_1^*, m_2^*)$ with $u_{(c)}(\theta^*)$ as given by (1.46).

1.5 Overview of Text

This text is intended to be accessible to most economic theorists. While it assumes that the reader is familiar with manifolds, it assumes no knowledge of integrability and the Frobenius Theorem, which are the fundamental mathematical topics here. The text is thus organized as follows. The classic problem that is depicted in Figure 1.4 is formalized in Chapter 2. Some fundamental concepts of calculus on manifolds are introduced in this chapter that are needed to study the model of mechanisms. Because this material is more extensively covered in a number of mathematics texts, proofs are discussed in this chapter only to the extent that doing so will help the reader to gain a deeper understanding of the work that follows concerning mechanisms. Chapter 2 is thus not intended to be a comprehensive treatment of these concepts. Spivak (1979) and Warner (1971) are among the best of the references for these topics. Specific results from these texts are cited wherever appropriate to compensate for the brevity of Chapter 2.

Chapter 3 concerns the model of mechanisms from a calculus perspective. Two examples are first presented to illustrate *Direct Sum, Product Structure,* and *Message Process.* After these three concepts are formalized, an extension of the Frobenius Theorem is proven that addresses the constraint of informational decentralization. This theorem is then applied to establish the local equivalence of *Direct Sum, Product Structure,* and *Message Process.* The limited sense in which this equivalence holds globally is also discussed.

Finally, in Chapter 4 this equivalence is applied to establish the first-order approach to constructing a mechanism that realizes a given real-valued C^∞ mapping F. This approach makes it possible to bound below the dimension of the message space needed to realize a given real-valued function f in terms of its derivatives, and also to characterize the mechanisms that realize a generic mapping F. These two results are then applied in a variety of economic models.

2

Classical Concepts and Results

There are three topics in this chapter: (i) integrability, which is a necessary and sufficient condition for the local equivalence of *Distribution, Foliation,* and *Mapping*; (ii) the Frobenius Theorem, which is the fundamental result for establishing this local equivalence; (iii) the obstacles to extending this local equivalence globally. An understanding of each of these three topics is needed for the discussion in Chapter 3 of the issues that arise from informational decentralization.

2.1 *Distribution, Foliation,* and *Mapping*

Let Θ denote an open subset of $\mathbb{R}^{d+c}$ for some $c, d > 0$. A *local coordinate system* at $\theta^* \in \Theta$ is a C^∞, nonsingular, one-to-one mapping u from an open neighborhood $O(\theta^*)$ of θ^* onto $(-\varepsilon, \varepsilon)^{d+c} \subset \mathbb{R}^{d+c}$ for some $\varepsilon > 0$ such that $u(\theta^*) = 0$. Given a mapping

$$u = (u_1, \ldots, u_{d+c}) : \Theta \to \mathbb{R}^{d+c},$$

define mappings $u_{(d)} : \Theta \to \mathbb{R}^d$ and $u_{(c)} : \Theta \to \mathbb{R}^c$ as $u_{(d)} \equiv (u_i)_{1 \le i \le d}$ and $u_{(c)} \equiv (u_i)_{d+1 \le i \le d+c}$. The mapping u can thus be written as $u = (u_{(d)}, u_{(c)})$. Similarly, a point $\theta \in \Theta$ will sometimes be written as $\theta = (\theta_{(d)}, \theta_{(c)})$, where $\theta_{(d)} \equiv (\theta_i)_{1 \le i \le d}$ and $\theta_{(c)} \equiv (\theta_i)_{d+1 \le i \le d+c}$.

Turning now to the main subject of this section, *Distribution, Foliation,* and *Mapping* in Figure 1.4 are now stated formally:

Distribution: A d-dimensional, integrable, C^∞ distribution $\mathcal{D}$ is defined on the open set $\Theta \subset \mathbb{R}^{d+c}$.

Foliation: The parameter space Θ can be expressed as the disjoint union of d-dimensional, C^∞ submanifolds of Θ, with the property that a C^∞

35

distribution $\mathcal{D}$ is defined by setting $\mathcal{D}(\theta)$ equal to the d-dimensional tangent plane to the unique submanifold that passes through θ.

Mapping: A C^∞ nonsingular mapping $u_{(c)} : \Theta \to \mathbb{R}^c$ is given.

Turning first to the terminology in *Distribution*, a C^∞ *vector field X on* Θ is a C^∞ mapping $X(\cdot)$ on Θ such that $X(\theta) \in T_\theta\Theta$ for each $\theta \in \Theta$. A vector field can be interpreted geometrically as assigning a vector to each point in Θ. A d-*dimensional distribution* $\mathcal{D}$ on Θ is a mapping that specifies a d-dimensional vector subspace of $T_\theta\Theta$ at each point $\theta \in \Theta$. A *vector field X lies in* $\mathcal{D}$ (or $X \in \mathcal{D}$) if $X(\theta) \in \mathcal{D}(\theta)$ for every $\theta \in \Theta$. The distribution $\mathcal{D}$ is C^∞ if there exists dC^∞ vector fields on Θ such that the vectors form a basis of the distribution at every point. A distribution is *integrable* if any pair of vector fields that lie within the distribution $\mathcal{D}$ satisfy a particular equation that is discussed below.

Turning now to *Foliation,* a *submanifold* of Θ *of dimension d* is a manifold $S \subset \Theta$ that has the following property:[1] for every $\theta^* \in S$, there exists a local coordinate system $u : O(\theta^*) \to \mathbb{R}^{d+c}$ such that

$$S \cap O(\theta^*) = u_{(c)}^{-1}(0). \tag{2.1}$$

An *integral manifold* of the distribution $\mathcal{D}$ through θ^* is a d-dimensional submanifold S of Θ containing the point θ^* whose tangent at any point θ in S is $\mathcal{D}(\theta)$.

The term "integrable" for the equation that vector fields within a distribution may satisfy is motivated by the Frobenius Theorem, which states that this equation is a necessary and sufficient condition for the existence of an integral manifold of the distribution through any point in Θ. This is the equivalence of *Distribution* and *Foliation*; the additional step of proving equivalence with *Mapping* follows locally from property (2.1) of a submanifold. The equation (or *integrability condition*) is thus the necessary and

---

[1] More precisely, this is the definition of an *imbedded* C^∞ submanifold. A C^∞ submanifold of Θ is a subset of Θ that has the structure of a manifold; "imbedded" refers to the existence of a mapping $u_{(c)}$ with the above property at each $\theta^* \in S$. The existence at each θ^* of such a mapping $u_{(c)}$ is in most treatments derived from a formal definition of an imbedded C^∞ submanifold as the image of a manifold H under an "imbedding" $i : H \to \mathbb{R}^{d+c}$. An *imbedding* i is a smooth one-to-one mapping that is a homeomorphism from H onto $i(H)$, where $i(H)$ has the topology induced from $\mathbb{R}^{d+c}$. I have chosen to use the equivalent definition of an imbedded C^∞ manifold that is given above because it is best suited to the purposes of this chapter. See Spivak (1979, pp. 62–65) or Warner (1971, pp. 22–29) for a thorough treatment of this subject. In particular, property (2.1) is discussed in Warner (1971, pp. 28–29), and Spivak (1979, p. 65) also uses "submanifold" to refer to an imbedded C^∞ submanifold. Property (2.1) will matter crucially in the discussions in Sections 2.7 and 3.6 of the sense in which *Distribution*⇒*Foliation* and *Direct Sum*⇒*Product Structure* hold globally.

sufficient condition for solving a differential equation in the geometric and analytic senses of Figure 1.4. The integrability condition will be discussed in the next three sections, followed by a discussion of the Frobenius Theorem in Section 2.4. Chapter 2 then concludes with a discussion of the difficulties encountered in trying to globalize the equivalence of *Distribution, Foliation,* and *Mapping.*

Before formalizing integrability in Section 2.2, it is worth pointing out the sense in which *Distribution* and *Foliation* restrict both Figure 1.4 and the general problem addressed in this book to fit the mathematical theory that is used here. The differentiability[2] of the distribution $\mathcal{D}$ is a key restriction in *Distribution* and *Foliation* above that is not stated in Figure 1.4. While differentiability is fundamental to the mathematical theory in this text, it is inessential both to the relationship depicted in Figure 1.4 and to the broader aims of the Hurwicz–Reiter research program concerning informational decentralization. This is illustrated by the following simple example.

2.1.1 Example: A Discontinuous Distribution $\mathcal{D}$ for Which the Equivalence in Figure 1.4 Holds

Let Θ be the open square

$$\Theta = \{(\theta_1, \theta_2) | 1 < \theta_1 < 2, 0 < \theta_2 < 1\}. \tag{2.2}$$

Define the 1-dimensional distribution $\mathcal{D}$ as the span of the vector field X, where

$$X(\theta) = \begin{cases} (1, 0) & \text{if } \theta_1 < \frac{3}{2}, \\ (0, 1) & \text{if } \theta_1 \geq \frac{3}{2}. \end{cases} \tag{2.3}$$

This vector field is discontinuous along the line $\theta_1 = 3/2$. An integral manifold of $\mathcal{D}$ exists through each $\theta^* = (\theta_1^*, \theta_2^*) \in \Theta$, however: if $\theta_1^* < 3/2$, then an integral manifold of $\mathcal{D}$ through θ^* is the horizontal open segment defined by $\theta_2 = \theta_2^*$, and if $\theta_1^* \geq 3/2$, then an integral manifold of $\mathcal{D}$ through θ^* is the vertical open segment defined by $\theta_1 = \theta_1^*$. Some integral manifolds of $\mathcal{D}$ are depicted in Figure 2.1. A function $u_{(c)}$ whose level sets are these integral manifolds is

$$u_{(c)}(\theta) = \begin{cases} \theta_2 & \text{if } \theta_1 < \frac{3}{2}, \\ \theta_1 & \text{if } \theta_1 \geq \frac{3}{2}. \end{cases} \tag{2.4}$$

---

[2] Much of the analysis that follows in this text could be carried out by assuming a weaker notion of differentiability than C^∞. The assumption of C^∞ is made here to avoid diverting attention throughout the text with a tedious bookkeeping of degrees of differentiability.

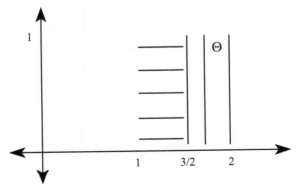

Figure 2.1. The integral manifolds of the distribution $\mathcal{D}$ in Subsection 2.1.1.

This example lies outside the mathematical theory developed in this text even though it illustrates the equivalence depicted in Figure 1.4. *Distribution and Mapping* as stated in Section 2.1 require that the distribution $\mathcal{D}$ and the mapping $u_{(c)}$ are smooth, which is not the case here. Notice also that *Foliation* as stated in Figure 1.4 assumes differentiability to the extent that the parameter space Θ is partitioned by smooth submanifolds of the same dimension. The partition in this example has this property. The formal statement of *Foliation* in Section 2.1 goes further, however, by requiring that the tangent space to these submanifolds varies smoothly not only along any one of the submanifolds in the partition (as it does in the example) but also throughout Θ (which is not true here).

2.2 Integrability

The standard basis of $\mathbb{R}^{d+c}$ defines $d + c$ vector fields,

$$\frac{\partial}{\partial \theta_1}, \dots, \frac{\partial}{\partial \theta_{d+c}}, \tag{2.5}$$

where $\partial/\partial \theta_i$ is a unit vector that points in the θ_i-direction at any point $\theta \in \Theta$. Any C^∞ vector field can be written as a linear combination of these vector fields using $d + c$ C^∞ real-valued functions on Θ as coefficients.

Definition 1: *Consider any two C^∞ vector fields*

$$X = \sum_{i=1}^{d+c} a_i(\theta) \frac{\partial}{\partial \theta_i} \quad and \quad Y = \sum_{i=1}^{d+c} b_i(\theta) \frac{\partial}{\partial \theta_i}.$$

The **Lie bracket** $[X, Y]$ of X and Y is the vector field on Θ defined by the formula

$$[X, Y] \equiv \sum_{j=1}^{d+c} \left(\sum_{i=1}^{d+c} a_i \frac{\partial b_j}{\partial \theta_i} - b_i \frac{\partial a_j}{\partial \theta_i} \right) \frac{\partial}{\partial \theta_j}. \tag{2.6}$$

The value of the vector field $[X, Y]$ at θ is denoted as $[X, Y](\theta)$.

The Lie bracket has some useful properties. It is easy to show using formula (2.6) that the Lie bracket is both *bilinear* and *skew-symmetric*:

Bilinearity: For any real numbers a and b, and any vector fields X, Y, and Z, $[aX + bY, Z] = a[X, Z] + b[Y, Z]$ and $[Z, aX + bY] = a[Z, X] + b[Z, Y]$.

Skew-symmetry: For any two vector fields X and Y, $[X, Y] = -[Y, X]$.

Skew-symmetry implies that $[X, X] = 0$ for any vector field X. The Lie bracket is also preserved under smooth mappings: given a C^∞ mapping $h : \Theta \to \mathbb{R}^k$ and letting $D_\theta h(\theta)$ denote the derivative of h at θ, the mapping h *preserves the Lie bracket* in the sense that

$$D_\theta h([X, Y])(\theta) = [D_\theta h(X), D_\theta h(Y)](h(\theta)) \tag{2.7}$$

for all θ.[3]

It is now possible to formally define the term "integrable", which is used in *Distribution*. A d-dimensional C^∞ distribution $\mathcal{D}$ is *integrable*[4] on Θ if the Lie bracket of any two vector fields that lie within $\mathcal{D}$ also lies within $\mathcal{D}$:

Definition 2: *The distribution $\mathcal{D}$ is* **integrable** *if and only if*

$$X, Y \in \mathcal{D} \Rightarrow [X, Y] \in \mathcal{D}. \tag{2.8}$$

Given vector fields $\{X_1, \ldots, X_d\}$ that define a basis for $\mathcal{D}$ at each θ, a necessary and sufficient condition for the integrability of $\mathcal{D}$ is that

$$[X_i, X_j] \in \mathcal{D} \tag{2.9}$$

for all $1 \le i, j \le d$.[5] The integrability of $\mathcal{D}$ thus reduces to a condition on any basis of $\mathcal{D}$, which makes it easier to verify integrability.

---

[3] See Spivak (1979, Prop. 3, p. 259) or Warner (1971, Prop. 1.55, p. 41).

[4] The term "involutive" is synonymous with "integrable" and is sometimes used in the literature (e.g., see Warner, 1971, p. 42).

[5] See Spivak (1979, Prop. 4, p. 261).

2.2.1 Example: Integrability and the Equality of Mixed Partials

With the goal of providing some insight into the integrability condition (2.8), consider the special case of $c = 1$, i.e., a d-dimensional distribution $\mathcal{D}$ in a $(d + 1)$-dimensional parameter space Θ. The mapping $u_{(c)}$ of *Mapping* is in this case a real-valued function whose level set at each point $\theta \in \Theta$ has $\mathcal{D}(\theta)$ as its tangent and whose gradient $\nabla u_{(c)}(\theta)$ at θ is perpendicular to $\mathcal{D}(\theta)$. There is a familiar mixed partial condition on a gradient that is necessary and sufficient for the local solvability of a partial differential equation. The integrability condition (2.8) is shown below to be strictly weaker than this mixed partial condition, reflecting the fact that integrating a distribution of codimension 1 is a relaxation of the problem of integrating a gradient.

Consider first the case of $c = d = 1$, i.e., a 1-dimensional distribution $\mathcal{D}$ on $\mathbb{R}^2$. Let the vector field $Y(\theta) \equiv (b_1(\theta), b_2(\theta))$ span $\mathcal{D}$. Skew-symmetry of the Lie bracket implies that $[Y, Y](\theta) = 0 \in \mathcal{D}(\theta)$ at every $\theta \in \Theta$, and the distribution $\mathcal{D}$ trivially satisfies the integrability condition.[6] If the equivalence depicted in Figure 1.4 is momentarily taken for granted, then for any $\theta \in \Theta$ there exists a function $u_{(c)}$ defined on a neighborhood of θ^* whose level sets are the integral manifolds of $\mathcal{D}$. Turning now to the problem of integrating a vector field, select a vector field $Z(\theta) \equiv (a_1(\theta), a_2(\theta))$ that is normal to $Y(\theta)$ and hence $\mathcal{D}(\theta)$ at every θ. There exists a function $u_{(c)}$ defined on a neighborhood of θ^* such that $\nabla u_{(c)}(\theta) = Z(\theta)$ if and only if Z satisfies the *mixed partial condition*

$$\frac{\partial a_1}{\partial \theta_2} = \frac{\partial a_2}{\partial \theta_1} \tag{2.10}$$

in some neighborhood of θ^*. Any 1-dimensional distribution $\mathcal{D}$ is integrable, which is not the case with each vector field Z. Integrating a gradient $Z(\theta)$ means finding a function $u_{(c)}(\theta)$ on some open subset of Θ whose gradient is $Z(\theta)$, while integrating a distribution that is perpendicular to $Z(\theta)$ means finding a function $u_{(c)}(\theta)$ on some open subset of Θ whose gradient points *in the same direction* as $Z(\theta)$. In this sense, integrating a distribution relaxes the problem of integrating a gradient, and the necessary and sufficient condition for integrating a distribution is thus weaker than the mixed partial condition.

---

[6] This argument shows that any 1-dimensional C^∞ distribution on $\mathbb{R}^{1+c}$ is integrable, regardless of the value of c.

Turning next to the case of an arbitrary value of d, let

$$Z(\theta) \equiv \sum_{i=1}^{d+c} a_i(\theta) \frac{\partial}{\partial \theta_i} \tag{2.11}$$

be a nonzero vector field that is normal to the distribution $\mathcal{D}(\theta)$ at each $\theta \in \Theta$. I now show that if Z satisfies the mixed partial condition, then the distribution $\mathcal{D}$ is integrable. The mixed partial condition is

$$\frac{\partial a_i}{\partial \theta_j} = \frac{\partial a_j}{\partial \theta_i} \tag{2.12}$$

for all $1 \leq i, j \leq d + c$. By assumption, near any $\theta' \in \Theta$ at least one $a_j(\theta)$ is nonzero. For notational convenience, we assume that $a_1(\theta) \neq 0$ near θ'. One basis for $\mathcal{D}(\theta)$ is

$$X_i(\theta) \equiv \left\{ a_i(\theta) \frac{\partial}{\partial \theta_1} - a_1(\theta) \frac{\partial}{\partial \theta_i} \,|\, 2 \leq i \leq d + c \right\}. \tag{2.13}$$

The distribution $\mathcal{D}$ is integrable if and only if $[X_i(\theta), X_j(\theta)] \in \mathcal{D}(\theta)$ for all $2 \leq i, j \leq d + c$. Applying formula (2.6), the Lie bracket $[X_i, X_j]$ reduces to

$$[X_i, X_j] = \left(a_i \frac{\partial a_j}{\partial \theta_1} - a_1 \frac{\partial a_j}{\partial \theta_i} - a_j \frac{\partial a_i}{\partial \theta_1} + a_1 \frac{\partial a_i}{\partial \theta_j} \right) \frac{\partial}{\partial \theta_1} \tag{2.14}$$

$$+ \left(a_j \frac{\partial a_1}{\partial \theta_1} - a_1 \frac{\partial a_1}{\partial \theta_j} \right) \frac{\partial}{\partial \theta_i} + \left(-a_i \frac{\partial a_1}{\partial \theta_1} + a_1 \frac{\partial a_1}{\partial \theta_i} \right) \frac{\partial}{\partial \theta_j}.$$

The vector $[X_i, X_j]$ lies in the span of the basis given in (2.13) if and only if it is orthogonal to $Z(\theta)$. Taking the inner product $[X_i, X_j] \cdot Z$ and then rearranging terms, it follows that $\mathcal{D}$ is integrable if and only if

$$0 = a_1^2 \left(\frac{\partial a_i}{\partial \theta_j} - \frac{\partial a_j}{\partial \theta_i} \right) + a_1 a_i \left(\frac{\partial a_j}{\partial \theta_1} - \frac{\partial a_1}{\partial \theta_j} \right) + a_1 a_j \left(\frac{\partial a_1}{\partial \theta_i} - \frac{\partial a_i}{\partial \theta_1} \right) \tag{2.15}$$

for all $2 \leq i, j \leq d + c$. The distribution $\mathcal{D}$ is thus integrable if Z satisfies the mixed partial condition.

The converse is false: an arbitrary vector field Z that is orthogonal to an integrable distribution $\mathcal{D}$ need not satisfy the mixed partial condition.[7] The Frobenius Theorem implies the existence locally of a function $u_{(c)}(\theta)$ such

---

[7] This is clear from noting that if a vector field Z exists that is orthogonal to $\mathcal{D}$ and also satisfies the mixed partial condition, then (i) every multiple $\lambda(\theta) \cdot Z(\theta)$ is also orthogonal to $Z(\theta)$, and (ii) every such multiple will not necessarily satisfy the mixed partial condition.

that $\nabla u_{(c)}(\theta)$ is perpendicular to $\mathcal{D}$. Integrability thus implies the existence of a multiple $\lambda(\theta) \cdot Z(\theta) = \nabla u_{(c)}(\theta)$ of the given vector field Z that satisfies the mixed partial condition.

2.3 A Geometric Interpretation of Integrability

Integrability is discussed in this section from a geometric perspective in the simple case of a 2-dimensional distribution $\mathcal{D}$ in $\mathbb{R}^3$ (i.e., $d = 2$ and $c = 1$). The following definition is needed for this discussion and in the remainder of the chapter. Given a C^∞ vector field X on Θ, an initial point $\theta^* \in \Theta$ determines a curve in Θ that is obtained by following the vector field X away from θ^* both forward in the direction of X and backward in the direction of $-X$. Formally, for a given θ^*, an *integral curve of* X *through* θ^* is a mapping

$$\rho(X, \theta^*, \cdot) : (a, b) \subset \mathbb{R} \cup \{-\infty, +\infty\} \to \mathbb{R}^{d+c} \qquad (2.16)$$

such that (i) $0 \in (a, b)$, (ii) $\rho(X, \theta^*, 0) = \theta^*$, and (iii) $d\rho/dt = X(\rho(X, \theta^*, t))$ for all $t \in (a, b)$. An integral curve of X through θ^* exists for each choice of θ^*. It is unique in the sense that any other mapping

$$\varpi(X, \theta^*, \cdot) : (a', b') \to \mathbb{R}^{d+c} \qquad (2.17)$$

for which $0 \in (a', b')$ and $d\varpi/dt = X(\varpi(X, \theta^*, t))$ for $t \in (a', b')$ necessarily satisfies

$$\rho(X, \theta^*, t) = \varpi(X, \theta^*, t) \qquad (2.18)$$

for $t \in (a, b) \cap (a', b')$.[8]

Turning now to the case of a 2-dimensional distribution $\mathcal{D}$ in $\mathbb{R}^3$, suppose the C^∞ vector fields X and Y lie within $\mathcal{D}$ and are linearly independent near $\theta' \in \Theta$. Start at the point θ' and trace out a small, four-sided path in the following way. As depicted in Figure 2.2a, follow the integral curve $\rho(X, \theta', \cdot)$ in the direction of X to the point $\theta^{(1)}$, then switch and follow the integral curve $\rho(Y, \theta^{(1)}, \cdot)$ in the direction of Y to the point $\theta^{(2)}$, then follow the integral curve $\rho(X, \theta^{(2)}, \cdot)$ in the direction of $-X$ to the point $\theta^{(3)}$, and finally follow an integral curve $\rho(Y, \theta^{(3)}, \cdot)$ in the direction of $-Y$ to the point $\theta^{(4)}$. If an integral manifold of $\mathcal{D}$ through θ' exists, then this

---

[8] Existence and uniqueness of integral curves is developed in Spivak (1979, pp. 188–198) and Warner, (1971, pp. 36–37).

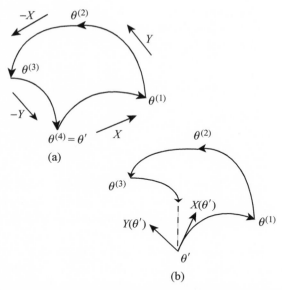

Figure 2.2. The vector fields X and Y lie within the distribution $\mathcal{D}$. As depicted in (a), if $\mathcal{D}$ is integrable, then it is possible to start at any point θ' and trace out a "curvy rectangle" by following the integral curves of X and Y. As depicted in (b), it may not be possible to do this if $\mathcal{D}$ is not integrable.

four-sided path lies entirely within this integral manifold because X and Y both lie within $\mathcal{D}$. By traversing appropriate distances along the four sides of the path, it is possible in this way to construct a "curvy rectangle" in the integral manifold that has θ' as a corner (i.e., $\theta' = \theta^{(4)}$). If an integral manifold through $\mathcal{D}$ does not exist, however, then it may not be possible to construct a rectangle in this way. This is illustrated in Figure 2.2(b).

2.3.1 Example: Integrable and Nonintegrable Distributions

Let the parameter space Θ be the subset of $\mathbb{R}^3$ defined by $\theta_1 > 0$. Consider first the distribution $\mathcal{D}$ that is defined at any point $\theta \in \Theta$ as the span of the vector fields $X(\theta)$ and $Y(\theta)$, where

$$X(\theta) \equiv -\theta_2 \frac{\partial}{\partial \theta_1} + \theta_1 \frac{\partial}{\partial \theta_2}, \tag{2.19}$$

$$Y(\theta) \equiv \frac{-\theta_3 \theta_1}{\sqrt{\theta_1^2 + \theta_2^2}} \frac{\partial}{\partial \theta_1} - \frac{-\theta_3 \theta_2}{\sqrt{\theta_1^2 + \theta_2^2}} \frac{\partial}{\partial \theta_2} + \sqrt{\theta_1^2 + \theta_2^2} \frac{\partial}{\partial \theta_3}. \tag{2.20}$$

One can show using formula (2.6) that $[X, Y] = 0 \in \mathcal{D}$ at every $\theta \in \Theta$, and so the distribution $\mathcal{D}$ is integrable. Alternatively, notice that $X(\theta)$ and $Y(\theta)$ are both orthogonal to the vector field

$$Z(\theta) \equiv \theta_1 \frac{\partial}{\partial \theta_1} + \theta_2 \frac{\partial}{\partial \theta_2} + \theta_3 \frac{\partial}{\partial \theta_3}, \tag{2.21}$$

which is the gradient of

$$f(\theta) = \frac{1}{2} \left(\theta_1^2 + \theta_2^2 + \theta_3^2 \right). \tag{2.22}$$

The integral manifolds of $\mathcal{D}$ are thus the level sets of f, which are the surfaces of spheres in Θ of arbitrary radius centered at the origin. By the Frobenius Theorem, the existence of integrable manifolds of $\mathcal{D}$ implies $[X, Y] \in \mathcal{D}$.

The vector field X was chosen so that its integral curve through a point $\theta^* \in \Theta$ that is γ units from the origin is the line of latitude through θ^* on the sphere of radius γ. Similarly, the integral curve of Y through θ^* is the line of longitude through θ^* on this sphere. These integral curves are parametrized as follows. Let $\pi(\theta_1, \theta_2) \equiv (r, \tau)$ be the mapping that represents the point (θ_1, θ_2) in polar coordinates,

$$\pi(\theta_1, \theta_2) = (r, \tau) \Leftrightarrow \begin{cases} \theta_1 = r \cos(\tau), \\ \theta_2 = r \sin(\tau), \end{cases} \tag{2.23}$$

and let $\sigma(\theta_1, \theta_2, \theta_3) = (\gamma, \varphi, \tau)$ be the mapping that represents the point $(\theta_1, \theta_2, \theta_3)$ in spherical coordinates,

$$\sigma(\theta_1, \theta_2, \theta_3) = (\gamma, \varphi, \tau) \Leftrightarrow \begin{cases} \theta_1 = \gamma \sin(\varphi) \cos(\tau), \\ \theta_2 = \gamma \sin(\varphi) \sin(\tau), \\ \theta_3 = \gamma \cos(\tau). \end{cases} \tag{2.24}$$

In particular, for the given point $\theta^* = (\theta_1^*, \theta_2^*, \theta_3^*)$, let $\pi(\theta_1^*, \theta_2^*) = (r^*, \tau^*)$ and $\sigma(\theta_1^*, \theta_2^*, \theta_3^*) = (\gamma^*, \varphi^*, \tau^*)$. The integral curve $\rho(X, \theta^*, t)$ determined by θ^* is given by the equations

$$\theta_1(t) = r^* \cos(t + \tau^*),$$
$$\theta_2(t) = r^* \sin(t + \tau^*), \tag{2.25}$$
$$\theta_3(t) = \theta_3^*.$$

These equations imply that a change Δt in t causes a change in longitude on the sphere of radius γ^* of Δt radians along a line of latitude in the direction

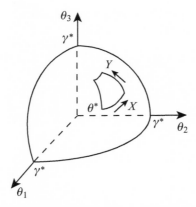

Figure 2.3. Lines of longitude and latitude define Euclidean coordinates near any point θ^* on the sphere.

determined by X. The integral curve $\rho(Y, \theta^*, t)$ of Y determined by θ^* is given by the equations

$$\theta_1(t) = \gamma^* \sin(\varphi^* - t) \cos(\tau^*),$$

$$\theta_2(t) = \gamma^* \sin(\varphi^* - t) \sin(\tau^*), \qquad (2.26)$$

$$\theta_3(t) = \gamma^* \cos(\varphi^* - t).$$

In these equations, a change Δt in t causes a change in latitude on the sphere of radius γ^* of Δt radians along a line of longitude in the direction determined by Y. As illustrated in Figure 2.3, one can trace out a rectangle of the form described above on the integral surface of $\mathcal{D}$ through θ^* by following lines of latitude and longitude in the indicated directions.

The condition $[X, Y] = 0$ that is satisfied here is in general a necessary and sufficient condition for the integral curves $\rho(X, \cdot, \cdot)$ and $\rho(Y, \cdot, \cdot)$ to define a local coordinate system near θ^* for the integral manifold through θ^*. In this example, the coordinates defined by X and Y for a point θ near θ^* are the radians of longitude and latitude that measure how far θ is from θ^* on the surface of the sphere of radius γ^*. In the case of an arbitrary 2-dimensional integral manifold, the coordinates (w_1, w_2) are assigned to a point θ^{**} near θ^* if θ^{**} is reached by starting at θ^* and following the integral of X through θ^* from $t = 0$ to $t = w_1$ and then following the integral curve of Y through $\rho(X, \theta^*, w_1)$ from $t = 0$ to $t = w_2$. The equation $[X, Y] = 0$ is a necessary and sufficient condition to insure that this numbering of points near θ^* is unambiguous. This will be discussed in more detail in Section 2.5.

The distribution $\mathcal{D}$ in this example is now altered so that it is no longer integrable. The vector field X^* is defined as

$$X^*(\theta) \equiv X - Y + \sqrt{\theta_1^2 + \theta_2^2}\, \frac{\partial}{\partial \theta_3}$$

$$= \left(-\theta_2 + \frac{\theta_3 \theta_1}{\sqrt{\theta_1^2 + \theta_2^2}} \right) \frac{\partial}{\partial \theta_1} + \left(\theta_1 + \frac{\theta_3 \theta_2}{\sqrt{\theta_1^2 + \theta_2^2}} \right) \frac{\partial}{\partial \theta_2}. \quad (2.27)$$

Define the distribution $\mathcal{D}^*(\theta)$ as the span of $\{X^*(\theta), Y(\theta)\}$ at every $\theta \in \Theta$. The bilinearity of the Lie bracket together with $[X, Y] = 0$ imply that

$$[X^*, Y] = \left[X - Y + \sqrt{\theta_1^2 + \theta_2^2}\, \frac{\partial}{\partial \theta_3}, Y \right]$$

$$= [X, Y] - [Y, Y] + \left[\sqrt{\theta_1^2 + \theta_2^2}\, \frac{\partial}{\partial \theta_3}, Y \right]$$

$$= \left[\sqrt{\theta_1^2 + \theta_2^2}\, \frac{\partial}{\partial \theta_3}, Y \right]. \quad (2.28)$$

Applying (2.6) and then simplifying produces

$$[X^*, Y] = -\theta_1 \frac{\partial}{\partial \theta_1} - \theta_2 \frac{\partial}{\partial \theta_2} + \theta_3 \frac{\partial}{\partial \theta_3}. \quad (2.29)$$

It is straightforward to show (e.g., by taking a determinant) that $[X^*, Y](\theta)$ does not lie in the span of $\{X^*(\theta), Y(\theta)\}$ at a generic value of θ. The distribution $\mathcal{D}^*$ is thus not integrable.

The relationship between the integral curves of X^*, Y and the nonexistence of integral manifolds of $\mathcal{D}^*$ is examined next. Notice first that θ_3 remains constant along any integral curve of X^* because the coefficient of $\partial/\partial \theta_3$ in X^* is zero. As before, let (r^*, τ^*) represent the point (θ_1^*, θ_2^*) in polar coordinates. The integral curve $\rho(X^*, \theta^*, t)$ of X^* through the point θ^* is given by the system of equations[9]

$$\theta_1(t) = (r^* + \theta_3^* t) \cos(t + \tau^*),$$

$$\theta_2(t) = (r^* + \theta_3^* t) \sin(t + \tau^*), \quad (2.30)$$

$$\theta_3(t) = \theta_3^*.$$

---

[9] While any vector field defines a unique integral curve through a given initial point, it is not generally possible to solve such a differential equation in *closed form* (i.e., to parametrize the curve with an explicit formula). It should be recognized that this example has been crafted so that it would be possible to solve for relatively simple formulas for the integral curves of X^* and Y. The rather complicated functions that define these vector fields were in fact selected to simplify the discussion of the integral curves.

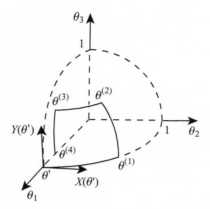

Figure 2.4. For the nonintegrable distribution $\mathcal{D}$ of Example 2.3.1 given by X^* (Eq. (2.27)) and Y (Eq. (2.20)), successively following the integral curves of X^* and Y does not lead back to the initial point $\theta' = (1, 0, 0)$.

The movement from θ^* to $\rho(X^*, \theta^*, \Delta t)$ along an integral curve of X^* can be separated into two components: (i) the movement along a line of latitude through θ^* that is r^* units from the θ_3-axis; (ii) a change in the distance from the θ_3-axis from r^* to $r^* + \theta_3^* \Delta t$. This second component distinguishes movement along an integral curve of X^* from movement along an integral curve of X.

Consider now the point $\theta' \equiv (\theta_1', \theta_2', \theta_3') = (1, 0, 0)$. Because $\theta_3' = 0$, the integral curve of X^* through this point is the same as the integral curve of X through it. As illustrated in Figure 2.4, it traces out the equator of the unit sphere. Follow this curve from $t = 0$ to $t = \varepsilon$ for arbitrary $\varepsilon > 0$. This traces out the integral curve from θ' to $\theta^{(1)}$, where

$$\theta^{(1)} \equiv (\cos(\varepsilon), \sin(\varepsilon), 0). \tag{2.31}$$

Recall that the integral curves of Y trace out the lines of longitude of the sphere. Follow the integral curve of Y determined by $\theta^{(1)}$ from $t = 0$ to $t = \varepsilon$. This traces out a curve from $\theta^{(1)}$ to $\theta^{(2)}$, where

$$\theta^{(2)} \equiv \left(\sin\left(\frac{\pi}{2} - \varepsilon\right) \cos(\varepsilon), \sin\left(\frac{\pi}{2} - \varepsilon\right) \sin(\varepsilon), \cos\left(\frac{\pi}{2} - \varepsilon\right) \right). \tag{2.32}$$

Now follow the integral curve through $\theta^{(2)}$ in the direction of $-X^*$ from $t = 0$ to $t = -\varepsilon$. The formulas in (2.30) imply that in this way a path from $\theta^{(2)}$ to $\theta^{(3)}$ is traced out, where

$$\theta^{(3)} \equiv \left(1 - \varepsilon \cos\left(\frac{\pi}{2} - \varepsilon\right) \sin\left(\frac{\pi}{2} - \varepsilon\right), 0, \cos\left(\frac{\pi}{2} - \varepsilon\right) \right). \tag{2.33}$$

This path starts at $\theta^{(2)}$ on the surface of the unit sphere and then proceeds into the interior of this sphere. Finally, follow the integral curve through $\theta^{(3)}$ in the direction of $-Y$ from $t = 0$ to $t = -\varepsilon$. This traces a path from $\theta^{(3)}$ to $\theta^{(4)}$, where

$$\theta^{(4)} \equiv \left(1 - \varepsilon \cos\left(\frac{\pi}{2} - \varepsilon\right), 0, 0\right). \tag{2.34}$$

If an integral manifold of $\mathcal{D}^*$ exists through $\theta' = (1, 0, 0)$, then all the points that lie on the paths that have been traced out lie within that integral manifold. Consequently, $\theta^{(4)}$ lies in the integral manifold through θ'. Recall that the value of ε is arbitrary, and notice that $\theta^{(4)}$ converges to $\theta' = (1, 0, 0)$ as $\varepsilon \to 0$. For small values of δ, all points of the form $(1 - \delta, 0, 0)$ therefore lie in this integral manifold, which implies that $\partial/\partial\theta_1(\theta') \in \mathcal{D}^*(\theta')$. Because $X^*(\theta') = \partial/\partial\theta_2(\theta')$ and $Y^*(\theta') = \partial/\partial\theta_3(\theta')$, however, the 2-dimensional plane $\mathcal{D}^*(\theta')$ does not contain $\partial/\partial\theta_1(\theta')$. This contradiction shows that an integral manifold of $\mathcal{D}^*$ does not exist through $\theta' = (1, 0, 0)$. A similar argument shows that an integral manifold of $\mathcal{D}^*$ does not exist through any other point in Θ.

2.4 The Frobenius Theorem

Figure 2.5 depicts the chain of implications that is used in this section to establish the local equivalence of *Distribution*, *Foliation*, and *Mapping*. This figure also shows whether an implication holds globally throughout Θ or instead only locally in a neighborhood $O(\theta^*)$ of any $\theta^* \in \Theta$. The implications *Distribution*$\Rightarrow$*Foliation* and *Distribution*$\Rightarrow$*Mapping* are established locally by the Frobenius Theorem, which is discussed below. The proofs that *Mapping*$\Rightarrow$*Foliation* and *Foliation*$\Rightarrow$*Distribution* hold globally involve showing that certain statements are true in a neighborhood $O(\theta^*)$ of an arbitrarily chosen point θ^*; this local proof immediately implies the global result. This pair of implications will be discussed at the end of this section. The sense in which *Distribution*$\Rightarrow$*Foliation* holds globally and the reasons why *Foliation*$\Rightarrow$*Mapping* and *Distribution*$\Rightarrow$*Mapping* are only true locally will be discussed in Sections 2.6 and 2.7.

Some notation is needed for the Frobenius Theorem and the discussion that follows: a point in the image $(-\varepsilon, \varepsilon)^{d+c}$ of a local coordinate system will be denoted as (w, m), where $w \equiv (w_i)_{1 \le i \le d} \in \mathbb{R}^d$ and $m \equiv (m_i)_{1 \le i \le c} \in \mathbb{R}^c$.

Theorem 3 (*Frobenius Theorem*): *Let $\mathcal{D}$ be a d-dimensional C^∞ distribution defined on the open subset Θ of $\mathbb{R}^{d+c}$ and let θ^* be any point in Θ. If $\mathcal{D}$ is*

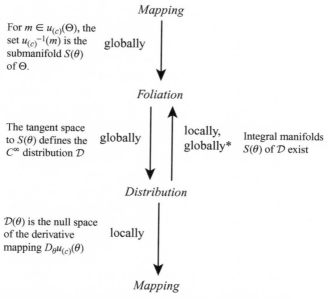

Figure 2.5. The sequence of logical implications that establishes the local equivalence of *Distribution*, *Foliation*, and *Mapping*. "Globally" and "locally" next to each implication indicates whether the result holds globally throughout Θ or only locally in a neighborhood of any given point $\theta \in \Theta$. The relationship that is established between two components is summarized alongside the implication. The "*" on "globally" next to the implication *Distribution*$\Rightarrow$*Foliation* indicates that while this implication always holds locally, it only holds globally with a weaker definition of an integral manifold than the one used throughout this text. This is discussed in Section 2.7.1.

integrable on Θ, then there exists an open neighborhood $O(\theta^*) \subset \Theta$ of θ^* and a local coordinate system $u : O(\theta^*) \to (-\varepsilon, \varepsilon)^{d+c} \subset \mathbb{R}^{d+c}$ with $u(\theta^*) = 0$ such that

(i) *a d-dimensional C^∞ integral manifold of $\mathcal{D}$ exists through each point $\theta^{**} \in O(\theta^*)$;*

(ii) *for any $m \in (-\varepsilon, \varepsilon)^c$, the level set $u_{(c)}^{-1}(m)$ of the mapping $u_{(c)}$ is an integral manifold of $\mathcal{D}$;*

(iii) *every connected integral manifold of $\mathcal{D}$ in $O(\theta^*)$ is a subset of a level set of $u_{(c)}$.*

The Frobenius Theorem generalizes familiar results on the local existence and uniqueness of a solution to an ordinary differential equation for each choice of the initial condition. The hypothesis of the theorem is the existence of an integrable distribution $\mathcal{D}$ on Θ, which is a generalized form of a differential equation. Part (i) of the theorem asserts the local existence of a geometric solution to the differential equation for any choice of an initial point $\theta^{**} \in O(\theta^*)$. Part (ii) states the existence locally of an analytic solution $u_{(c)}$ to the differential equation: for each choice of an initial point $\theta^{**} \in O(\theta^*)$, the level set $u_{(c)}^{-1}(u_{(c)}(\theta^{**}))$ is an integral manifold of $\mathcal{D}$ through the initial point θ^{**}. Because any open subset of a manifold is itself a manifold, there is more than one integral manifold of $\mathcal{D}$ through the initial point θ^{**}. Part (iii), however, states that all such connected integral manifolds in $O(\theta^*)$ are subsets of $u_{(c)}^{-1}(u_{(c)}(\theta^{**}))$. The manifold $u_{(c)}^{-1}(u_{(c)}(\theta^{**}))$ is thus the unique largest connected integral manifold of $\mathcal{D}$ in $O(\theta^*)$ that contains the initial point θ^{**}, and the solution of the differential equation is unique in this sense. Parts (ii) and (iii) thus assert the local existence and uniqueness of a solution to the differential equation for each choice of the initial point.

The Frobenius Theorem has a geometric interpretation that is worth noting. By property (2.1) in the definition of a submanifold, the integral manifold of the d-dimensional distribution $\mathcal{D}$ through the point θ^* can be "flattened" near θ^*, i.e., it can be identified with the d-dimensional coordinate plane $m = 0$ in $\mathbb{R}^{d+c}$ through an appropriate selection of the local coordinate system at θ^*. This is depicted in Figure 2.6(a). The Frobenius Theorem goes further by asserting the existence of a local coordinate system at the given point θ^* that simultaneously flattens all the integral manifolds of $\mathcal{D}$ near θ^*. This is depicted in Figure 2.6(b).

It is straightforward to apply the Frobenius Theorem to show that *Distribution*$\Rightarrow$*Foliation* and *Distribution*$\Rightarrow$*Mapping* hold locally. The hypothesis of the theorem is *Distribution*, and the sets in $\{u_{(c)}^{-1}(m) | m \in u_{(c)}(O(\theta^*))\}$ clearly partition $O(\theta^*)$ in the manner described in *Foliation*. The mapping $u_{(c)}$ is nonsingular on $O(\theta^*)$ because u is a local coordinate system on this set, and so *Mapping* also follows from the Frobenius Theorem.

The implications *Mapping*$\Rightarrow$*Foliation*$\Rightarrow$*Distribution* are now shown to hold globally. To establish *Mapping*$\Rightarrow$*Foliation*, it is sufficient to prove (i) that the level sets of $u_{(c)}$ are submanifolds of Θ, and (ii) the tangent spaces to these submanifolds vary smoothly over Θ. Part (i) of this statement is an elementary result from the theory of manifolds,[10] and part (ii) follows immediately from the smoothness of the mapping $u_{(c)}$.

---

[10] See Spivak (1965, Thm. 5-1, p. 111) or Warner (1971, Thm. 1.38, p. 31).

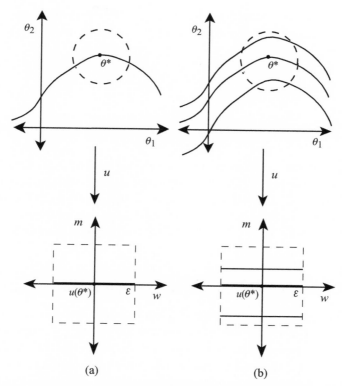

Figure 2.6. By property (2.1) in the definition of a d-dimensional submanifold $S(\theta^*)$ containing θ^*, there exists a local coordinate system $u : O(\theta^*) \to \mathbb{R}^{d+c}$ that "flattens" $S(\theta^*) \cap O(\theta^*)$ in the sense that $u(S(\theta^*) \cap O(\theta^*))$ is a d-dimensional rectangle. This is depicted in (a). As depicted in (b), the Frobenius Theorem asserts the existence of a local coordinate system u that simultaneously flattens all the integral manifolds of the integrable distribution $\mathcal{D}$ within the domain of u.

Turning next to *Foliation⇒Distribution*, the only part of *Distribution* that is not obvious from *Foliation* is the integrability of the distribution $\mathcal{D}$ defined by the submanifolds. The *necessity* of the integrability condition for the existence of integral manifolds for a distribution thus remains to be established. Consider any two C^∞ vector fields X, Y that lie in $\mathcal{D}$. Let S be one of the submanifolds mentioned in *Foliation*, and let θ^* denote a point in S. It is sufficient to prove that $[X, Y](\theta^*) \in \mathcal{D}(\theta^*)$. Property (2.1) of a submanifold asserts the existence of a local coordinate system u defined on the open neighborhood $O(\theta^*)$ of θ^* such that $S \cap O(\theta^*) = u_{(c)}^{-1}(0)$. The nonsingularlity of u implies that the derivative mapping $D_\theta u(\theta)$ is an isomorphism at every $\theta \in O(\theta^*)$. Because $S \cap O(\theta^*) = u_{(c)}^{-1}(0)$, for

$\theta \in S \cap O(\theta^*)$ the derivative $D_\theta u(\theta)$ maps $\mathcal{D}(\theta)$ onto the tangent space at $u(\theta)$ to the coordinate plane $\{(w, m) \in \mathbb{R}^{d+c} | m = 0\}$, i.e.,

$$D_\theta u(\theta)(\mathcal{D}(\theta)) = \left\{ \sum_{i=1}^d \lambda_i \frac{\partial}{\partial w_i} \, | \lambda_i \in \mathbb{R}, 1 \le i \le d \right\}. \tag{2.35}$$

Therefore,

$$D_\theta u(\theta)([X, Y])(\theta) = [D_\theta u(X), D_\theta u(Y)] \, (u(\theta)) \in D_\theta u(\theta)(\mathcal{D}(\theta)). \tag{2.36}$$

The equality follows from the fact that the Lie bracket is preserved under smooth mappings (Eq. (2.7)), while the inclusion follows from applying the characterization (2.35) of $D_\theta u(\mathcal{D}(\theta))$ to $D_\theta u(X)$ and $D_\theta u(Y)$ in formula (2.6) for the Lie bracket. Because $D_\theta u(\theta^*)$ is an isomorphism, it follows from (2.36) that $[X, Y](\theta^*) \in \mathcal{D}(\theta^*)$, which completes the proof that $\mathcal{D}$ is integrable.

2.5 The Proof of the Frobenius Theorem

The Frobenius Theorem is a central result in differential geometry whose proof can be found in almost any text on this subject.[11] A rigorous proof is thus not needed here. It is important, however, that the reader have some understanding of the construction of the local coordinate system u in the proof of this theorem because the equivalence of *Direct Sum*, *Product Structure*, and *Message Process* will be proven in Chapter 3 by adapting this construction to the model of mechanisms. I thus begin this section by sketching the construction in the simple case of $c = 1$ and $d = 2$. The construction in the general case will then be outlined.

2.5.1 The Case of $c = 1$ and $d = 2$

I first state a necessary and sufficient condition in this special case for a set of vector fields to define coordinates near a point θ^*. Let X and Y be vector fields on $\Theta = \mathbb{R}^3$ that span $\mathcal{D}$ at every point. Through a linear change of coordinates on $\mathbb{R}^3$, one can assume without loss of generality that at the point θ^* the vectors X and Y point in the direction of the coordinate axes θ_1 and θ_2, i.e.,

$$X(\theta^*) = \frac{\partial}{\partial \theta_1}(\theta^*) \tag{2.37}$$

[11] See Spivak (1979, Thm. 5, p. 262) or Warner (1971, Thm. 1.60, p. 42).

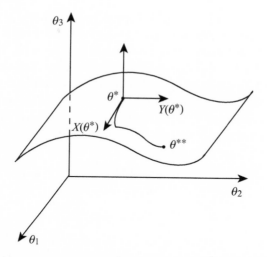

Figure 2.7. Starting at θ^*, follow the integral curve of X from $t = 0$ to $t = w_1$ and then follow the integral curve of Y from $t = 0$ to $t = w_2$.

and

$$Y(\theta^*) = \frac{\partial}{\partial \theta_2}(\theta^*). \tag{2.38}$$

Starting at θ^*, follow the integral curve $\rho(X, \theta^*, t)$ from $t = 0$ to $t = w_1$ and then follow the integral curve $\rho(Y, \rho(X, \theta^*, w_1), t)$ from $t = 0$ to $t = w_2$. Define $\theta^{**}(w_1, w_2)$ as the point at which one stops,

$$\theta^{**}(w_1, w_2) \equiv \rho(Y, \rho(X, \theta^*, w_1), w_2). \tag{2.39}$$

This is illustrated in Figure 2.7. Alternatively, start at θ^*, follow first the integral curve $\rho(Y, \theta^*, t)$ from $t = 0$ to $t = w_2$ and then follow the integral curve $\rho(X, \rho(Y, \theta^*, w_2), t)$ from $t = 0$ to $t = w_1$. This leads to the point $\theta^{***}(w_1, w_2)$, where

$$\theta^{***}(w_1, w_2) \equiv \rho(X, \rho(Y, \theta^*, w_2), w_1). \tag{2.40}$$

If an integral manifold of $\mathcal{D}$ exists through θ^*, then both θ^{**} and θ^{***} lie in this manifold. An additional property is sought here: it is desired that the parameters w_1 and w_2 in the integral curves of X and Y serve as coordinates for points in the integral manifold near θ^*. These parameters unambiguously number the points in this manifold near θ^* if and only if $\theta^{**}(w_1, w_2) = \theta^{***}(w_1, w_2)$ for small values of w_1 and w_2. As stated in the Frobenius Theorem, a necessary and sufficient condition for the existence of an integral manifold of the distribution spanned by X and Y through each point θ is $[X, Y] \in \mathcal{D}$; as Theorem 4 below states, a necessary and sufficient condition for the integral curves of X and Y to define coordinates locally on each such manifold is the stronger condition $[X, Y] = 0$.

Assuming that vector fields X and Y can be found that span $\mathcal{D}$ at every point and such that $[X, Y] = 0$, the coordinate system u in the Frobenius Theorem is constructed near θ^* as follows. Recall that $X(\theta^*)$ and $Y(\theta^*)$ point in the directions of the θ_1- and the θ_2-axes, respectively. The vector field $\partial/\partial\theta_3$ thus lies outside $\mathcal{D}$ near θ^*. Vary the initial point away from θ^* in the θ_3-direction, i.e., along the line $\{(\theta_1^*, \theta_2^*, m + \theta_3^*)|m \in \mathbb{R}\}$. The coordinates (w_1, w_2, m) are assigned by u to the point $\theta = (\theta_1, \theta_2, \theta_3)$ if and only if

$$\theta = \rho(Y, \rho(X, (\theta_1^*, \theta_2^*, m + \theta_3^*), w_1), w_2) \qquad (2.41)$$

$$= \rho(X, \rho(Y, (\theta_1^*, \theta_2^*, m + \theta_3^*), w_2), w_1).$$

Holding m constant and varying w_1 and w_2 traces out an integral manifold of $\mathcal{D}$.[12] The value m thus numbers the integral manifolds of $\mathcal{D}$ near θ^* and the parameters w_1, w_2 of the integral curves of X and Y provide coordinates on each of these integral manifolds of $\mathcal{D}$. This local coordinate system has the form described in the Frobenius Theorem, with $u_{(d)}(\theta) \equiv (w_1(\theta), w_2(\theta))$ and $u_{(c)}(\theta) \equiv m(\theta)$ as defined implicitly by (2.41). Notice that

$$(D_\theta u)^{-1}\left(\frac{\partial}{\partial w_1}\right) = X \qquad (2.42)$$

and

$$(D_\theta u)^{-1}\left(\frac{\partial}{\partial w_2}\right) = Y. \qquad (2.43)$$

Equation (2.42) holds because the w_1 coordinate measures through the coordinate system u movement along an integral curve of X. Equation (2.43) is explained similarly using w_2 and Y.

2.5.2 The General Case

For the construction of the coordinate system in the general case, the condition $[X, Y] = 0$ is extended in Theorem 4 below to form a necessary and sufficient condition for a set of vector fields to define coordinates near a point θ^*. With (2.42)–(2.43) in mind, some notation is needed. Given a local

---

[12] This is a crucial step in the proof of Theorem 4 that captures the importance of the integrability condition $[X, Y] \in \mathcal{D}$. Similarly, Equations (2.42) and (2.43) below, while seemingly obvious in this intuitive discussion, require the condition $[X, Y] = 0$ for a formal proof.

coordinate system u at θ^*, define the vector field $\partial/\partial u_i$ for $1 \leq i \leq d + c$ as

$$\frac{\partial}{\partial u_i} \equiv (D_\theta u)^{-1} \left(\frac{\partial}{\partial e_i} \right), \tag{2.44}$$

where e_i denotes the ith coordinate relative to the standard basis for the range of u (i.e., $e_i \equiv w_i$ for $1 \leq i \leq d$ and $e_i \equiv m_i$ for $d + 1 \leq i \leq d + c$).

Theorem 4 (*Necessary and Sufficient Conditions for a Set of Linearly Independent Vector Fields to Define a Local Coordinate System*):

Necessity. If u is a local coordinate system at θ^*, then

$$\left[\frac{\partial}{\partial u_i}, \frac{\partial}{\partial u_j} \right] = 0$$

for all $1 \leq i, j \leq d + c$.

Sufficiency. If the vector fields $X_1, \ldots, X_d$ defined near θ^* are linearly independent and satisfy $[X_i, X_j] = 0$ for all $1 \leq i, j \leq d$, then there exists a local coordinate system u at θ^* such that $X_i = \partial/\partial u_i$ near θ^* for $1 \leq i \leq d$.

Necessity follows immediately from the fact that the Lie bracket is preserved under changes of coordinates: for any $1 \leq i, j \leq d + c$,

$$\left[\frac{\partial}{\partial u_i}, \frac{\partial}{\partial u_j} \right] = \left[(D_\theta u)^{-1} \left(\frac{\partial}{\partial e_i} \right), (D_\theta u)^{-1} \left(\frac{\partial}{\partial e_j} \right) \right] \tag{2.45}$$

$$= (D_\theta u)^{-1} \left[\frac{\partial}{\partial e_i}, \frac{\partial}{\partial e_j} \right]$$

$$= (D_\theta u)^{-1} (0) = 0.$$

The proof of *Sufficiency* generalizes the argument presented above in the case of $c = 1$ and $d = 2$ to arbitrary c and d.[13] Let $\mathcal{D}$ denote the distribution spanned by the vector fields $X_1, \ldots, X_d$. Assume for simplicity that each X_i points in the direction of the θ_i-axis at θ^* (i.e., $X_i(\theta^*) = \partial/\partial\theta_i(\theta^*)$ for $1 \leq i \leq d + c$). The c-dimensional plane at θ^* spanned by

$$\left\{ \frac{\partial}{\partial\theta_i}(\theta^*) | d + 1 \leq i \leq d + c \right\} \tag{2.46}$$

is transverse to $\mathcal{D}(\theta^*)$. For θ near θ^*, the coordinate system u assigns coordinates $u(\theta) = (w, m)$ to θ if and only if θ is reached by starting at the

---

[13] The following discussion is drawn from Spivak (1979, Thm. 14, p. 219).

initial point $(\theta^*_{(d)}, \theta^*_{(c)} + m)$ and successively following the integral curve of X_1 from $t = 0$ to $t = w_1$, then following the integral curve of X_2 from $t = 0$ to $t = w_2, \ldots,$ and finally following the integral curve of X_d from $t = 0$ to $t = w_d$. Formally, $u(\theta) = (w, m)$ if and only if[14]

$$\theta = \rho(X_d, \rho(X_{d-1}, (\ldots, \rho(X_1, (\theta^*_{(d)}, \theta^*_{(c)} + m), w_1)), w_{d-1}), w_d). \quad (2.47)$$

An integral manifold of $\mathcal{D}$ is a level set of the last c coordinates $u_{(c)}$ of this coordinate system u, and $u_{(c)}(\theta) = m$ if and only if the integral manifold of $\mathcal{D}$ through θ intersects the c-dimensional plane $\{(\theta^*_{(d)}, \theta_{(c)}) | \theta_{(c)} \in \mathbb{R}^c\}$ at $\theta_{(c)} = \theta^*_{(c)} + m$.

The coordinate system u in the statement of *Sufficiency* in Theorem 4 has all the properties required by the coordinate system whose existence is established in the Frobenius Theorem. The proof of the Frobenius Theorem is thus completed by proving the following theorem.

Theorem 5: *Given a d-dimensional, C^∞, integrable distribution $\mathcal{D}$ on Θ and a point $\theta^* \in \Theta$, there exists d vector fields $X_1, \ldots, X_d$ on some open neighborhood $O(\theta^*)$ of θ^* such that*

  (i) $X_1, \ldots, X_d$ span $\mathcal{D}(\theta)$ at each $\theta \in O(\theta^*)$;
  (ii) $[X_i, X_j] = 0$ on $O(\theta^*)$ for all $1 \le i, j \le d$.

Proof: This proof follows a construction in Spivak (1979, pp. 262–263). Let $Y_1, \ldots, Y_d$ be any set of d vector fields that span $\mathcal{D}(\theta)$ at each θ near θ^*. After a linear change of coordinates in $\mathbb{R}^{d+c}$, it can be assumed that $Y_i(\theta^*) = \partial/\partial\theta_i(\theta^*)$ for $1 \le i \le d$. Let $\pi_{(d)} : \mathbb{R}^{d+c} \to \mathbb{R}^d$ denote the projection mapping onto the first d coordinates,

$$\pi_{(d)}(\theta) = \theta_{(d)}. \quad (2.48)$$

Because $\mathcal{D}(\theta^*)$ is spanned by

$$\{Y_1(\theta^*), Y_2(\theta^*), \ldots, Y_d(\theta^*)\} = \left\{\frac{\partial}{\partial\theta_1}(\theta^*), \ldots, \frac{\partial}{\partial\theta_d}(\theta^*)\right\}, \quad (2.49)$$

the restriction of the derivative mapping $D_\theta \pi_{(d)}(\theta)$ to $\mathcal{D}(\theta)$ is an isomorphism for θ near θ^*. Each of the vector fields

$$X_i(\theta) \equiv \left(D_\theta \pi_{(d)}(\theta)\right)^{-1} \left(\frac{\partial}{\partial\theta_i}(\theta_{(d)})\right) \bigcap \mathcal{D}(\theta) \quad (2.50)$$

---

[14] Warner (1971, Thm. 1.60, p. 42) avoids the awkwardness of expressions such as (2.47) by proving the Frobenius Theorem through induction on the dimension d of the distribution $\mathcal{D}$.

for $1 \leq i \leq d$ is thus well defined for θ near θ^*. The vector fields $(X_i(\theta))_{1 \leq i \leq d}$ are obviously linearly independent and thus span $\mathcal{D}$. Notice that

$$D_\theta \pi_{(d)}(\theta)([X_i, X_j]) = \left[D_\theta \pi_{(d)}(\theta)(X_i), D_\theta \pi_{(d)}(\theta)(X_j) \right] \qquad (2.51)$$

$$= \left[\frac{\partial}{\partial \theta_i}, \frac{\partial}{\partial \theta_j} \right] = 0$$

for all $1 \leq i, j \leq d$. Because $D_\theta \pi_{(d)}(\theta)$ is an isomorphism on $\mathcal{D}(\theta)$ for θ near θ^*, it follows from the integrability of $\mathcal{D}$ (i.e., $[X_i, X_j] \in \mathcal{D}$) together with (2.51) that $[X_i, X_j] = 0$ for all $1 \leq i, j \leq d$. ∎

2.6 Obstacles to Global Equivalence

The main conclusion of this section is that *Distribution⇔Foliation⇔ Mapping* holds globally in Θ only if strong assumptions are placed on the region Θ, the distribution $\mathcal{D}$, and/or the numbers c and d. As depicted in Figure 2.5, the obstacle to establishing this equivalence globally is *Distribution⇒Mapping*,[15] which is the statement of existence and uniqueness of an analytic solution to a differential equation as formulated in *Distribution*. There is a sense in which *Distribution⇒Foliation* holds globally. This implication asserts the existence and uniqueness of a geometric solution to a differential equation. It holds globally only with a weaker notion of a submanifold (or solution to the differential equation) than is used in the local version and elsewhere in this text. This topic is discussed below in Subsections 2.6.2 and 2.6.3.

The equivalence *Distribution⇔Foliation⇔Mapping* holds globally in some special mathematical settings, and economic issues sometimes sufficiently restrict the mathematical model so that a global result can be proven. The example in Subsection 1.3.1 of a distribution defined by a demand function is one such special case in which a global result can be proven. This is discussed below in Subsection 2.7.1. Globalization is meaningful in mechanism design, especially when an agent's parameter space Θ_i determines the range of his preferences; globalization in this case is the familiar problem of determining the domain of preferences over which a mechanism can be successfully defined. All the problems in globalization that are discussed in this section can arise in the model of mechanisms that is

---

[15] The obstacles to proving *Distribution⇒Mapping* globally also prevent a global proof of *Foliation⇒Mapping*. I focus on *Distribution⇒Mapping* here because it is the link in Figure 2.5 that is needed to prove the global equivalence of *Distribution, Foliation,* and *Mapping*.

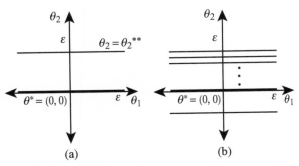

Figure 2.8. In (a), the two segments are subsets of a single integral manifold of $\mathcal{D}$ in Θ that appear within $O(\theta^*) = (-\varepsilon, \varepsilon)^2$ as distinct integral manifolds of the distribution. As depicted in (b), an infinite number of such segments that appear distinct within $(-\varepsilon, \varepsilon)^2$ may all be subsets of the same integral manifold of $\mathcal{D}$ in Θ. Example 2.6.1 demonstrates that this can prevent the existence of a mapping $u_{(c)}$ that globally numbers the integral manifolds of the distribution $\mathcal{D}$.

discussed in Chapter 3. My objective in this section is thus to help the reader to appreciate the mathematical difficulties that arise in trying to establish *Distribution*⇔*Foliation*⇔*Mapping* globally, with the added goal that he may recognize solutions to these difficulties when analyzing particular economic models.

A difficulty in globalizing *Distribution*⇒*Mapping* is illustrated in Figure 2.8, which depicts a 1-dimensional distribution $\mathcal{D}$ in $\mathbb{R}^2$. Applying the Frobenius Theorem, the integral manifolds of $\mathcal{D}$ in a neighborhood $O(\theta^*)$ of the point θ^* can be regarded after a suitable choice of coordinates as the horizontal line segments indexed by the points on the θ_2-axis with θ^* identified with the origin of coordinates and $O(\theta^*)$ with the open square $(-\varepsilon, \varepsilon)^2$. Suppose one follows the integral manifold of $\mathcal{D}$ through θ^* in the direction of increasing θ_1. It is conceivable that after leaving $O(\theta^*)$ one could return to $O(\theta^*)$ at a different value of θ_2 (Figure 2.8(a)). The segments

$$\{(\theta_1, \theta_2)| - \varepsilon < \theta_1 < \varepsilon, \theta_2 = \theta_2^* = 0\} \tag{2.52}$$

and

$$\{(\theta_1, \theta_2)| - \varepsilon < \theta_1 < \varepsilon, \theta_2 = \theta_2^{**}\}, \tag{2.53}$$

which appear as different integral manifolds of $\mathcal{D}$ within $O(\theta^*)$, might thus be part of the same integral manifold of $\mathcal{D}$ from a global perspective. A function $u_{(c)} : \Theta \to \mathbb{R}$ whose level sets are the integral manifolds of $\mathcal{D}$ must assign the same value to each of these segments. Defining such a function is thus not simply a matter of extending the function $u_{(c)}$ of the Frobenius

Theorem from $O(\theta^*)$ to Θ, for this function assigns different values to each of these segments.

Continuing along an integral manifold of $\mathcal{D}$, it is possible that one leaves and returns to the neighborhood $O(\theta^*)$ again and again, each time crossing the θ_2-axis at different values. From a global perspective, all these segments are subsets of the same integral manifold of $\mathcal{D}$ through θ^*. It may be possible to return in this way to $O(\theta^*)$ a finite or even an infinite number of times. The union of all the horizontal segments in $O(\theta^*)$ that one crosses can even form a dense subset of $O(\theta^*)$.[16] If an integral manifold of $\mathcal{D}$ returns to the neighborhood $O(\theta^*)$ of θ^* again and again, regardless of the size of $O(\theta^*)$, then a nonsingular function $u_{(c)}$ that globally numbers the integral manifolds of $\mathcal{D}$ may not exist. The implication *Distribution*$\Rightarrow$*Mapping* thus does not hold globally in all problems.

2.6.1 Example: The Nonexistence Globally of the Mapping $u_{(c)}$

Samuelson (1950) developed the following example to illustrate that *Distribution*$\Rightarrow$*Mapping* need not hold globally.[17] Let $\Theta = \mathbb{R}^2 \setminus \{(0, 0)\}$ and represent points in Θ using polar coordinates (i.e., $\theta_1 = r \cos(\tau)$, $\theta_2 = r \sin(\tau)$). Let $\mathcal{D}$ be the 1-dimensional distribution spanned by the vector field X, where[18]

$$X(r, \tau) = \left(\frac{dr}{dt}, \frac{d\tau}{dt} \right) \equiv (1 - r, 1). \tag{2.54}$$

The integral curve $\rho(X, (r^*, \tau^*), t)$ of the vector field X through a given point (r^*, τ^*) is defined by the equations

$$r(t) = (r^* - 1)e^{-t} + 1, \tag{2.55}$$

$$\tau(t) = t + \tau^*.$$

---

[16] This is illustrated below in Example 2.6.3.
[17] This example was further analyzed by Debreu (1972, pp. 607–609), who altered it to show that it does not fundamentally depend on the nonconvexity of Θ.
[18] Expressed in Euclidean coordinates (θ_1, θ_2), the vector field X is

$$X(\theta) \equiv \left(\theta_1 \left(\frac{1}{\sqrt{\theta_1^2 + \theta_2^2}} - 1 \right) - \theta_2, \theta_2 \left(\frac{1}{\sqrt{\theta_1^2 + \theta_2^2}} - 1 \right) + \theta_1 \right)$$

at the point θ that is determined by the polar coordinates (r, τ). Although this example could be worked using Euclidean coordinates, this formula suggests why it is simpler to use polar coordinates.

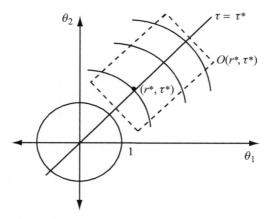

Figure 2.9. The integral manifold of $\mathcal{D}$ through a point outside the unit circle spirals inward toward this circle, while the integral manifold of $\mathcal{D}$ through a point inside the unit circle spirals outward toward this circle. While a mapping $u_{(c)}$ exists that numbers the integral manifolds of $\mathcal{D}$ near any nonzero point, such a mapping does not exist on any open set that contains the unit circle.

The graph of the integral curve $\rho(X, (r^*, \tau^*), t)$ of X through (r^*, τ^*) is the integral manifold of $\mathcal{D}$ through (r^*, τ^*). If $r^* = 1$, then the integral manifold of $\mathcal{D}$ through (r^*, τ^*) is the unit circle $r = 1$. If $r^* < 1$, then the integral curve of X through (r^*, τ^*) spirals outward toward the unit circle as $t \to \infty$ and it converges inward to the origin as $t \to \ln(1\text{-}r^*)$. If $r^* > 1$, then the integral curve of X through (r^*, τ^*) spirals inward toward the unit circle as $t \to \infty$ and it spirals outward as $t \to -\infty$.

Consider now the existence of a mapping $u_{(c)}$ whose level sets are the integral manifolds of $\mathcal{D}$. In a neighborhood $O(r^*, \tau^*)$ of a given point (r^*, τ^*), the integral manifold of $\mathcal{D}$ through (r^*, τ^*) is an arc that appears to lie along a circle centered at the origin with radius equal to r^*. This arc actually lies along such a circle only if $r^* = 1$, while if $r^* \neq 1$ the arc moves toward the unit circle as it is followed in a counterclockwise direction (i.e., the direction of increasing t in (2.55)). This is illustrated in Figure 2.9. As suggested by the proof of the Frobenius Theorem, the value of the function $u_{(c)}$ at (r^{**}, τ^{**}) near (r^*, τ^*) can be defined as the difference $r - r^*$, where r is the radius of the point at which the integral manifold of $\mathcal{D}$ through (r^{**}, τ^{**}) crosses the ray $\tau = \tau^*$. The following argument shows, however, that the local existence of the function $u_{(c)}$ cannot be extended to a global result. Consider the value of $u_{(c)}$ on the unit circle. The integral manifold of $\mathcal{D}$ through any point (r^*, τ^*) in Θ converges to the unit circle. If the function $u_{(c)}$ assigns different values to each integral manifold of $\mathcal{D}$, then it clearly cannot be continuous at points in the unit circle. Throughout this chapter, the function $u_{(c)}$ that numbers the integral manifolds of $\mathcal{D}$ is required to be both smooth and nonsingular. In this example, however, while such a function can exist locally, nonexistence is proven globally even for continuous functions $u_{(c)}$.[19]

2.6.2 A Subtlety of Submanifolds

As part of addressing *Distribution⇒Mapping* and *Distribution⇒Foliation* from a global perspective, it is necessary to discuss the more fundamental issue of what is meant by "the integral manifold through θ^* in Θ." The subtle point here is the sense in which this set is a manifold, which is closely related to the existence locally of the desired mapping $u_{(c)}$. Given the integrable distribution $\mathcal{D}$ and a point $\theta^* \in \Theta$, there exists a unique largest connected d-dimensional manifold $S(\theta^*)$ that contains θ^* and whose tangent at each $\theta \in S(\theta^*)$ is $\mathcal{D}(\theta)$.[20] This manifold $S(\theta^*)$ is the *maximal integral manifold* of $\mathcal{D}$ through θ^*. The main point here is that $S(\theta^*)$ may not be a submanifold of Θ in the sense defined in Section 2.1. At issue is the defining property (2.1) of a submanifold, which requires that there exists for every $\theta^{**} \in S(\theta^*)$ a local coordinate system $u : O(\theta^{**}) \to \mathbb{R}^{d+c}$ such that $S(\theta^*) \cap O(\theta^{**}) = u_{(c)}^{-1}(0)$. It may be the case that such a local coordinate system u does not exist locally near some $\theta^{**} \in S(\theta^*)$. The desired mapping $u_{(c)}$ may thus not exist locally, let alone globally.

The problem is illustrated in Figure 2.8(b). Suppose in this figure that there exists a sequence $(\theta_{2,i})_{i\in\mathbb{N}}$ such that $\lim_{i\to\infty} \theta_{2,i} = 0$ and each of the horizontal segments

$$\{(\theta_1, \theta_{2,i})| -\varepsilon < \theta_1 < \varepsilon\}$$

in $O(\theta^*)$ together with the horizontal segment

$$\{(\theta_1, 0)| -\varepsilon < \theta_1 < \varepsilon\}$$

all lie in the same maximal integral manifold $S(\theta^*)$ of $\mathcal{D}$ in Θ. Assume that $S(\theta^*)$ is a submanifold of Θ and let u denote a local coordinate system defined on $O(\theta^*)$ such that $u_{(c)}$ is zero on $S(\theta^*) \cap O(\theta^*)$. The derivative $\nabla u_{(c)}(\theta^*)$ of $u_{(c)}$ at θ^* is (i) nonzero near θ^*, else u would not be a local

---

[19] The set of integral manifolds of a smooth distribution $\mathcal{D}$ has the same cardinality as the set of real numbers, and hence they can always be numbered in a discontinuous manner using $\mathbb{R}$. I am unaware of results that describe the properties weaker than continuity that such numbering schemes may have.

[20] See Spivak (1979, Thm. 6, p. 264).

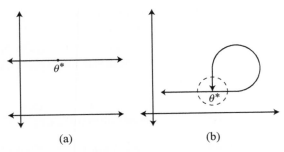

Figure 2.10. The line in (a) is an imbedded submanifold of $\mathbb{R}^2$ while the line in (b) is an immersed submanifold of $\mathbb{R}^2$.

coordinate system; (ii) perpendicular to the θ_1-axis because $u_{(c)}(\theta_1, 0) = 0$ for θ_1 near 0. The function $u_{(c)}$ thus either strictly increases or strictly decreases along the θ_2-axis near $\theta = \theta^*$, which cannot be true because $\lim_{i \to \infty} \theta_{2,i} = 0$ and $u_{(c)}(0, \theta_{2,i}) = 0$ for all i. The contradiction implies that a suitable local coordinate system u does not exist. The manifold $S(\theta^*)$ is thus not a submanifold of Θ in the sense defined in Section 2.1.

Formally, the distinction here is between an "imbedded submanifold of Θ" that is taken as the definition of a submanifold in Section 2.1 and the weaker notion of an "immersed submanifold of Θ"; the maximal integral manifold $S(\theta^*)$ is an immersed submanifold of Θ but not necessarily an imbedded submanifold of Θ.[21] The distinction is reflected in the topology on $S(\theta^*)$ relative to which this set is a manifold. In the case of an imbedded submanifold of Θ, the topology on $S(\theta^*)$ is the induced topology from the ambient space Θ, while in the case of an immersed submanifold of Θ, the topology is any topology relative to which the inclusion mapping $i : S(\theta^*) \to \Theta$ is smooth and nonsingular at every $\theta \in S(\theta^*)$. The distinction is illustrated in Figure 2.10(a) and 2.10(b), both of which concern 1-dimensional submanifolds of $\Theta = \mathbb{R}^2$. The line in Figure 2.10(a) is an imbedded submanifold, with $u_{(c)}(\theta) = \theta_2 - \theta_2^*$ near any point θ^*. The standard topology on this line is identical to induced topology from the ambient space Θ. Figure 2.10(b) depicts a line that has been bent back on itself. This is an immersed submanifold but not an imbedded submanifold, for any C^∞ mapping $u_{(c)}$ that is zero on $S(\theta^*) \cap O(\theta^*)$ is necessarily zero throughout $O(\theta^*)$. The standard topology that is retained by this line as it is bent back on itself is distinct from the induced topology from $\mathbb{R}^2$, for

---

[21] The discussion here focuses on how this distinction affects the existence of the mapping $u_{(c)}$ that indexes the integral manifold of $\mathcal{D}$. A more general discussion of these two notions of a submanifold can be found in Spivak (1979, pp. 60–65).

any neighborhood of θ^* in the induced topology contains an unbounded subinterval of the line.

The distinction between immersed and imbedded submanifolds is illustrated in Figure 2.8(b) as follows. In the topology relative to which $S(\theta^*)$ is a manifold (the topology of an immersed submanifold), the subinterval

$$\{(\theta_1, 0)| - \varepsilon < \theta_1 < \varepsilon\}$$

of the θ_1-axis is an open subset of $S(\theta^*)$. In the topology induced on $S(\theta^*)$ from Θ (the topology of an imbedded submanifold), this subinterval is not an open set because every open neighborhood of $\theta^* = (0, 0)$ in $S(\theta^*)$ in the induced topology intersects an infinite number of the horizontal subintervals[22]

$$\{(\theta_1, \theta_{2,i})| - \varepsilon < \theta_1 < \varepsilon\}.$$

In summary, *Distribution*$\Rightarrow$*Foliation* holds globally only if the term "submanifold" in *Foliation* is weakened to "immersed submanifold" instead of "imbedded submanifold," which it is taken to mean everywhere else in this text. The issue is property (2.1) of an imbedded submanifold, i.e., whether or not each maximal integral manifold of $\mathcal{D}$ can be represented locally as the level set of a mapping $u_{(c)} : O(\theta^*) \to \mathbb{R}^c$. If such a function does not exist locally near some point θ^* in some example, then of course it is also the case that *Distribution*$\Rightarrow$*Mapping* does not hold globally.

2.6.3 Example: A Maximal Integral Manifold Need Not Be a Submanifold

The problem identified in Subsection 2.6.2 is illustrated formally in this subsection. Let Θ be the torus,[23] i.e., $\Theta = S^1 \times S^1$, where S^1 is the unit circle in $\mathbb{R}^2$. Local coordinates near any point in Θ are provided by a pair of

---

[22] Although the example of Figure 2.8(b) may resemble the cycling curves of Example 2.6.1, the problem discussed here is different. Each maximal integral manifold of $\mathcal{D}$ in Example 2.6.1 is an imbedded submanifold of Θ (i.e., in a sufficiently small neighborhood in Θ of any point θ^*, the maximal integral manifold of $\mathcal{D}$ through θ^* approximates an arc of a circle). The issue addressed in this subsection is whether or not a *particular* maximal integral manifold can be represented locally as the level set of a smooth mapping $u_{(c)}$; the issue in Example 2.6.1 is whether or not *distinct* maximal integral manifolds can be assigned distinct values under some smooth mapping $u_{(c)}$.

[23] This well-known example is sometimes called the *skew line on the torus* (e.g., see Spivak, 1979, p. 62, or Warner, 1971, p. 51, Ex. 21). It is assumed for simplicity throughout this text that Θ is an open subset of $\mathbb{R}^{d+c}$, which is not true of the torus. This example can be extended to an open subset of $\mathbb{R}^3$ by varying the thickness of the torus in Figure 2.11.

Classical Concepts and Results

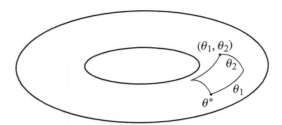

Figure 2.11. Local coordinates on the torus $\Theta = S^1 \times S^1$ as measured from a point θ^* are provided by a pair of numbers (θ_1, θ_2), where θ_i measures the angle in radians along the ith circle starting from the given point θ^*.

numbers (θ_1, θ_2), where each θ_i measures the angle in radians along the ith circle starting from the given point. This is illustrated in Figure 2.11. The distribution $\mathcal{D}$ is a 1-dimensional distribution that is spanned at each point θ by the vector field

$$X(\theta) = \frac{\partial}{\partial \theta_1} + \lambda \frac{\partial}{\partial \theta_2}, \tag{2.56}$$

where λ is a fixed number that will be selected below. The integral curve $\rho(X, \theta^*, t)$ is given by the equation

$$\rho(X, \theta^*, t) = (\theta_1^* + t, \theta_2^* + \lambda t). \tag{2.57}$$

The image of $\rho(X, \theta^*, t)$ as t varies between $-\infty$ and ∞ is the integral manifold of $\mathcal{D}$ through θ^*.

The integral curve $\rho(X, \theta^*, t)$ has a simple geometric interpretation that is illustrated in Figure 2.12. By following the integral curve from $t = 0$ to $t = 2\pi$, a path is traced that starts at θ^* and proceeds all the way around the torus and back to the cross-sectional circle indexed by θ_1^*. The number λ determines how many times this integral curve winds around the torus as t

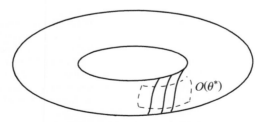

Figure 2.12. In the case of an irrational number λ, the integral manifold of the distribution $\mathcal{D}$ through θ^* is dense in any open neighborhood $O(\theta^*)$ of θ^*.

increases from 0 to 2π. For example, if $\lambda = 1$, then the curve wraps around the torus exactly once and $\rho(X, \theta^*, t) = \rho(X, \theta^*, 2\pi) = \theta^*$. If $\lambda \geq 2$, then the integral curve wraps around the torus at least twice. If $\lambda < 1$, then the integral curve does not completely make it around the torus as t changes from 0 to 2π.

The rationality or irrationality of λ determines the topological nature of the integral manifolds of $\mathcal{D}$. If λ is rational, then $\rho(X, \theta^*, t) = \theta^*$ has a countably infinite number of solutions $t \in \mathbb{R}$. In this case, the integral curve $\rho(X, \theta^*, t)$ retraces itself again and again as t varies from $-\infty$ and ∞, and the maximal integral manifold of $\mathcal{D}$ through any θ^* is a simple closed curve. Each maximal integral manifold of $\mathcal{D}$ is thus an imbedded submanifold of Θ and *Distribution* ⇒ *Foliation* holds globally.

The case of irrational λ is most interesting for the purpose of this example. In this case, an integral curve $\rho(X, \theta^*, t)$ cycles endlessly as t varies, never retracing itself. It can be shown that each maximal integral manifold of $\mathcal{D}$ is in fact dense in Θ. Figure 2.12 depicts a "rectangle" $O(\theta^*)$ on the torus in which the integral manifold of $\mathcal{D}$ through θ^* has the properties depicted in Figure 2.8(b) and analyzed in Subsection 2.6.2. Each maximal integral manifold of $\mathcal{D}$ is an immersed submanifold of Θ but not an imbedded submanifold of Θ. *Distribution* ⇒ *Foliation* thus holds globally in the case of irrational λ only with this weaker concept of submanifold.

2.7 A Global Construction of *Mapping*

It has been shown in the preceding section that *Distribution* ⇒ *Foliation* holds globally only if the definition of a submanifold is relaxed so that a mapping $u_{(c)}$ satisfying property (2.1) need not exist in a neighborhood of each $\theta^* \in \Theta$. It was argued above that *Mapping* ⇒ *Foliation* ⇒ *Distribution* holds globally, while *Distribution* ⇒ *Mapping* may not. The key issue in the global relationship among *Distribution*, *Foliation*, and *Mapping* is thus the existence of a smooth, nonsingular mapping $u_{(c)}$ whose level sets are the maximal integral manifolds of $\mathcal{D}$.

One approach to constructing such a mapping $u_{(c)}$ globally is to follow the construction in the proof of *Sufficiency* in Theorem 4, which is the crucial step in proving the Frobenius Theorem. The idea of this construction is quite simple. A c-dimensional plane P is selected that transversally intersects the d-dimensional integral manifolds of the distribution $\mathcal{D}$. The points in P index locally the submanifolds in *Foliation*. The value of $u_{(c)}(\theta)$ is defined as the unique point in P at which the maximal integral manifold $S(\theta)$ of

$\mathcal{D}$ through θ intersects this plane. This construction in general succeeds only in defining $u_{(c)}$ locally. It may fail globally either because (i) a c-dimensional plane does not exist that intersects every maximal integral manifold of $\mathcal{D}$ or (ii) any such plane intersects some maximal integral manifold of $\mathcal{D}$ more than once and thus fails to number these submanifolds in an unambiguous fashion. Problem (i) is illustrated in Subsection 2.7.2 below while problem (ii) was addressed in Section 2.6.

In some instances, however, this construction successfully defines $u_{(c)}$ throughout Θ. I explore this construction in some depth in two examples below because it is so elementary in its approach. It has clear parallels in the construction of mechanisms in noncalculus settings, including cases in which Θ and M are finite or countably infinite. Understanding the potential and the limitations of this construction can thus provide insight into the construction of mechanisms beyond the calculus-based model of this text.[24] Subsection 2.7.1 returns to the problem posed in Subsection 1.3.1 of deriving preferences and a utility function that rationalize a given mapping as a consumer's inverse demand. This example demonstrates how modeling considerations can insure that the construction successfully defines $u_{(c)}$ over the entire set Θ. It also illustrates the significance of integrability within a central problem of microeconomics. As mentioned above, the second example in Subsection 2.7.2 illustrates how the construction may fail because a c-dimensional plane does not exist that intersects every maximal integral manifold of the distribution $\mathcal{D}$.

2.7.1 Example: Consumer Demand

Recall the problem posed in Subsection 1.3.1.[25] A vector $\theta \in \Theta = \mathbb{R}^n_{++}$ denotes a bundle of $n \geq 2$ goods. A C^∞ mapping $p : \Theta \to \mathbb{R}^n_{++}$ is given.

---

[24] The *flagpole method* of Hurwicz and Reiter (2006) for constructing a message process from a partition of Θ is essentially the construction that is used to prove the Frobenius Theorem. The use of this construction in a mechanism design context originates in an insight of Leonard Shapiro. The *method of transversals* of Hurwicz and Reiter (2006) involves selecting a representative element from each set in a covering of Θ as a means of constructing a message process from the covering (e.g., in the same way that a transverse plane to a foliation determines or "selects" a point of intersection with each manifold in the foliation). It abstracts the geometric insight that underlies the construction of the Frobenius Theorem to noncalculus settings.

[25] The discussion that follows is largely drawn from Hurwicz (1971), which addresses the properties of demand and inverse demand functions far more generally than this subsection.

At issue is whether or not there exist preferences for a consumer on Θ for which p is the inverse demand mapping. Preferences are thus sought relative to which each bundle $\theta^* \in \Theta$ is optimal among all $\theta \in \Theta$ that satisfy the budget constraint

$$p(\theta^*) \cdot \theta \leq p(\theta^*) \cdot \theta^* \tag{2.58}$$

determined by the endowment θ^*.

The problem is first normalized by selecting good n as a numéraire. Because $p_n(\theta) > 0$ by assumption, the given mapping p can be replaced by the function $(\widetilde{p}, 1)$ defined by

$$(\widetilde{p}, 1) = \left(\frac{p_1}{p_n}, \frac{p_2}{p_n}, \ldots, \frac{p_{n-1}}{p_n}, 1 \right) \tag{2.59}$$

without altering the solution set of (2.58). For notational convenience, the "~" is dispensed with below and it is simply assumed that a C^∞ mapping $p : \Theta \to \mathbb{R}_{++}^{n-1}$ is given; the problem now to determine whether or not preferences exist for which $(p, 1)$ represents inverse demand. With the normalization, the consumer's budget equation becomes

$$p(\theta^*) \cdot \theta_{-n} + \theta_n = p(\theta^*) \cdot \theta_{-n}^* + \theta_n^* \tag{2.60}$$

given the endowment θ^*, where $\theta_{-n} = (\theta_1, \theta_2, \ldots, \theta_{n-1})$.

An $(n-1)$-dimensional distribution $\mathcal{D}$ is defined as the normal hyperplane to $(p(\theta), 1)$ at each $\theta \in \Theta$,

$$\mathcal{D}(\theta) = \{X(\theta) | (p(\theta), 1) \cdot X(\theta) = 0\}. \tag{2.61}$$

A basis for $\mathcal{D}$ is $(X_t)_{1 \leq t \leq n-1}$, where

$$X_t = -\frac{\partial}{\partial \theta_t} + p_t \frac{\partial}{\partial \theta_n}. \tag{2.62}$$

As depicted in Figure 1.5, the consumer's indifference surfaces that are sought here are the integral manifolds of a foliation defined by $\mathcal{D}$. A necessary and sufficient condition for the existence of this foliation is provided by the Frobenius Theorem, together with the observation that the integrability of $\mathcal{D}$ can be verified using the basis $(X_t)_{1 \leq t \leq n-1}$:

$$\left[X_i, X_j \right] \in \mathcal{D} \tag{2.63}$$

for all $1 \leq i, j \leq n-1$.

Condition (2.63) is now reduced to obtain a condition directly in terms of p. Applying the bilinearity of the Lie bracket together with its formula (2.6) implies

$$
\begin{aligned}
[X_i, X_j] &= \left[-\frac{\partial}{\partial \theta_i} + p_i \frac{\partial}{\partial \theta_n}, -\frac{\partial}{\partial \theta_j} + p_j \frac{\partial}{\partial \theta_n} \right] \\
&= -\left[\frac{\partial}{\partial \theta_i}, p_j \frac{\partial}{\partial \theta_n} \right] - \left[p_i \frac{\partial}{\partial \theta_n}, \frac{\partial}{\partial \theta_j} \right] + \left[p_i \frac{\partial}{\partial \theta_n}, p_j \frac{\partial}{\partial \theta_n} \right] \\
&= -\frac{\partial p_j}{\partial \theta_i} \frac{\partial}{\partial \theta_n} + \frac{\partial p_i}{\partial \theta_j} \frac{\partial}{\partial \theta_n} + \left(p_i \frac{\partial p_j}{\partial \theta_n} - p_j \frac{\partial p_i}{\partial \theta_n} \right) \frac{\partial}{\partial \theta_n} \\
&= \left(\frac{\partial p_i}{\partial \theta_j} - \frac{\partial p_j}{\partial \theta_i} + p_i \frac{\partial p_j}{\partial \theta_n} - p_j \frac{\partial p_i}{\partial \theta_n} \right) \frac{\partial}{\partial \theta_n}.
\end{aligned}
\tag{2.64}
$$

Noting the $-\partial/\partial \theta_t$ term in each X_t, it is clear from (2.64) that $[X_i, X_j]$ can be expressed as a linear combination of the basis $(X_t)_{1 \le t \le n-1}$ if and only if

$$
\frac{\partial p_i}{\partial \theta_j} - \frac{\partial p_j}{\partial \theta_i} + p_i \frac{\partial p_j}{\partial \theta_n} - p_j \frac{\partial p_i}{\partial \theta_n} = 0,
\tag{2.65}
$$

or equivalently,

$$
\frac{\partial p_i}{\partial \theta_j} - p_j \frac{\partial p_i}{\partial \theta_n} = \frac{\partial p_j}{\partial \theta_i} - p_i \frac{\partial p_j}{\partial \theta_n}.
\tag{2.66}
$$

Equation (2.66) holding for all $1 \le i, j \le n-1$ is thus necessary and sufficient for the integrability of $\mathcal{D}$. This reduced form of the integrability condition is commonly expressed as the requirement that the *Antonelli substitution matrix*

$$
A = \left(\frac{\partial p_i}{\partial \theta_j} - p_j \frac{\partial p_i}{\partial \theta_n} \right)_{1 \le i, j \le n-1}
\tag{2.67}
$$

is symmetric.[26]

This symmetry condition is necessary and sufficient for the existence of a foliation with the property that the integral manifold $S(\theta^*)$ is tangent to the budget hyperplane (2.60) at θ^*. Interpreting $S(\theta^*)$ as an indifference surface of the preferences, tangency between $S(\theta^*)$ and the budget hyperplane is necessary but not sufficient to insure that θ^* is optimal in the budget set relative to the preferences. Sufficiency of the tangency condition is insured

---

[26] This integrability condition was first identified by Antonelli (1886) with later clarification by Samuelson (1950). In particular, Samuelson showed that the symmetry of the Antonelli substitution matrix is equivalent to the symmetry of the Slutsky substitution matrix when quantity demanded is an invertible function of price.

if the Antonelli substitution matrix (2.67) is also negative semidefinite, for this condition insures convexity of the indifference surfaces.[27] Symmetry of A is thus necessary for $(p, 1)$ to be an inverse demand mapping, while symmetry and negative semidefiniteness of A are together sufficient to insure that $(p, 1)$ is an inverse demand mapping.

A Utility Function That Represents the Preferences

Following the proof of Theorem 4, a function U whose level sets are the integral manifolds of $\mathcal{D}$ is constructed by selecting a line that transversally intersects the integral manifolds. Debreu (1972) selects the line

$$\theta_1 = \theta_2 = \cdots = \theta_n. \tag{2.68}$$

For $y \in \mathbb{R}$, let $\bar{y} \in \mathbb{R}^n$ denote the vector $\bar{y} = (y, y, \ldots, y)$. The utility $U(\theta)$ thus equals the value of $y \in \mathbb{R}$ such that

$$S(\theta) = S(\bar{y}), \tag{2.69}$$

i.e., θ and $\bar{y}$ lie on the same indifference surface and are consequently equivalent. This is depicted in Figure 2.13(a). The assumption that $p(\theta) \in \mathbb{R}^n_{++}$ for all θ insures that U is well defined globally on Θ.

For $\theta^* \in \Theta$, an alternative approach of Samuelson (1950) and Hurwicz (1971) selects the line

$$\left\{ \left(\theta^*_{-n}, \theta_n \right) \mid \theta_n > 0 \right\} \tag{2.70}$$

as the transverse hyperplane. As depicted in Figure 2.13(b), $U^*(\theta)$ is defined as the point $(\theta^*_{-n}, U^*(\theta))$ at which $S(\theta)$ intersects this line.

2.7.2 Example: A Transverse Plane May Not Exist Globally

The construction that proves *Sufficiency* in Theorem 4 fails in this example because no c-dimensional plane transversally intersects each integral manifold of $\mathcal{D}$. More generally, it will be shown that a mapping $u_{(c)}$ cannot be defined globally despite the example's simplicity. The parameter space Θ is the open unit square $(0, 1)^2 \subset \mathbb{R}^2$ and the distribution $\mathcal{D}$ is spanned at each point by the vector field

$$X(\theta) = \left(-1, 2 \left(\theta_1 - \frac{1}{2} \right) \right). \tag{2.71}$$

---

[27] See, for instance, Hurwicz (1971, p. 194).

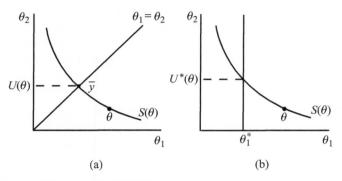

(a)   (b)

Figure 2.13. Graph (a) depicts the definition in Debreu (1972) of a utility function U that indexes the indifference surfaces $S(\theta)$ of a consumer. In the case of $n = 2$ goods depicted here, $U(\theta) = y$ if the consumer is indifferent between θ and $\bar{y} = (y, y)$, i.e., $\bar{y} \in S(\theta)$. Graph (b) depicts the approach of Samuelson (1950) and Hurwicz (1971) in which the indifference surfaces are indexed using the vertical line $\theta_1 = \theta_1^*$: $U^*(\theta)$ is the value of θ_2 such that the consumer is indifferent between θ and $(\theta_1^*, U^*(\theta))$, i.e., $(\theta_1^*, U^*(\theta)) \in S(\theta)$. In terms of the proof of Theorem 4, graph (a) depicts the numbering of the submanifolds in a foliation using the diagonal line $\theta_1 = \theta_2$ as the transverse plane to the submanifolds, while graph (b) depicts this numbering using the vertical line $\theta_1 = \theta_1^*$ as the transverse plane.

The maximal integral manifold of $\mathcal{D}$ through θ^* is the image of the integral curve

$$\rho(X, \theta^*, t) = \left(\theta_1^* - t, \theta_2^* - \left(\theta_1^* - t - \frac{1}{2} \right)^2 + \left(\theta_1^* - \frac{1}{2} \right)^2 \right),$$

where t is restricted to some open real interval containing 0 so that this integral curve goes to the boundary of the unit square Θ but does not cross it. Several maximal integral manifolds of $\mathcal{D}$ are depicted in Figure 2.14. It is clear from this figure that no line can intersect each maximal integral manifold of $\mathcal{D}$ exactly once. The construction that proves *Sufficiency* in Theorem 4 thus fails in this example.

The integral manifolds in this example are the intersection with the unit square Θ of the level sets of the function

$$f(\theta_1, \theta_2) = \theta_2 + \left(\theta_1 - \frac{1}{2} \right)^2. \tag{2.72}$$

The integral manifolds of $\mathcal{D}$ are obtained by graphing the parabola $f(\theta) = 0$ and translating it vertically. This function f does not index the maximal integral manifolds of $\mathcal{D}$ because it assigns the same number to distinct

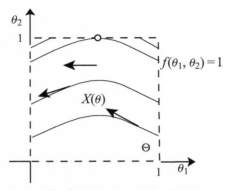

Figure 2.14. A line does not exist that crosses each integral manifold of $\mathcal{D}$ exactly once.

integral manifolds (i.e., the distinct connected components of the intersection of certain level sets of f with Θ). It is clear that a continuous function $u_{(c)}$ does not exist that numbers the maximal integral manifolds because approaching the level set $f(\theta) = 1$ from below implies that $u_{(c)}$ must assign the same value to each of the two distinct maximal integral manifolds of $\mathcal{D}$ that lie in this level set.

The reader may be dissatisfied with this example because it seems to rest on the rather contrived restriction of the function f to the open unit square. The point of example is primarily to illustrate that the method of the proof of *Sufficiency* in Theorem 4 may not work globally, even if the parameter space Θ is elementary. It is also true that the open unit square is diffeomorphic to the positive orthant $\mathbb{R}^2_{++} = \{(\theta_1, \theta_2)|\theta_1, \theta_2 > 0\}$: there exists smooth, one-to-one, and surjective mappings $\varsigma : \mathbb{R}^2_{++} \to \Theta$. The mapping ς can be chosen so that $\lim_{\theta_2 \to 1} |\varsigma^{-1}(\theta)| = \infty$.[28] The composition $\mathcal{D} \circ \varsigma$ defines a smooth, integrable, distribution on $\mathbb{R}^2_{++}$ that may not in any respect appear contrived. The existence of a continuous mapping $u_{(c)} : \mathbb{R}^2_{++} \to \mathbb{R}$ that properly numbers the maximal integral manifolds of $\mathcal{D} \circ \varsigma$ would imply that the mapping $u_{(c)} \circ \varsigma^{-1}$ properly numbers the integral manifolds of $\mathcal{D}$. The above argument thus shows that no such mapping $u_{(c)}$ exists on $\mathbb{R}^2_{++}$.

It is assumed throughout this text that Θ is open to avoid the complications that can arise at boundary points. It is now shown, however, that this example does not depend on the assumption that Θ is open: a suitable

---

[28] One example is

$$\varsigma(\theta) = \left(1 - \frac{1}{1 + \theta_1}, 1 - \frac{1}{1 + \theta_2}\right).$$

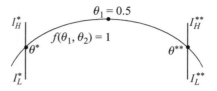

Figure 2.15. The vertical intervals I_L^*, I_H^*, I_L^{**}, and I_H^{**} are inside Θ.

function $u_{(c)}$ does not exist even if the foliation defined by $\mathcal{D}$ is extended to the closed unit square $\overline{\Theta}$. Suppose for the sake of contradiction that a continuous mapping $u_{(c)}$ exists that assigns a unique value to each integral manifold of $\mathcal{D}$ in $\overline{\Theta}$. A translation allows us to assume that $u_{(c)}$ equals 0 on $f^{-1}(1)$. As illustrated in Figure 2.15, select $\theta^*, \theta^{**} \in f^{-1}(1) \cap \Theta$ such that $\theta_1^* < 0.5 < \theta_2^{**}$. It was crucial in the above proof of nonexistence of $u_{(c)}$ on Θ that θ^* and θ^{**} are in distinct integral manifolds of $\mathcal{D}$ in Θ; θ^* and θ^{**}, however, lie in the same integral manifold of $\mathcal{D}$ in $\overline{\Theta}$ and $u_{(c)}(\theta^*) = u_{(c)}(\theta^{**}) = 0$. Choose $\varepsilon > 0$ so that the vertical closed intervals

$$I_L^* = \left\{ (\theta_1^*, \theta_2) \, \middle| \, \theta_2 \in [\theta_2^* - \varepsilon, \theta_2^*] \right\},$$

$$I_H^* = \left\{ (\theta_1^*, \theta_2) \, \middle| \, \theta_2 \in [\theta_2^*, \theta_2^* + \varepsilon] \right\},$$

$$I_L^{**} = \left\{ (\theta_1^{**}, \theta_2) \, \middle| \, \theta_2 \in [\theta_2^{**} - \varepsilon, \theta_2^{**}] \right\},$$

$$I_H^{**} = \left\{ (\theta_1^{**}, \theta_2) \, \middle| \, \theta_2 \in [\theta_2^{**}, \theta_2^{**} + \varepsilon] \right\}$$

all lie in Θ. The continuity of $u_{(c)}$ implies that

$$u_{(c)}\left(I_L^*\right), \quad u_{(c)}\left(I_H^*\right), \quad u_{(c)}\left(I_L^{**}\right), \quad \text{and} \quad u_{(c)}\left(I_H^{**}\right) \tag{2.73}$$

are closed subintervals of $\mathbb{R}$. Each of the subintervals in (2.73) has nonempty interior because its elements index a countable set of integral manifolds of $\mathcal{D}$ in $\overline{\Theta}$. The assumption that $u_{(c)}$ unambiguously numbers the integral manifolds of $\mathcal{D}$ implies that

$$\begin{aligned} \{0\} &= u_{(c)}\left(I_L^*\right) \cap u_{(c)}\left(I_H^*\right) \\ &= u_{(c)}\left(I_L^{**}\right) \cap u_{(c)}\left(I_H^{**}\right) \\ &= u_{(c)}\left(I_H^*\right) \cap u_{(c)}\left(I_H^{**}\right). \end{aligned} \tag{2.74}$$

Assume without loss of generality that $u_{(c)}(\theta) \leq 0$ for $\theta \in I_L^* \cup I_L^{**}$. Consequently, $u_{(c)}(\theta) \geq 0$ for $\theta \in I_H^* \cup I_H^{**}$. It is therefore the case that each of the sets $u_{(c)}(I_H^*)$ and $u_{(c)}(I_H^{**})$ is a closed subinterval of $[0, \infty)$ with nonempty interior that contains 0. It follows that $u_{(c)}(I_H^*) \cap u_{(c)}(I_H^{**})$ has a nonempty interior, which contradicts the last equality of (2.74). A continuous mapping $u_{(c)}$ therefore does not exist on $\overline{\Theta}$ that indexes the integral manifolds of $\mathcal{D}$.

It is worth noting that the global nonexistence of the mapping $u_{(c)}$ in this example does not depend on a maximal integral manifold of $\mathcal{D}$ returning again and again to an arbitrarily small neighborhood of a point θ^* (as nonexistence did in the examples of Subsections 2.6.1 and 2.6.3). In this example, a neighborhood $O(\theta^*)$ of any θ^* can be chosen so that any maximal integral manifold of $\mathcal{D}$ intersects $O(\theta^*)$ at most once. Each maximal integral manifold of $\mathcal{D}$ is an imbedded submanifold of Θ, and so *Distribution*$\Rightarrow$*Foliation* holds in this example without weakening the definition of a submanifold in *Foliation*. The "cycling" of a maximal integral manifold that was discussed in Section 2.6 is thus not the only factor that prevents the nonexistence of a global numbering scheme $u_{(c)}$.

3

Application to Mechanisms

3.1 Two Examples

Having discussed integrability, the Frobenius Theorem, and the equivalence of *Distribution, Manifold,* and *Mapping* at some length in Chapter 2, it is appropriate to begin the analysis of mechanisms with two examples that illustrate how decentralization changes Figure 1.4. These examples highlight the mathematical issues that arise when the equivalence of Figure 1.4 is investigated in the context of mechanisms. They are drawn from two classic models of microeconomics – Cournot competition and trade in a Walrasian equilibrium. The informal presentation of *Direct Sum, Product Structure,* and *Message Process* in Section 1.4 provides sufficient background for understanding these examples.

Some notation that will be used throughout the remainder of the text is first summarized. Agent i's *parameter vector* θ_i will be written as

$$\theta_i \equiv (\theta_{i,t})_{1 \leq t \leq d_i + c_i} \in \Theta_i \subset \mathbb{R}^{d_i + c_i} \tag{3.1}$$

for some $d_i, c_i > 0$, where agent i's *parameter space* Θ_i is an open subset of $\mathbb{R}^{d_i + c_i}$. A parameter vector θ_i will sometimes be written as

$$\theta_i \equiv \left(\theta_{(i,d_i)}, \theta_{(i,c_i)}\right), \tag{3.2}$$

where

$$\theta_{(i,d_i)} \equiv (\theta_{i,t})_{1 \leq t \leq d_i} \tag{3.3}$$

and

$$\theta_{(i,c_i)} \equiv (\theta_{i,t})_{d_i + 1 \leq t \leq d_i + c_i}. \tag{3.4}$$

An integral manifold of the distribution $\mathcal{D}$ through θ will continue to be denoted as $S(\theta)$ and an integral manifold of the distribution $\mathcal{D}_i$ will be written as $S_i(\theta)$. The submanifold $S_i(\theta)$ is a subset of $\Theta_i \times \{\theta_{-i}\}$; $S_i^*(\theta)$ will denote its projection into Θ_i. Notice that $S_i^*(\theta)$ is a submanifold of Θ_i and that

$$S_i(\theta) = S_i^*(\theta) \times \{\theta_{-i}\}. \tag{3.5}$$

Finally, there are three points that the reader should have in mind as he or she works through these examples:

- The main purpose of these examples is to introduce the reader to *Product Structure*. *Product Structure* adds a requirement to *Foliation* that concerns how the parameter space Θ is partitioned by d-dimensional submanifolds: in *Product Structure*, the submanifold $S(\theta)$ through the point θ can be written as a Cartesian product

$$S(\theta) = \prod_{i=1}^{n} S_i^*(\theta),$$

where $S_i^*(\theta)$ is a d_i-dimensional submanifold of Θ_i and $d \equiv \Sigma_{i=1}^n d_i$.
- The submanifold $S_i^*(\theta)$ can depend on the parameters θ_{-i} of the other agents besides agent i. A message process thus does not typically define a unique partition of each agent's parameter space Θ_i, for the partition of Θ_i may vary with the parameters θ_{-i} of the other agents. It is this feature that makes *Product Structure* a far richer and more complicated geometric structure than it may appear at first glance.
- The examples in Subsections 3.1.1 and 3.1.2 both start with a *Message Process* and then derive the corresponding *Product Structure* and *Direct Sum*. Proceeding in the direction *Message Process*⇒*Product Structure*⇒*Direct Sum* is routine and it is followed here to familiarize the reader with the topic. The implication *Direct Sum*⇒*Message Process* is the real objective of this theory because it represents the first-order approach to constructing mechanisms. It is also the most difficult step in establishing the local equivalence of *Direct Sum*, *Product Structure*, and *Message Process*.

3.1.1 Example: Cournot Duopoly with Quadratic Cost

This example is a special case of the classic model of Cournot concerning competition among firms. The parameters of the general model satisfy $n = 2$ and $c_1 = c_2 = d_1 = d_2 = 1$ in this example.

There are two firms that produce the same product. For $i = 1, 2$, let $m_i \geq 0$ measure the output of firm i. The price p at which the total output $m_1 + m_2$ of the two firms is sold is given by the inverse demand function

$$p(m_1 + m_2) = \begin{cases} 10 - (m_1 + m_2) & \text{if } m_1 + m_2 \leq 10, \\ 0 & \text{if } m_1 + m_2 > 10 \end{cases} \tag{3.6}$$

The cost $C_i(m_i, \theta_i)$ to firm i of manufacturing the output m_i is

$$C_i(m_i, \theta_i) \equiv \frac{\theta_{i,1}}{2} m_i^2 + \theta_{i,2} m_i, \tag{3.7}$$

where $\theta_i = (\theta_{i,1}, \theta_{i,2})$ is the privately known technology of firm i. In order to insure the existence of an interior solution below, it is assumed that

$$\Theta_i = \{\theta_i | 0 < \theta_{i,1}, \theta_{i,2} < 2\}$$

for $i = 1, 2$.

The message space $M = \{(m_1, m_2) | m_1, m_2 \geq 0\}$ is the strategy space of the Cournot competition game in which each firm i chooses its output m_i to maximize its profit given its cost function $C_i(m_i, \theta_i)$ and the output m_{-i} of the other firm. The profit $P_i(m_1, m_2, \theta_i)$ of firm i is its revenue minus its cost,

$$P_i(m_1, m_2, \theta_i) = (10 - m_i - m_{-i}) m_i - \left(\frac{\theta_{i,1}}{2} m_i^2 + \theta_{i,2} m_i \right). \tag{3.8}$$

The first-order condition for selecting m_i to maximize $P_i(\cdot, m_{-i}, \theta_i)$ is

$$0 = \frac{\partial P_i}{\partial m_i} = (10 - m_{-i} - \theta_{i,2}) - (2 + \theta_{i,1}) m_i. \tag{3.9}$$

The first derivative test implies that the solution m_i to (3.9) maximizes firm i's profit given the vector θ_i and the output m_{-i} of the other firm.

As analyzed by Cournot (1838), the first-order condition (3.9) suggests the following message adjustment rule for each firm. Given its vector θ_i and the output $m(t) = (m_1(t), m_2(t))$ of the two firms at time t, firm i chooses its output $m_i(t + 1)$ for the $(t + 1)$'s message adjustment rule is thus

$$m_i(t + 1) - m_i(t) \equiv \alpha_i(m(t), \theta_i) \equiv \frac{10 - m_i(t) - \theta_{i,2}}{2 + \theta_{i,1}} - m_i(t). \tag{3.10}$$

Our focus in this text is on the equilibrium in which neither firm wants to change its output. Equilibrium is defined by the pair of equations

$$0 = \alpha_1(m, \theta_1) = \frac{10 - m_2 - \theta_{1,2}}{2 + \theta_{1,1}} - m_1, \tag{3.11}$$

and

$$0 = \alpha_2(m, \theta_2) = \frac{10 - m_1 - \theta_{2,2}}{2 + \theta_{2,1}} - m_2, \tag{3.12}$$

or equivalently,

$$m_1 = \frac{(10 - \theta_{1,2})(2 + \theta_{2,1}) - (10 - \theta_{2,2})}{(2 + \theta_{2,1})(2 + \theta_{1,1}) - 1}, \tag{3.13}$$

and

$$m_2 = \frac{(10 - \theta_{2,2})(2 + \theta_{1,1}) - (10 - \theta_{1,2})}{(2 + \theta_{2,1})(2 + \theta_{1,1}) - 1}. \tag{3.14}$$

The pair (m_1, m_2) in (3.13)–(3.14) is a Cournot–Nash equilibrium.

I now discuss this equilibrium from the perspective of the equivalence that will be established later in this chapter. The value $u_{(c)}(\theta)$ of the mapping in *Message Process* is the equilibrium pair (m_1, m_2) given by the formulas in (3.13)–(3.14). Given $\theta^* \in \Theta$, the level set $u_{(c)}^{-1}(u_{(c)}(\theta^*))$ consists of all values of θ for which $m^* = u_{(c)}(\theta^*)$ is an equilibrium. It can be shown that the derivative $D_\theta u_{(c)}(\theta^*)$ has rank equal to 2 at every $\theta^* \in \Theta$. The level set $u_{(c)}^{-1}(u_{(c)}(\theta^*))$ is thus a 2-dimensional C^∞ submanifold of Θ.

It is not obvious from a glance at formulas (3.13)–(3.14) that every level set of $u_{(c)}$ has a special structure that reflects the fact that this mapping defines the equilibrium of a message process. As in *Message Process*, $u_{(c)}(\theta) = m$ solves a system of the form

$$(0, 0) = \alpha(\theta, m) = (\alpha_1(\theta_1, m), \alpha_2(\theta_2, m)).$$

For a given m^* in the image of $u_{(c)}$, the level set $u_{(c)}^{-1}(m^*)$ consists of all values of θ that solve the two equations $0 = \alpha_1(\theta_1, m^*)$ and $0 = \alpha_2(\theta_2, m^*)$. The equation $0 = \alpha_1(\theta_1, m^*)$ restricts the value of θ_1 but not the value of θ_2, while the equation $0 = \alpha_2(\theta_2, m^*)$ restricts the value of θ_2 but not the value of θ_1. The level set $u_{(c)}^{-1}(m^*)$ is therefore a Cartesian product of two 1-dimensional C^∞ manifolds, i.e., the solution set in Θ_1 of the equation $0 = \alpha_1(\cdot, m^*)$ and the solution set in Θ_2 of the equation $0 = \alpha_2(\cdot, m^*)$:

$$u_{(c)}^{-1}(m^*) = \{\theta \in \Theta | \alpha(\theta, m^*) = 0\}$$

$$= \{\theta_1 \in \Theta_1 | \alpha_1(\theta_1, m^*) = 0\} \times \{\theta_2 \in \Theta_2 | \alpha_2(\theta_2, m^*) = 0\} \tag{3.15}$$

$$= \left\{ \theta_1 \in \Theta_1 \Big| 0 = \frac{10 - m_2^* - \theta_{1,2}}{2 + \theta_{1,1}} - m_1^* \right\}$$

$$\times \left\{ \theta_2 \in \Theta_2 \Big| 0 = \frac{10 - m_1^* - \theta_{2,2}}{2 + \theta_{2,1}} - m_2^* \right\}.$$

This is the *Product Structure* that is discussed in Section 1.4.

Product Structure partitions the subset Θ of $\mathbb{R}^4$ as a union of 2-dimensional submanifolds by partitioning both Θ_1 and Θ_2 as unions of 1-dimensional submanifolds (in this case, open line segments). As noted before, however, there is not necessarily a single partition of each parameter space, for the partition of Θ_1 can vary with the value of θ_2 and the partition of Θ_2 can vary with the value of θ_1. Consider the 1-dimensional submanifold in Θ_1 that is defined by the equation $\alpha_1(\theta_1, m) = 0$. Rewriting formula (3.11) for α_1 implies that this submanifold is the line in Θ_1 given by the equation

$$\theta_{1,2} = -m_1\theta_{1,1} + (10 - m_2 - 2m_1). \tag{3.16}$$

Let $\theta_1^* = (1, 1)$ and $\theta_2^* = (1, 1)$. It follows from (3.13)–(3.14) that

$$u_{(c)}(\theta_1^*, \theta_2^*) = (m_1^*, m_2^*) = \left(\frac{9}{4}, \frac{9}{4}\right). \tag{3.17}$$

The submanifold of Θ_1 through θ_1^* determined by θ_2^* is thus the line segment given by

$$\theta_{1,2} = -\frac{9}{4}\theta_{1,1} + \frac{13}{4}. \tag{3.18}$$

Vary θ_2 away from θ_2^*. From (3.13)–(3.14), the value of $u_{(c)}(\theta_1^*, \theta_2)$ for an arbitrary value of θ_2 is given by

$$m_1 = \frac{8 + 9\theta_{2,1} + \theta_{2,2}}{5 + 3\theta_{2,1}} \tag{3.19}$$

and

$$m_2 = \frac{21 - 3\theta_{2,2}}{5 + 3\theta_{2,1}}. \tag{3.20}$$

It is clear from (3.19)–(3.20) together with (3.16) that the slope and the intercept of the line through θ_1^* in (3.18) can be made to vary away from their respective values of $-9/4$ and $13/4$ at $\theta_2^* = (1, 1)$ by changing the value of θ_2 away from θ_2^*. From (3.16), in fact, it is clear that changing the value of θ_2 away from θ_2^* fails to alter the submanifold of Θ_1 through θ_1^* only if θ_2 is changed without altering the values of m_1^* and m_2^*, i.e., only if θ_2 continues to satisfy $\alpha_2(\theta_2, m^*) = 0$.

Having noted *Product Structure* in this setting and the sense in which the equilibrium mapping $u_{(c)}$ satisfies *Message Process*, this example is now completed with a discussion of the sense in which the tangent space to a level set of $u_{(c)}$ is a distribution that satisfies *Direct Sum*. It follows from

(3.13)–(3.14) that the derivative $D_\theta u_{(c)}(\theta)$ of $u_{(c)}$ at $\theta \in \Theta$ is given by the 2×4 matrix

$$D_\theta u_{(c)}(\theta) = \frac{1}{(2 + \theta_{2,1})(2 + \theta_{1,1}) - 1}$$

$$\times \begin{pmatrix} -(2 + \theta_{2,1})\lambda_1 & -(2 + \theta_{2,1}) & \lambda_2 & 1 \\ \lambda_1 & 1 & -(2 + \theta_{1,1})\lambda_2 & -(2 + \theta_{1,1}) \end{pmatrix},$$

$$(3.21)$$

where

$$\lambda_1 = \frac{(10 - \theta_{1,2})(2 + \theta_{2,1}) - (10 - \theta_{2,2})}{(2 + \theta_{2,1})(2 + \theta_{1,1}) - 1}$$

and

$$\lambda_2 = \frac{(10 - \theta_{2,2})(2 + \theta_{1,1}) - (10 - \theta_{1,2})}{(2 + \theta_{2,1})(2 + \theta_{1,1}) - 1}.$$

The tangent plane at θ to the level set $u_{(c)}^{-1}(u_{(c)}(\theta))$ is the null space of this derivative mapping. This null space is 2-dimensional because this matrix has rank 2 at every point $\theta \in \Theta$. While it may not be obvious from a glance at (3.21), this null space has a special feature that reflects the informational decentralization: the null space of $D_\theta u_{(c)}(\theta)$ intersects each of the 2-dimensional coordinate planes spanned by

$$\left\{ \frac{\partial}{\partial \theta_{1,1}}(\theta), \frac{\partial}{\partial \theta_{1,2}}(\theta) \right\} \tag{3.22}$$

and

$$\left\{ \frac{\partial}{\partial \theta_{2,1}}(\theta), \frac{\partial}{\partial \theta_{2,2}}(\theta) \right\}, \tag{3.23}$$

respectively, in a line. This is notable because a generic 2-dimensional vector subspace of $\mathbb{R}^4$ intersects each of these 2-dimensional coordinate planes only at the origin of coordinates.

Two vectors in the null space of $D_\theta u_{(c)}(\theta)$ are (for instance)

$$X_1(\theta) \equiv \frac{\partial}{\partial \theta_{1,1}} + \left(\frac{-(10 - \theta_{1,2})(2 + \theta_{2,1}) - (10 - \theta_{2,2})}{(2 + \theta_{2,1})(2 + \theta_{1,1}) - 1} \right) \frac{\partial}{\partial \theta_{1,2}} \tag{3.24}$$

and

$$X_2(\theta) \equiv \frac{\partial}{\partial \theta_{2,1}} + \left(\frac{-(10 - \theta_{2,2})(2 + \theta_{1,1}) - (10 - \theta_{1,2})}{(2 + \theta_{2,1})(2 + \theta_{1,1}) - 1} \right) \frac{\partial}{\partial \theta_{2,2}}. \quad (3.25)$$

Define the 2-dimensional distribution $\mathcal{D}(\theta)$ as the tangent space at θ to the level set $u_{(c)}^{-1}(u_{(c)}(\theta))$. The above remarks imply that $X_1(\theta)$ and $X_2(\theta)$ are a basis of $\mathcal{D}(\theta)$ at each $\theta \in \Theta$. The vector field X_i lies in the $(\partial/\partial\theta_{i,1}, \partial/\partial\theta_{i,2})$ coordinate plane; at a given point θ with $u_{(c)}(\theta) = m$, $X_i(\theta)$ spans the tangent space of the 1-dimensional submanifold $\{\theta_i | \alpha_i(\theta_i, m) = 0\}$ of Θ_i that is the intersection of $u_{(c)}^{-1}(m)$ and the plane $\Theta_i \times \{\theta_{-i}\}$. Let $\mathcal{D}_i(\theta)$ denote the 1-dimensional distribution spanned by $X_i(\theta)$. Because $\{X_1(\theta), X_2(\theta)\}$ is a basis of $\mathcal{D}(\theta)$, each vector in $\mathcal{D}(\theta)$ can be expressed in a unique way as a sum of a vector in $\mathcal{D}_1(\theta)$ plus a vector in $\mathcal{D}_2(\theta)$. Every sum of such vectors also lies within $\mathcal{D}$. The distribution $\mathcal{D}$ is thus the direct sum of the distributions $\mathcal{D}_1$ and $\mathcal{D}_2$,

$$\mathcal{D} \equiv \mathcal{D}_1 \oplus \mathcal{D}_2. \quad (3.26)$$

3.1.2 Example: Exchange Economy with Quadratic Utility

This example concerns the Walrasian equilibrium of an exchange economy in which there are two agents and two commodities. As in the previous example, $n = 2$ and $c_1 = c_2 = d_1 = d_2 = 1$. The initial endowments of agents 1 and 2 are $w_1 = (1, 0)$ and $w_2 = (0, 1)$, respectively. The utility function of agent i is the quadratic function

$$U_i(x_{i1}, x_{i2}) \equiv \theta_{i,1} x_{i1} + \theta_{i,2} x_{i2} - \frac{x_{i1}^2}{2} - \frac{x_{i2}^2}{2}, \quad (3.27)$$

where x_{ij} denotes agent i's consumption of good j and $\theta_i = (\theta_{i,1}, \theta_{i,2}) \in \Theta_i$ is a vector that determines his preferences for the two goods. The sets Θ_1 and Θ_2 are

$$\Theta_1 \equiv \{(\theta_{1,1}, \theta_{1,2}) \in \mathbb{R}^2 | 1 < \theta_{1,2} < \theta_{1,1} < 2\} \quad (3.28)$$

and

$$\Theta_2 \equiv \{(\theta_{2,1}, \theta_{2,2}) \in \mathbb{R}^2 | 1 < \theta_{2,1} < \theta_{2,2} < 2\}. \quad (3.29)$$

The constraints on θ_1 and θ_2 in (3.28) and (3.29) insure the monotonicity of preferences over the set of feasible allocations.

It can be shown that the price of good 2 in a Walrasian equilibrium of this exchange economy is nonzero for all $\theta_1 \in \Theta_1$ and $\theta_2 \in \Theta_2$. Good 2 can thus serve as the *numèraire*, i.e., the price of good 2 is fixed at one while the price of good 1 is a nonnegative real number p. Given the price vector $(p, 1)$, agent 1's utility is maximized subject to his budget constraint $px_{11} + x_{12} = p$ at

$$x_{11} = \frac{\theta_{1,1} + p(p - \theta_{1,2})}{1 + p^2}, \tag{3.30}$$

$$x_{12} = p(1 - x_{11}) = p\left(1 - \frac{\theta_{1,1} + p(p - \theta_{1,2})}{1 + p^2}\right), \tag{3.31}$$

and agent 2's utility is maximized subject to his budget constraint $px_{21} + x_{22} = 1$ at

$$x_{21} = \frac{\theta_{2,1} + p(p - \theta_{2,2})}{1 + p^2}, \tag{3.32}$$

$$x_{22} = 1 - px_{21} = 1 - p\left(\frac{\theta_{2,1} + p(1 - \theta_{2,2})}{1 + p^2}\right). \tag{3.33}$$

The formulas in (3.30)–(3.33) present each agent i's demand for the two goods as a function of his vector θ_i and the price p of good 1.

For given values of θ_1 and θ_2, a *Walrasian equilibrium* is a five-tuple

$$(x_{11}, x_{12}, x_{21}, x_{22}, p)$$

that satisfies (3.30)–(3.33) and the following constraints of *feasibility*:

$$x_{21} = 1 - x_{11},$$

$$x_{22} = 1 - x_{12},$$

$$0 \leq x_{11}, x_{12} \leq 1.$$

There exists a unique Walrasian equilibrium for each choice of $\theta_1 \in \Theta_1$ and $\theta_2 \in \Theta_2$. The equilibrium price p is

$$p = \frac{\theta_{1,1} + \theta_{2,1} - 1}{\theta_{1,2} + \theta_{2,2} - 1}. \tag{3.34}$$

With the restrictions imposed on θ_1 and θ_2 in (3.28) and (3.29), it can be shown that the equilibrium allocation lies in the interior of the set of feasible allocations (i.e., $0 < x_{i1}, x_{i2} < 1$ for $i = 1, 2$).

Consider the *competitive message process* whose equilibrium state for each choice of θ_1 and θ_2 is the Walrasian equilibrium that is determined by these parameters. An element of the message space M^* consists of a positive value of p together with positive consumption bundles for the two agents:

$$M^* = \left\{ (x_{11}, x_{12}, x_{21}, x_{22}, p) \in \mathbb{R}^5 \mid x_{11}, x_{12}, x_{21}, x_{22}, p > 0 \right\}. \quad (3.35)$$

Letting $x_{11}(t)$, $x_{12}(t)$, $x_{21}(t)$, $x_{22}(t)$, and $p(t)$ denote the state of the system at time t, agent 1 adjusts his bundle $(x_{11}(t), x_{12}(t))$ toward the bundle in (3.30)–(3.31) that is optimal for him given his budget constraint $p(t)x_{11} + x_{12} = p(t)$:

$$\dot{x}_{11}(t) = \frac{\theta_{1,1} + p(t)(p(t) - \theta_{1,2})}{1 + (p(t))^2} - x_{11}(t), \quad (3.36)$$

$$\dot{x}_{12}(t) = p(t)\left(1 - \frac{\theta_{1,1} + p(t)(p(t) - \theta_{1,2})}{1 + (p(t))^2}\right) - x_{12}(t). \quad (3.37)$$

Similarly, agent 2 adjusts his bundle $(x_{21}(t), x_{22}(t))$ toward the bundle given in (3.32)–(3.33) that is optimal for him given his budget constraint $p(t)x_{21} + x_{22} = 1$:

$$\dot{x}_{21}(t) = \frac{\theta_{2,1} + p(t)(1 - \theta_{2,2})}{1 + (p(t))^2} - x_{21}(t), \quad (3.38)$$

$$\dot{x}_{22}(t) = 1 - p(t)\left(\frac{\theta_{2,1} + p(t)(1 - \theta_{2,2})}{1 + (p(t))^2}\right) - x_{22}(t). \quad (3.39)$$

Agent 2 can also serve as the *auctioneer* who adjusts the price $p(t)$ of good 1 according to the excess demand at time t for good 1:

$$\dot{p}(t) = x_{11}(t) + x_{21}(t) - 1. \quad (3.40)$$

In an equilibrium $(x_{11}, x_{12}, x_{21}, x_{22}, p)$ for fixed values of θ_1 and θ_2, agent 1's bundle (x_{11}, x_{12}) and agent 2's bundle (x_{21}, x_{22}) satisfy (3.30)–(3.31) and (3.32)–(3.33), respectively, which means that each agent's bundle maximizes his utility subject to the budget constraint that is determined by the equilibrium value of p. It is also clear from (3.40) that the equilibrium value of p clears the market in the sense that $x_{11} + x_{21} = 1$ (the total initial endowment of good 1). This fact together with the fact that both budget constraints hold in equilibrium imply that $x_{12} + x_{22} = 1$. An equilibrium of this message adjustment process is thus a Walrasian equilibrium, and hence the equilibrium p is the function of θ_1 and θ_2 that is given in Eq. (3.34).

The five-tuples $(x_{11}, x_{12}, x_{21}, x_{22}, p)$ that are Walrasian equilibria for some choice of θ_1 and θ_2 satisfy the equations $x_{11} + x_{21} = 1$, $x_{12} + x_{22} = 1$, $px_{11} + x_{12} = p$, and $px_{21} + x_{22} = 1$. All such five-tuples are thus elements of the 2-dimensional submanifold of M^* that forms the solution set of these equations. This reflects the redundancy (i.e., the linear dependence) of the five message rules of (3.36)–(3.40) in their equilibrium state: for fixed values of θ_1 and θ_2, the values of x_{11} and x_{22} from the equations in (3.30) and (3.32) are sufficient to calculate the remaining three numbers in the Walrasian equilibrium for θ_1 and θ_2 (i.e., $x_{12} = 1 - x_{22}$, $x_{21} = 1 - x_{11}$, and $p = (1 - x_{22})/(1 - x_{11})$).

Because our focus is on the equilibrium state of message processes, it is appropriate to let the message space M consist of just the two variables x_{11} and x_{22}, which are now relabeled as m_1 and m_2, respectively. The message space and the message rules are as follows for the remainder of this example:

$$M = \{(m_1, m_2)|m_1, m_2 > 0\},$$

$$\alpha_1(\theta_1, m) = \frac{\theta_{1,1} + p(p - \theta_{1,2})}{1 + p^2} - m_1, \tag{3.41}$$

and

$$\alpha_2(\theta_2, m) = 1 - p\left(\frac{\theta_{2,1} + p(1 - \theta_{2,2})}{1 + p^2}\right) - m_2.$$

The value of p in these formulas can be written in terms of m_1 and m_2 as

$$p = \frac{1 - x_{22}}{1 - x_{11}} = \frac{1 - m_2}{1 - m_1}. \tag{3.42}$$

The message adjustment rules α_1 and α_2 were obtained from the adjustment rules for x_{11} and x_{22} in (3.36) and (3.39) by replacing x_{11} and x_{22} with m_1 and m_2.

The example is now expressed in terms of *Direct Sum*, *Product Structure*, and *Message Process*. Beginning with *Message Process*, $u_{(c)} : \Theta \rightarrow M$ is the mapping whose value m at $\theta \in \Theta$ is the solution to $\alpha_1(\theta_1, m) = \alpha_2(\theta_2, m) = 0$. As explained above, the ordered pair $u_{(c)}(\theta) = (m_1, m_2)$ consists of agent 1's equilibrium allocation $m_1 = x_{11}$ of good 1 together with agent 2's equilibrium allocation m_2 of good 2. The formulas that define $u_{(c)}(\theta)$ are obvious from the formulas for α_1 and α_2 in (3.41) and (3.42), respectively, once formula (3.34) for the equilibrium value of p as a function of θ is substituted into these equations:

$$u_{(c)}(\theta) = \left(\frac{\theta_{1,1} + p(p - \theta_{1,2})}{1 + p^2}, 1 - p \left(\frac{\theta_{2,1} + p(1 - \theta_{2,2})}{1 + p^2} \right) \right), \quad (3.43)$$

where the value of p is given by (3.34).

Consider next *Product Structure*. For a particular value of $m^* = (m_1^*, m_2^*)$ in the image of $u_{(c)}$, the level set $u_{(c)}^{-1}(m^*)$ consists of all values of θ for which m_1^* is agent 1's demand for good 1 and m_2^* is agent 2's demand for good 2 when the price of good 1 is $p^* = (1 - m_2^*)/(1 - m_1^*)$. Let $x_{ij}(\theta_i, p)$ denote agent i's demand for good j when θ_i is his vector and p is the price of good 1. The level set $u_{(c)}^{-1}(m^*)$ is the Cartesian product

$$u_{(c)}^{-1}(m^*) = \left\{ \theta_1 \in \Theta_1 | x_{11}(\theta_1, p^*) = m_1^* \right\} \times \left\{ \theta_2 \in \Theta_2 | x_{22}(\theta_2, p^*) = m_2^* \right\}. \quad (3.44)$$

Using the formulas in (3.43), this level set can be written as

$$\left\{ \theta_1 \in \Theta_1 | \left(1 + (p^*)^2 \right) m_1^* - (p^*)^2 = \theta_{1,1} - p^* \theta_{1,2} \right\} \quad (3.45)$$

$$\times \left\{ \theta_2 \in \Theta_2 \left| \frac{1 + (p^*)^2}{p^*} (1 - m_2^*) - p^* = \theta_{2,1} - p^* \theta_{2,2} \right. \right\},$$

i.e., it is the product of two lines. As in the case of Cournot competition considered in Subsection 3.1.1, the submanifold of Θ_i that passes through θ_i depends on the value of θ_{-i} only to the extent that changing the value of θ_{-i} affects the equilibrium messages (m_1^*, m_2^*).

At a point $\theta = (\theta_1, \theta_2)$ in the level set (3.45), the line in the $\Theta_i \times \{\theta_{-i}\}$ plane through θ points in the direction of $(p^*, 1)$. With this in mind, it is clear that the 2-dimensional distribution $\mathcal{D}$ whose value at θ is the tangent plane to the submanifold $u_{(c)}^{-1}(u(\theta))$ is spanned by the vectors

$$X_1(\theta) \equiv p(\theta) \frac{\partial}{\partial \theta_{1,1}} + \frac{\partial}{\partial \theta_{1,2}} = \left(\frac{\theta_{1,1} + \theta_{2,1} - 1}{\theta_{1,2} + \theta_{2,2} - 1} \right) \frac{\partial}{\partial \theta_{1,1}} + \frac{\partial}{\partial \theta_{1,2}}$$

and

$$X_2(\theta) \equiv p(\theta) \frac{\partial}{\partial \theta_{2,1}} + \frac{\partial}{\partial \theta_{2,2}} = \left(\frac{\theta_{1,1} + \theta_{2,1} - 1}{\theta_{1,2} + \theta_{2,2} - 1} \right) \frac{\partial}{\partial \theta_{2,1}} + \frac{\partial}{\partial \theta_{2,2}},$$

where the value of $p(\theta)$ is from (3.34). Letting $\mathcal{D}_i$ denote the 1-dimensional distribution spanned by $X_i(\theta)$, it follows that

$$\mathcal{D} \equiv \mathcal{D}_1 \oplus \mathcal{D}_2, \quad (3.46)$$

which illustrates *Direct Sum*.

3.2 *Direct Sum, Product Structure, and Message Process*

I begin with formal statements of *Direct Sum*, *Product Structure*, and *Message Process*:

Direct Sum: For $1 \leq i \leq n$, a d_i-dimensional, integrable, C^∞ distribution $\mathcal{D}_i$ is defined on Θ such that

(i) $\mathcal{D}_i(\theta)$ lies in the span of $\{\partial/\partial\theta_{i,t}\}_{1 \leq t \leq d_i + c_i}$, the set of $d_i + c_i$ coordinate vectors associated with the standard basis for $\mathbb{R}^{d_i + c_i}$;

(ii) the direct sum $\mathcal{D} \equiv \oplus_{i=1}^n \mathcal{D}_i$ is integrable.

Product Structure: For each $1 \leq i \leq n$, Θ is partitioned by d_i-dimensional C^∞ submanifolds, with $S_i(\theta^*)$ denoting the unique submanifold that contains θ^* in the ith partition. These submanifolds have the following properties:

(i) $S_i(\theta^*)$ lies within the $(d_i + c_i)$-dimensional plane $\Theta_i \times \theta^*_{-i}$;

(ii) the distribution $\mathcal{D}_i$ whose value at θ is the tangent space to $S_i(\theta)$ at θ is C^∞ on Θ;

(iii) Θ is partitioned by the C^∞ submanifolds

$$S(\theta) = \prod_{i=1}^n S_i^*(\theta),$$

where $S_i^*(\theta)$ is the projection of $S_i(\theta)$ into Θ_i.

Message Process: A message process $\mathcal{M}P = (\Theta, M, (\mu_i)_{1 \leq i \leq n})$ is given with the following properties:

(i) for each $1 \leq i \leq n$ and each $\theta_i \in \Theta_i$, agent i's equilibrium message set $\mu_i(\theta_i)$ is the solution set in M of an equation $\alpha_i(\theta_i, m) = 0$, where $\alpha_i : \Theta_i \times M \to \mathbb{R}^{c_i}$ is a C^∞ mapping;

(ii) there exists a C^∞ mapping $u_{(c)} : \Theta \to M$ that determines the unique equilibrium message for each $\theta \in \Theta$, i.e.,

$$m \in \bigcap_{i=1}^n \mu_i(\theta_i) \Leftrightarrow u_{(c)}(\theta) = m;$$

(iii) for each $1 \leq i \leq n$ and each $\theta \in \Theta$, the $c_i \times (d_i + c_i)$ matrix $D_{\theta_i}\alpha_i(\theta_i, m)$ has rank c_i at $m = u_{(c)}(\theta)$.

The main ideas of *Direct Sum*, *Product Structure*, and *Message Process* should by now be clear, though the purpose of some regularity assumptions may not become evident until the relationship among *Direct Sum, Product*

Structure, and *Message Process* is investigated formally.[1-3] A restriction has been added in *Message Process* that was not addressed explicitly in the general discussion of Section 1.1. Property (ii) assumes uniqueness of the equilibrium message $u_{(c)}(\theta)$ for each $\theta \in \Theta$. Mulitiple equilibria are common in games, and multiple equilibria are needed if the goal is to realize every value of a correspondence. Attention is thus restricted in this text to a special case in which there is a rule $u_{(c)}$ for selecting an equilibrium for each θ. Uniqueness of equilibrium is assumed here because it simplifies the construction of message processes. In the equivalence of *Message Process* and *Product Structure*, the level sets of the equilibrium rule $u_{(c)}$ are the sets $S(\theta)$ in *Product Structure*. Uniqueness of equilibrium is captured in Property (iii) of *Product Structure*, which requires that each $\theta^* \in \Theta$ belongs to only one of these sets. The next two subsections address the duality between the Property (ii) of *Direct Sum* and Property (iii) of *Product Structure*. These two properties are therefore, respectively, first-order and geometric formulations of uniqueness of equilibrium.

3.2.1 The Duality between Integrability Condition (ii) of *Direct Sum* and Partitioning Condition (iii) of *Product Structure*

Direct Sum is redundant in the sense that the integrability of $\mathcal{D}$ in Property (ii) together with Property (i) implies the integrability of each distribution

---

[1] Property (iii) of *Message Process* prevents redundancy in agent i's system of message equations $\alpha_i(\theta_i, m)$. Chen (1992, pp. 252–253) shows that a mechanism that realizes the objective F and that does not satisfy this condition can be replaced by a mechanism that realizes F with a message space of smaller dimension and that also satisfies the condition. A mechanism that satisfies this condition is therefore deemed *efficient* by Chen. See also Saari (1984, p. 254; 1995, p. 231) for a formulation of efficiency in this sense in terms of regularity conditions on a message process.

[2] It is useful to notice that (iii) of *Message Process* implies that the equilibrium message mapping $u_{(c)}$ is nonsingular. Letting $\alpha(\theta, m) = (\alpha_i(\theta_i, m))_{1 \le i \le n}$, differentiation of $\alpha(\theta, u_{(c)}(\theta)) = 0$ with respect to θ produces

$$0 = D_\theta \alpha + D_m \alpha \cdot D_\theta u_{(c)} \Leftrightarrow D_m \alpha \cdot D_\theta u_{(c)} = -D_\theta \alpha.$$

Property (iii) together with the independence of each $\alpha_i(\theta, m)$ of θ_{-i} implies that rank $D_\theta \alpha = \dim \Theta$, which must therefore also hold for $D_\theta u_{(c)}$.

[3] It is worthwhile at this point to identify some sources for *Direct Sum*, *Product Structure*, and *Message Process* in Hurwicz et al. (1978). In the language of this manuscript, *Product Structure* asserts the existence of a "parameter-indexed product structure" and *Message Process* numbers the sets in this product stucture, producing a "message-indexed product structure." The main ideas of *Product Structure* are identified in Theorem 1 (p. 2) and Theorem 2 (p. 6) of the manuscript. The implication *Product Structure⇒Message Process* is addressed in its Lemma A′ (p. 9) and Lemmas B″₁–B″₃ (pp. 21–32). *Direct Sum* is formulated in Theorem 6 (p. 64) of the manuscript, which states an equivalence of *Direct Sum* and *Product Structure*. As noted in the Preface of this text, each of these results in Hurwicz et al. (1978) are stated in the context of realizing a function f.

$\mathcal{D}_i$. This is shown by the following argument. For $X, Y \in \mathcal{D}_i$, formula (2.6) for the Lie bracket along with (i) implies[4]

$$[X, Y](\theta) \in T_\theta (\Theta_i \times \{\theta_{-i}\}). \qquad (3.47)$$

Because $\mathcal{D}$ is integrable and $\mathcal{D}_i \subset \mathcal{D}$, $[X, Y](\theta) \in \mathcal{D}(\theta)$. Because

$$T_\theta (\{\theta_{-i}\} \times \Theta_i) \cap \mathcal{D}(\theta) = \mathcal{D}_i(\theta), \qquad (3.48)$$

it follows that $[X, Y](\theta) \in \mathcal{D}_i(\theta)$, which verifies the integrability of $\mathcal{D}_i$.

The integrability of each $\mathcal{D}_i$ is explicitly assumed in *Direct Sum* in order to emphasize the significance of the integrability of $\mathcal{D}$ over and above the integrability of $\mathcal{D}_1, \ldots, \mathcal{D}_n$. The significance of the integrability of $\mathcal{D}$ in Property (ii) of *Direct Sum* and its relationship to Property (iii) of *Product Structure* is the subject of this subsection and the next.

For the moment, remove Property (ii) from *Direct Sum* and Property (iii) from *Product Structure*. Also, relax the term "submanifold" in *Product Structure* from "imbedded submanifold" (as is standard in this text) to the weaker "immersed submanifold" for the remainder of this subsection. With this qualification, *Direct Sum* excluding its Property (ii) is equivalent to *Product Structure* excluding its Property (iii): *Direct Sum* excluding (ii) implies the existence of n partitions $\{S_i(\theta)|\theta \in \Theta\}_{1 \le i \le n}$ of Θ having all of the properties of *Product Structure* except its Property (iii), and conversely, *Product Structure* excluding its Property (iii) defines distributions $\mathcal{D}_1, \ldots, \mathcal{D}_n$ that satisfy *Direct Sum* excluding its Property (ii).[5]

Property (i) of both *Direct Sum* and *Product Structure* implies that the projection $S_i^*(\theta)$ of $S_i(\theta)$ into Θ_i is a submanifold of Θ_i. Each product $\Pi_{i=1}^n S_i^*(\theta)$ is also therefore a submanifold of Θ, regardless of whether one starts with *Direct Sum* excluding its Property (ii) or *Product Structure* excluding its Property (iii). The issue of interest in either case is whether or not

$$\left\{ \prod_{i=1}^n S_i^*(\theta)|\theta \in \Theta \right\} \qquad (3.49)$$

---

[4] This step is inspired by a calculation in the proof of Proposition 1 in Hurwicz et al. (1978, pp. 68–69).

[5] As discussed in Subsection 2.6.2, the integral manifolds $S_i(\theta)$ arising from the distributions in *Direct Sum* may only be immersed as submanifolds in Θ instead of imbedded. The submanifolds in *Product Structure* are assumed to be imbedded in Θ. The discussion in this subsection and the next concerns the partitioning of Θ by integral manifolds and not the derivation of a message process from either *Direct Sum* or *Product Structure*. The distinction between immersed and imbedded submanifolds is thus immaterial here and therefore ignored.

is a partition of Θ, for while every θ surely lies within the submanifold $\Pi_{i=1}^{n} S_i^*(\theta)$, some points θ may lie within distinct submanifolds of this form. This is illustrated in an example in Subsection 3.2.2 below. It is explicitly assumed in (iii) of *Product Structure* that (3.49) partitions Θ. This property follows from (ii) in *Direct Sum* once it is proven that each integral manifold $S(\theta)$ of $\mathcal{D}$ satisfies

$$S(\theta) = \prod_{i=1}^{n} S_i^*(\theta), \qquad (3.50)$$

which is shown later in this chapter to follow from *Direct Sum* $\Rightarrow$ *Product Structure*.

The point of this discussion is the duality between Property (ii) of *Direct Sum* and Property (iii) of *Product Structure*. This duality reveals a set theoretic aspect of the integrability condition (ii) of *Direct Sum* in partitioning Θ with the integral manifolds of the distribution $\mathcal{D}$. The partitioning of Θ by Cartesian products of the form (3.50) is fundamental in mechanism construction. Integrability and smoothness are only means and not the objective in a more abstract approach to this problem. The set theoretic aspect of the integrability condition (ii) of *Direct Sum* is thus emphasized here as a way of connecting the first-order approach of this text to mechanism construction in its most fundamental sense.

As the dual to the integrability condition (ii) of *Direct Sum*, Property (iii) of *Product Structure* is also an integrability condition. Starting from *Product Structure*, define $\mathcal{D}(\theta)$ as the tangent space to the submanifold $\Pi_{i=1}^{n} S_i^*(\theta)$ at θ. It is clear that $\mathcal{D}(\theta) = \oplus_{i=1}^{n} \mathcal{D}_i(\theta)$ for the distributions $\mathcal{D}_1, \ldots, \mathcal{D}_n$ defined in (ii) of *Product Structure*. The following argument derives the integrability of $\mathcal{D}$ from Property (iii). This property imposes the following condition on the submanifolds $\Pi_{i=1}^{n} S_i^*(\theta)$: for all $\theta, \theta^* \in \Theta$,

$$\prod_{i=1}^{n} S_i^*(\theta^*) \cap \prod_{i=1}^{n} S_i^*(\theta) \neq \emptyset \Rightarrow \prod_{i=1}^{n} S_i^*(\theta^*) = \prod_{i=1}^{n} S_i^*(\theta). \qquad (3.51)$$

By definition, the tangent space to $\Pi_{i=1}^{n} S_i^*(\theta)$ at θ is $\mathcal{D}(\theta)$. Statement (3.51) insures that $\mathcal{D}$ also defines the tangent space to the submanifold $\Pi_{i=1}^{n} S_i^*(\theta)$ at all other points θ^* that lie within it (not just θ). This is true because by (3.51),

$$\theta^* \in \prod_{i=1}^{n} S_i^*(\theta) \Rightarrow \prod_{i=1}^{n} S_i^*(\theta^*) = \prod_{i=1}^{n} S_i^*(\theta), \qquad (3.52)$$

and as just noted, the tangent to $\Pi_{i=1}^n S_i^*(\theta^*)$ at θ^* is $\mathcal{D}(\theta^*)$. Consequently, the submanifolds of the form $\Pi_{i=1}^n S_i^*(\theta)$ are the integral manifolds of $\mathcal{D}$ and so $\mathcal{D}$ must be integrable.

If Property (iii) is not imposed in *Product Structure* and (3.51) therefore does not hold for all $\theta, \theta^* \in \Theta$, then the tangent to $\Pi_{i=1}^n S_i^*(\theta)$ at θ^* need not equal $\mathcal{D}(\theta^*)$ and $\Pi_{i=1}^n S_i^*(\theta)$ need not be an integral manifold of the direct sum $\mathcal{D}$. This is illustrated in the following example.

3.2.2 Example: Nonintegrability of the Direct Sum $\mathcal{D}$ and the Failure of the Product Sets to Partition Θ

This example concerns distributions $\mathcal{D}_1$ and $\mathcal{D}_2$ that satisfy Property (i) of *Direct Sum* but not (ii). The corresponding integral manifolds S_1 and S_2 satisfy Properties (i) and (ii) of *Product Structure* but not (iii).

Let $\Theta_1 = \Theta_2 = \mathbb{R}_{++}^2$. The submanifold $S_1(\theta^*)$ is

$$S_1(\theta^*) \equiv \{(\theta_1, \theta_2^*) | (\theta_{1,2} - \theta_{1,2}^*) = \theta_{2,1}^*(\theta_{1,1} - \theta_{1,1}^*)\}, \tag{3.53}$$

and the submanifold $S_2(\theta^*)$ is

$$S_2(\theta^*) \equiv \{(\theta_1^*, \theta_2) | (\theta_{2,2} - \theta_{2,2}^*) = \theta_{1,1}^*(\theta_{2,1} - \theta_{2,1}^*)\}, \tag{3.54}$$

i.e., $S_i(\theta^*)$ is the line in $\Theta_i \times \{\theta_{-i}^*\}$ through θ^* whose slope is $\theta_{-i,1}^*$. The distributions $\mathcal{D}_1$ and $\mathcal{D}_2$ are spanned by X_1 and X_2, respectively, where

$$X_1(\theta) \equiv \frac{\partial}{\partial \theta_{1,1}} + \theta_{2,1} \frac{\partial}{\partial \theta_{1,2}} \tag{3.55}$$

and

$$X_2(\theta) \equiv \frac{\partial}{\partial \theta_{2,1}} + \theta_{1,1} \frac{\partial}{\partial \theta_{2,2}}. \tag{3.56}$$

Applying formula (2.6), the Lie bracket $[X_1, X_2]$ is

$$[X_1, X_2] = -\frac{\partial}{\partial \theta_{1,2}} + \frac{\partial}{\partial \theta_{2,2}}, \tag{3.57}$$

which lies outside the span of X_1 and X_2 at all values of $\theta \in \Theta$. The direct sum $\mathcal{D} \equiv \mathcal{D}_1 \oplus \mathcal{D}_2$ is thus not integrable.

Consider next the Cartesian product $S(\theta) \equiv S_1^*(\theta) \times S_2^*(\theta)$ and let $\theta_1^* = \theta_2^* = (4, 4)$. The submanifold $S(\theta^*)$ is a 2-dimensional plane through θ^*,

$$S(\theta^*) = S_1^*(\theta^*) \times S_2^*(\theta^*) \tag{3.58}$$

$$= \{(\theta_{1,1}, \theta_{1,2}) | \theta_{1,2} = 4\theta_{1,1} - 12\} \times \{(\theta_{2,1}, \theta_{2,2}) | \theta_{2,2} = 4\theta_{2,1} - 12\}.$$

There are many different products $S(\theta^{**})$, however, that contain θ^* and yet are distinct from $S(\theta^*)$. Consider, for instance, $\theta_1^{**} = \theta_2^{**} = (1, 1)$. The product $S(\theta^{**})$ is the plane

$$S(\theta^{**}) \equiv S_1^*(\theta^{**}) \times S_2^*(\theta^{**}) \tag{3.59}$$

$$= \{(\theta_{1,1}, \theta_{1,2}) | \theta_{1,1} = \theta_{1,2}\} \times \{(\theta_{2,1}, \theta_{2,2}) | \theta_{2,1} = \theta_{2,2}\},$$

which contains (θ_1^*, θ_2^*). It is clear, however, that $S(\theta^*) \neq S(\theta^{**})$; Θ is thus not partitioned by the Cartesian products of the form $S(\theta) = S_1^*(\theta) \times S_2^*(\theta)$. Note also that the tangent plane to $S(\theta^*)$ at θ^{**} is distinct from $\mathcal{D}(\theta^{**})$, which is the tangent plane to $S(\theta^{**})$ at θ^{**}. The product $S(\theta^*)$ is thus not an integral manifold of the direct sum $\mathcal{D}$.

3.3 *Message Process*⇒*Product Structure*⇒*Direct Sum*

Figure 3.1 depicts the argument that will be followed in Sections 3.3–3.6 to investigate the equivalence of *Direct Sum*, *Product Structure*, and *Message Process*. It mirrors the argument depicted in Figure 2.5 and followed in Chapter 2 to investigate the equivalence of *Distribution*, *Foliation*, and *Mapping*. *Direct Sum*, *Product Structure*, and *Message Process* have been formulated in the preceding section to make it straightforward to prove that *Message Process*⇒*Product Structure*⇒*Direct Sum* holds globally. I thus begin by proving this pair of implications. The local equivalence of *Direct Sum*, *Product Structure*, and *Message Process* is then completed with the proof that *Direct Sum*⇒*Message Process* holds locally. This implication is proven in Sections 3.4 and 3.5. Finally, Section 3.6 concerns the sense in which the implication *Direct Sum*⇒*Product Structure* holds globally.

Proof: Message Process⇒*Product Structure* **Holds Globally.** Fix $\theta^* \in \Theta$ and for $1 \leq i \leq n$ define

$$S_i(\theta^*) \equiv \{(\theta_i, \theta_{-i}^*) | \theta_i \in \Theta_i, \alpha_i(\theta_i, u_{(c)}(\theta^*)) = 0\}. \tag{3.60}$$

$S_i(\theta^*)$ lies within the plane $\Theta_i \times \{\theta_{-i}^*\}$ and regularity assumption (ii) in *Message Process* insures that it is a d_i-dimensional C^∞ submanifold of Θ.[6] Recall from *Product Structure* that $\mathcal{D}_i(\theta)$ is defined as the distribution whose value at θ is the tangent space to $S_i(\theta)$ at θ. $\mathcal{D}_i(\theta^*)$ is the null space of the $(c_i \times \dim \Theta_i)$ matrix $D_{\theta_i} \alpha_i(\theta_i, m)$ at $\theta_i = \theta_i^*$ and $m = u_{(c)}(\theta^*)$; because $u_{(c)}$ and α_i are both C^∞, it follows that $\mathcal{D}_i$ is also C^∞.

---

[6] See Spivak (1979, Prop. 12, p. 65) or Warner (1971, Thm. 1.38, p. 31).

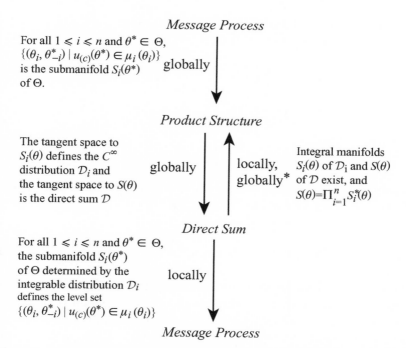

Message Process

For all $1 \leqslant i \leqslant n$ and $\theta^* \in \Theta$,
$\{(\theta_i, \theta^*_{-i}) \mid u_{(c)}(\theta^*) \in \mu_i(\theta_i)\}$
is the submanifold $S_i(\theta^*)$ globally
of Θ.

Product Structure

The tangent space to
$S_i(\theta)$ defines the C^∞
distribution $\mathcal{D}_i$ and   globally   locally,   Integral manifolds
the tangent space to $S(\theta)$ globally* $S_i(\theta)$ of $\mathcal{D}_i$ and $S(\theta)$
is the direct sum $\mathcal{D}$ of $\mathcal{D}$ exist, and
        $S(\theta) = \Pi^n_{i=1} S^*_i(\theta)$

Direct Sum

For all $1 \leqslant i \leqslant n$ and $\theta^* \in \Theta$,
the submanifold $S_i(\theta^*)$
of Θ determined by the   locally
integrable distribution $\mathcal{D}_i$
defines the level set
$\{(\theta_i, \theta^*_{-i}) \mid u_{(c)}(\theta^*) \in \mu_i(\theta_i)\}$

Message Process

Figure 3.1. Starting with *Message Process* at the top, the sequence of logical implications that establish the local equivalence of *Direct Sum*, *Product Structure*, and *Message Process* is depicted in the center of the figure. The relationship between two components is summarized alongside the implication. The asterisk "*" on "globally" next to the implication *Direct Sum⇒ Product Structure* indicates that while this implication always holds locally, it only holds globally with a weaker definition of an integral manifold than the one used throughout this text. This is discussed in Section 3.6.

It is clear that $\theta \in S_i(\theta)$. To show that the sets in $\{S_i(\theta) \mid \theta \in \Theta\}$ partition Θ, it is thus sufficient to show that $\theta^* \in S_i(\theta') \Rightarrow S_i(\theta^*) = S_i(\theta')$. Because $S_i(\theta') \subset \{(\theta_i, \theta'_{-i}) \mid \theta_i \in \Theta_i\}$, $\theta^* \in S_i(\theta')$ implies that θ^* and θ' differ only in their ith component, i.e., $\theta^*_{-i} = \theta'_{-i}$. For $j \neq i$, it follows that

$$\alpha_j(\theta^*_j, u_{(c)}(\theta')) = \alpha_j(\theta'_j, u_{(c)}(\theta')) = 0. \qquad (3.61)$$

Because $\theta^* \in S_i(\theta')$, θ^* also satisfies $\alpha_i(\theta^*_i, u_{(c)}(\theta')) = 0$ and so $\alpha(\theta^*, u_{(c)}(\theta')) = 0$. Property (iii) of *Message Process* asserts that $u_{(c)}(\theta^*) = m$ is the unique solution to the equation $\alpha(\theta^*, m) = 0$, and so $u_{(c)}(\theta^*) = u_{(c)}(\theta')$. It follows immediately from the definition of S_i that $S_i(\theta^*) = S_i(\theta')$.

It remains to be shown that the Cartesian products of the form $S(\theta) \equiv \prod_{i=1}^{n} S_i^*(\theta)$ partition Θ. It is clear that

$$S(\theta^*) \equiv \prod_{i=1}^{n} S_i^*(\theta^*)$$

$$= \prod_{i=1}^{n} \{\theta_i \in \Theta_i \,|\, \alpha_i\left(\theta_i, u_{(c)}(\theta^*)\right) = 0\} \qquad (3.62)$$

$$= \{\theta \in \Theta \,|\, \alpha(\theta, u_{(c)}(\theta^*)) = 0\}.$$

Because $u_{(c)}(\theta)$ is the unique value of m that solves the equation $\alpha(\theta, m) = 0$, it follows from the last line of (3.62) that

$$S(\theta^*) = u_{(c)}^{-1}(u_{(c)}(\theta^*)). \qquad (3.63)$$

It is obvious from (3.63) that the sets in $\{S(\theta)|\theta \in \Theta\}$ partition Θ. ∎

Proof: Product Structure⇒Direct Sum Holds Globally. For each $1 \leq i \leq n$, *Product Structure* implies the existence of a C^∞ distribution $\mathcal{D}_i$ on Θ such that an integral manifold $S_i(\theta^*)$ of $\mathcal{D}_i$ exists through each point $\theta^* \in \Theta$. The distribution $\mathcal{D}_i$ is thus integrable, and $\mathcal{D}_i(\theta^*)$ lies in the span of $\{\partial/\partial\theta_{i,t}\}_{1\leq i\leq d_i+c_i}$ because $S_i(\theta^*) \subset \Theta_i \times \{\theta_{-i}^*\}$.

To establish the integrability of the direct sum $\mathcal{D}$, it is sufficient to show that the Cartesian products of the form $S(\theta) \equiv \prod_{i=1}^{n} S_i^*(\theta)$ are the integral manifolds of this distribution, i.e., the tangent space to $S(\theta)$ at $\theta^* \in S(\theta)$ is $\mathcal{D}(\theta^*)$. Because the sets in $\{S(\theta)|\theta \in \Theta\}$ partition Θ,

$$\theta^* \in S(\theta) \Rightarrow S(\theta) = S(\theta^*) \equiv \prod_{i=1}^{n} S_i^*(\theta^*). \qquad (3.64)$$

The tangent space to $S(\theta)$ at θ^* is thus the tangent space to

$$S(\theta^*) \equiv \prod_{i=1}^{n} S_i^*(\theta^*) \qquad (3.65)$$

at θ^*, which equals the direct sum $\mathcal{D}(\theta^*)$. ∎

3.4 A Modified Frobenius Theorem

Recall from Section 2.4 that the Frobenius Theorem is the key to proving that *Distribution⇒Mapping* holds locally. Given $\theta^* \in \Theta$ and an integrable,

d-dimensional, C^∞ distribution $\mathcal{D}$ on Θ, the Frobenius Theorem asserts the existence of a local coordinate system at θ^* that simultaneously "flattens" all the integral manifolds of $\mathcal{D}$: the integral manifolds of $\mathcal{D}$ appear as d-dimensional coordinate planes in this new coordinate system and the remaining c coordinates of this local coordinate system define the mapping $u_{(c)}$ whose values index these integral manifolds. The key to proving that *Direct Sum*$\Rightarrow$*Message Process* holds locally is a reformulation of the Frobenius Theorem that incorporates features of message processes. Specifically, this modified Frobenius Theorem asserts the existence of a local coordinate system u at θ^* that simultaneously flattens the integral manifolds of each of the distributions $\mathcal{D}_1, \ldots, \mathcal{D}_n$ while retaining the separation of parameters among the n agents: relative to the new coordinates and for $1 \le i \le n$, each integral manifold $S_i(\theta)$ of $\mathcal{D}_i$ appears as a d_i-dimensional coordinate plane within $\mathbb{R}^{d_i+c_i}$.

This reformulation of the Frobenius Theorem is presented in Theorem 6.[7] The notation used in this theorem and in the proof that *Direct Sum*$\Rightarrow$*Message Process* is summarized in Table 3.1. As in the discussion of the standard Frobenius Theorem, the image $(-\varepsilon, \varepsilon)^{d+c}$ of the local coordinate system u is regarded as a subset of $W \times M$, where W is an open subset of $\mathbb{R}^d$ and M is an open subset of $\mathbb{R}^c$. An element $w \in W$ will now be written as $w = (w_1, \ldots, w_n)$ and an element $m \in M$ will be written as $m = (m_1, \ldots, m_n)$, where, for $1 \le i \le n$, $w_i \in \mathbb{R}^{d_i}$ and $m_i \in \mathbb{R}^{c_i}$.

Theorem 6 (*Frobenius Theorem for Mechanism Design*): *Let $\mathcal{D}_1, \ldots, \mathcal{D}_n$ be C^∞ distributions on the open subset Θ of $\mathbb{R}^{d+c}$ that have the properties stated in* Direct Sum *and let θ^* be any point in Θ. There exists an open neighborhood $O(\theta^*) \subset \Theta$ of θ^*, a local coordinate system $u : O(\theta^*) \to (-\varepsilon, \varepsilon)^{d+c} \subset W \times M$, and an inverse mapping $v \equiv u^{-1} : (-\varepsilon, \varepsilon)^{d+c} \to O(\theta^*)$ such that the following statement holds for each $\theta' \in O(\theta^*)$ and $(w', m') \equiv u(\theta')$:*

(i) A maximal, connected, d-dimensional C^∞ integral manifold $S(\theta')$ of the direct sum $\mathcal{D}$ exists through θ' in $O(\theta^*)$, and it satisfies

$$S(\theta') = \{\theta \in O(\theta^*) \mid u_{(c)}(\theta) = u_{(c)}(\theta')\} \tag{3.66}$$

$$= \{\theta = v(w, m') \mid w \in (-\varepsilon, \varepsilon)^d\}. \tag{3.67}$$

---

[7] This theorem originates in Williams (1981, Lem. 1 and Lem. 1A). It appears as Theorem 1 in Williams (1982a) as applied to the realization problem. See also Spivak (1979, Ex. 5, p. 270) for a related exercise.

Table 3.1. *The notation used in the Frobenius*
Theorem for Mechanism Design.

$$u \equiv \left(u_{(i,d_i)}, u_{(i,c_i)}\right)_{1 \le i \le n}$$

$$u_{(i,d_i)} : O(\theta^*) \rightarrow W_i \subset R^{d_i}$$

$$u_{(i,c_i)} : O(\theta^*) \rightarrow M_i \subset R^{c_i}$$

$$u_{(d)} = \left(u_{(i,d_i)}\right)_{1 \le i \le n} : O(\theta^*) \rightarrow W \equiv \prod_{i=1}^{n} W_i$$

$$u_{(c)} = \left(u_{(i,c_i)}\right)_{1 \le i \le n} : O(\theta^*) \rightarrow M \equiv \prod_{i=1}^{n} M_i$$

$$O(\theta^*) \subset \Theta \subset R^{d+c}.$$

$$u : O(\theta^*) \rightarrow (-\varepsilon, \varepsilon)^{d+c} \subset \prod_{i=1}^{n} (W_i \times M_i)$$

$$u^{-1} = v \equiv \left(v_{(i)}, v_{(-i)}\right)$$

$$v_{(i)} : (-\varepsilon, \varepsilon)^{d+c} \rightarrow \Theta_i$$

$$v_{(-i)} : (-\varepsilon, \varepsilon)^{d+c} \rightarrow \prod_{j \ne i} \Theta_j$$

Moreover, the following statements hold for each $1 \le i \le n$:

(ii) *A maximal, connected,* d_i-*dimensional* C^∞ *integral manifold* $S_i(\theta')$ *of* $\mathcal{D}_i$ *exists through* θ' *in* $O(\theta^*)$, *and it satisfies*

$$S_i(\theta') = \{(\theta_i, \theta'_{-i}) \in O(\theta^*)| \, u_{(i,c_i)}(\theta_i, \theta'_{-i}) = m'_i\} \qquad (3.68)$$

$$= \{\theta | u_{(c)}(\theta) = m', u_{(j,d_j)}(\theta) = w'_j \text{ for } j \ne i\} \qquad (3.69)$$

$$= \{\theta = v((w_i, w'_{-i}), m')| \, w_i \in (-\varepsilon, \varepsilon)^{d_i}\}. \qquad (3.70)$$

(iii) *The derivative* $D_{\theta_i} u_{(i,c_i)}$ *has rank equal to* c_i *on* $O(\theta^*)$.

(iv) *The mapping* $v_{(i)} : (-\varepsilon, \varepsilon)^{d+c} \rightarrow \Theta_i$ *depends only on the values of* w_i *and* m *and not on the value of* w_{-i}.

The new coordinates (w, m) have the following interpretation. The integral manifolds $S(\theta)$ of the direct sum $\mathcal{D}$ are placed by the mapping u in a one-to-one correspondence with the d-dimensional planes in $(-\varepsilon, \varepsilon)^{d+c}$ of the form

$$\{(w, m')| w \in (-\varepsilon, \varepsilon)^d\}, \qquad (3.71)$$

where each choice of m' determines a particular plane. This is the content of (3.66) and (3.67). For each $1 \le i \le n$, the integral manifolds $S_i(\theta)$ of $\mathcal{D}_i$

are placed by u in a one-to-one correspondence with the d_i-dimensional planes of the form

$$\{((w_i, w'_{-i}), m')|w_i \in (-\varepsilon, \varepsilon)^{d_i}\}, \tag{3.72}$$

where each choice of

$$w'_{-i} \in (-\varepsilon, \varepsilon)^{\Sigma_{j\neq i}d_j} \text{ and } m' \in (-\varepsilon, \varepsilon)^c \tag{3.73}$$

determines one such plane. This is the content of (3.69) and (3.70). In (3.68) the θ_{-i} coordinates are fixed at $\theta_{-i} = \theta'_{-i}$; u will be constructed so that the c_i equations $u_{(i,c_i)}(\theta_i, \theta'_{-i}) = m'_i$ on the $(d_i + c_i)$-dimensional space Θ_i have as their solution the d_i-dimensional integral manifold $S_i(\theta')$. Finally, statements (iii) and (iv) of the theorem are features of the local coordinate system u that are useful below in the proof that *Direct Sum⇒Message Process* holds locally. Theorem 6 itself will be proven in Section 3.5.

As depicted in Figure 3.1, *Direct Sum⇒Product Structure* locally follows from *Direct Sum⇒Message Process* locally together with *Message Process⇒Product Structure* globally. *Direct Sum⇒Message Process* locally is proven below in Subsection 3.4.1 and *Message Process⇒Product Structure* globally was proven in Section 3.3. It is worth noting, however, that *Direct Sum⇒Product Structure* locally follows directly from Theorem 6 by a simple argument. Although this argument is unnecessary in the chain of implications depicted in Figure 3.1 for establishing the local equivalence of *Direct Sum*, *Product Structure*, and *Message Process*, it is included here to familiarize the reader with Theorem 6.[8]

Proof: Direct Sum⇒Product Structure Locally. The following sequence of equalities follow from the conclusions of Theorem 6: for $\theta' \in O(\theta^*)$ such that $u(\theta') = (w', m')$,

$$S(\theta') = \{\theta = v(w, m')| w \in (-\varepsilon, \varepsilon)^d\} \tag{3.74}$$

$$= \{(\theta_i)_{1\leq i\leq n}| \text{ each } \theta_i = v_i(w_i, m'), w_i \in (-\varepsilon, \varepsilon)^{d_i}\} \tag{3.75}$$

$$= \prod_{i=1}^{n}\{\theta_i = v_i(w_i, m')| w_i \in (-\varepsilon, \varepsilon)^{d_i}\} \tag{3.76}$$

$$= \prod_{i=1}^{n} S_i^*(\theta'). \tag{3.77}$$

---

[8] This result originates in Theorems 1 and 2 of Williams (1981).

The first equality is (3.67), the second follows from (iv) in the statement of the theorem, the third simply rewrites (3.75), and the last follows from (3.70) together with (iv). ■

3.4.1 *Direct Sum*⇒*Message Process* Locally

The primary role in this text of the Frobenius Theorem for Mechanism Design is in proving *Direct Sum*⇒*Message Process* locally.[9] Except for issues related to the global equivalence of *Direct Sum*, *Product Structure*, and *Message Process* that are addressed in Section 3.6, this proof completes the chain of implications in Figure 3.1.

Proof: Direct Sum⇒*Message Process Locally.* Given $\theta^* \in \Theta$, the proof relies on properties of the coordinate system $u : O(\theta^*) \to (-\varepsilon, \varepsilon)^{d+c}$ described in Theorem 6. The notation of this theorem is used below. Reflecting the informational decentralization, the domain in a message process has the form $(\Pi_{i=1}^{n} O(\theta_i^*)) \times M'$, where M' is an open subset of $\mathbb{R}^c$ and each $O(\theta_i^*)$ is an open subset of $\Theta_i \subset \mathbb{R}^{c_i}$ that contains θ_i^*. Because $O(\theta^*)$ is not necessarily a Cartesian product of this form, sets $\Pi_{i=1}^{n} O(\theta_i^*) \subset O(\theta^*)$ and $M' \subset M$ are constructed in the next paragraph with several properties that are used below to define the message adjustment rules.

Choose $0 < \varepsilon' \leq \varepsilon$ such that

$$\prod_{i=1}^{n} v_{(i)}((-\varepsilon', \varepsilon')^{d+c}) \subset O(\theta^*). \tag{3.78}$$

Such an ε' exists because each $v_{(i)}$ is continuous. The message space M' for $\alpha(\theta, m)$ will be

$$M' \equiv (-\varepsilon', \varepsilon')^c. \tag{3.79}$$

The open subset $\Pi_{i=1}^{n} O(\theta_i^*) \subset O(\theta^*)$ is now defined. Notice that

$$v((-\varepsilon', \varepsilon')^{d+c}) \subset \prod_{i=1}^{n} v_{(i)}((-\varepsilon', \varepsilon')^{d+c}), \tag{3.80}$$

and that $v((-\varepsilon', \varepsilon')^{d+c})$ is an open subset of $O(\theta^*)$ because $v \equiv u^{-1}$ and u is a local coordinate system. It is thus possible to select open sets

---

[9] The proof below originates in Williams (1982b), which establishes *Product Structure*⇒*Message Process* locally (Lemma A′ of Hurwicz et al., 1978, p. 9). The local equivalence of *Direct Sum* and *Product Structure* allows this argument to be used here.

$O(\theta_1^*), \ldots, O(\theta_n^*)$ such that

$$\prod_{i=1}^{n} O(\theta_i^*) \subset v((-\varepsilon', \varepsilon')^{d+c}) \Leftrightarrow u\left(\prod_{i=1}^{n} O(\theta_i^*)\right) \subset (-\varepsilon', \varepsilon')^{d+c}. \quad (3.81)$$

Statement (3.81) establishes that

$$\theta \in \prod_{i=1}^{n} O(\theta_i^*) \Rightarrow u_{(c)}(\theta) \in M', \quad (3.82)$$

which is necessary for $u_{(c)}$ to satisfy *Message Process*.

The message adjustment rules $(\alpha_i)_{1 \le i \le n}$ are now constructed, which is the central task of the proof. Let $u(\theta^*) \equiv (w^*, m^*) = 0$. Define $\alpha_i : O(\theta_i^*) \times M' \to \mathbb{R}^{c_i}$ by the formula

$$\alpha_i(\theta_i, m) \equiv u_{(i, c_i)}(\theta_i, v_{(-i)}(w_{-i}^*, m)) - m_i. \quad (3.83)$$

For α_i to be well defined, it is necessary that $(\theta_i, v_{(-i)}(w_{-i}^*, m)) \in O(\theta^*)$, the domain of $u_{(i, c_i)}$, for $(\theta_i, m) \in O(\theta_i^*) \times M'$. This follows from the construction above of $\Pi_{i=1}^{n} O(\theta_i^*)$ and M': Statement (3.81) implies

$$\theta_i \in O(\theta_i^*) \subset v_{(i)}((-\varepsilon', \varepsilon')^{d+c})), \quad (3.84)$$

and consequently

$$(\theta_i, v_{(-i)}(w_{-i}^*, m)) \in \prod_{j=1}^{n} v_{(j)}((-\varepsilon', \varepsilon')^{d+c}) \subset O(\theta^*), \quad (3.85)$$

where the last inclusion follows from (3.78).

Property (iii) of Theorem 6 implies

$$\text{rank } D_{\theta_i} \alpha_i(\theta_i, m) = c_i \text{ at } m = u_{(c)}(\theta) \quad (3.86)$$

for all $1 \le i \le n$, as required in (iii) of *Message Process*. It remains to be shown that $\alpha(\theta, m) = (\alpha_i(\theta_i, m))_{1 \le i \le n}$ has the following property for $(\theta, m) \in (\Pi_{i=1}^{n} O(\theta_i^*)) \times M'$:

$$\alpha(\theta, m) = 0 \text{ if and only if } m = u_{(c)}(\theta). \quad (3.87)$$

The proof that *Direct Sum⇒Message Process* is completed by establishing (3.87) in the following two steps. ∎

Proof of **Sufficiency in** (3.87): Let θ denote an element of $\Pi_{i=1}^{n} O(\theta_i^*)$ and let $u(\theta) \equiv (w, m)$. Using the equality

$$m_i = u_{(i, c_i)}(\theta) \quad (3.88)$$

for $1 \leq i \leq n$, the goal is to prove that $\alpha_i(\theta_i, m) = 0$ for each i, or equivalently

$$m_i = u_{(i,c_i)}(\theta_i, v_{(-i)}(w^*_{-i}, m)). \tag{3.89}$$

Equation (3.89) is established through the following sequence of equalities:

$$m_i = u_{(i,c_i)}(\theta) = u_{(i,c_i)}(v(w, m)) \tag{3.90}$$

$$= u_{(i,c_i)}(v(w_i, w_{-i}, m)) \tag{3.91}$$

$$= u_{(i,c_i)}(v(w_i, w^*_{-i}, m)) \tag{3.92}$$

$$= u_{(i,c_i)}(v_{(i)}(w_i, m), v_{(-i)}(w^*_{-i}, m)) \tag{3.93}$$

$$= u_{(i,c_i)}(\theta_i, v_{(-i)}(w^*_{-i}, m)). \tag{3.94}$$

Statement (3.90) is a consequence of $u(\theta) \equiv (w, m)$. Statement (3.91) follows from (3.90) by writing $w = (w_i, w_{-i})$. Statement (3.92) follows from (3.91) because $u \equiv v^{-1}$: changing w from (w_i, w_{-i}) to (w_i, w^*_{-i}) corresponds, through v, to a movement within a level set of $u_{(c)}$ (and hence within a level set of $u_{(i,c_i)}$). Statement (3.93) follows from the fact that $v_{(i)}$ does not depend on w_{-i} (Statement (iii) in Theorem 6). Statement (3.94) then follows from the equivalence

$$u(\theta) = (w, m) \Leftrightarrow \theta = v(w, m) \tag{3.95}$$

$$\Leftrightarrow \theta_i = v_{(i)}(w_i, m) \text{ for } 1 \leq i \leq n.$$

∎

***Proof of* Necessity in (3.87):** For $\theta \in \Pi_{i=1}^n O(\theta_i^*)$ and $m \in M'$, the hypothesis is equivalent to

$$m_i = u_{(i,c_i)}(\theta_i, v_{(-i)}(w^*_{-i}, m)) \tag{3.96}$$

holding for all $1 \leq i \leq n$. The desired conclusion is equivalent to $u_{(i,c_i)}(\theta) = m_i$ for each i. This is established by working upward along the sequence of equalities in (3.94)–(3.90): the last line (3.94) equals m_i (by assumption), and proving that the last line equals the first line establishes the desired equality.

To work upward through this sequence of equalities, all that is needed is a value $w \in (-\varepsilon, \varepsilon)^d$ such that

$$\theta = v(w, m) \Leftrightarrow \theta_i = v_{(i)}(w_i, m) \text{ for } 1 \leq i \leq n, \tag{3.97}$$

where $\theta = (\theta_i)_{1 \leq i \leq n}$ and m are the given values that solve (3.96) for $1 \leq i \leq n$. The existence of this w follows from the equality of the sets (3.68) and

(3.70) in Theorem 6: letting $\theta' = v(w^*, m)$ and θ'' a variable, the equality of these sets implies

$$\{(\theta_i'', \theta_{-i}') \in O(\theta^*)| \ u_{(i,c_i)}(\theta_i'', \theta_{-i}') = m_i\} = \tag{3.98}$$

$$\{\theta'' = v((w_i, w_{-i}^*), m)| \ w_i \in (-\varepsilon, \varepsilon)^{d_i}\}, \tag{3.99}$$

where $w^* = u_{(d)}(\theta')$ has been substituted. The given θ is in the set (3.98) because it satisfies (3.96). Because θ therefore lies in (3.99), there exists $w_i \in (-\varepsilon, \varepsilon)^{d_i}$ such that

$$\theta_i = v_i((w_i, w_{-i}^*), m) = v_i(w_i, m), \tag{3.100}$$

where the second equality comes from (iv) of Theorem 6. ∎

3.5 Proof of the Theorem for Mechanism Design

A d-dimensional integrable distribution $\mathcal{D}$ is assumed both in the standard Frobenius Theorem and in the Frobenius Theorem for Mechanism Design, and both theorems assert for each $\theta^* \in \Theta$ the existence of a local coordinate system $u \equiv (u_{(d)}, u_{(c)})$ on a neighborhood $O(\theta^*)$ of θ^* such that the level sets of $u_{(c)}$ are the maximal integral manifolds of $\mathcal{D}$ in $O(\theta^*)$. The Frobenius Theorem for Mechanism Design differs from the standard Frobenius Theorem in assuming the special structure of the distribution $\mathcal{D}$ in *Direct Sum* and then asserting properties of u that are not in the standard theorem. The strategy followed below for proving the Frobenius Theorem for Mechanism Design is to modify the construction of the local coordinate system in the proof of the standard Frobenius Theorem to take into account the special structure of the distribution $\mathcal{D}$ in *Direct Sum* and then to construct a local coordinate system with the desired features. It should be kept in mind in this construction that the standard Frobenius Theorem has already been proven. The objective below is thus to adapt the proof of the standard theorem as needed without reproving its conclusions. In particular, the existence of the integral manifolds defined by the integrable distributions $\mathcal{D}_1, \ldots, \mathcal{D}_n$ and $\mathcal{D}$ that is stated in the Frobenius Theorem for Mechanism Design need not be reproven.

Recall from Section 2.5 the construction of u in the standard Frobenius Theorem:

(i) A set of C^∞ vector fields $\{X_i | 1 \leq i \leq d\}$ is selected that spans $\mathcal{D}(\theta)$ at every θ near θ^* and with the property that $[X_j, X_h] = 0$ for $1 \leq j, h \leq d$.

(ii) A c-dimensional plane P through θ^* is selected that transversally intersects the integral manifolds of $\mathcal{D}$ near θ^*. After reindexing the standard coordinates in $\Theta \subset \mathbb{R}^d$, it can be assumed without loss of generality that $P = \{(\theta^*_{(d)}, \theta_{(c)}) | \theta_{(c)} \in \mathbb{R}^c\}$.

Near θ^*, the points in P index the integral manifolds of $\mathcal{D}$ and the vector fields $\{X_i | 1 \leq i \leq d\}$ define coordinates within each of these integral manifolds: for θ near θ^*, the coordinates $(w, m) \in \mathbb{R}^{d+c}$ are assigned to θ by u if and only if θ is reached by starting at the initial point $(\theta^*_{(d)}, m + \theta^*_{(c)})$ in P and following the integral curve of X_1 from $t = 0$ to $t = w_1$, then following the integral curve of X_2 from $t = 0$ to $t = w_2, \ldots$, and finally following the integral curve of X_d from $t = 0$ to $t = w_d$.

This construction is adapted below to prove the Frobenius Theorem for Mechanism Design by selecting the basis of $\mathcal{D}$ and the transverse plane P to the integral manifolds of $\mathcal{D}$ in the following way:

(i) A set of d vector fields $\{X_{i,h} | 1 \leq i \leq n, 1 \leq h \leq d_i\}$ is selected that span $\mathcal{D}(\theta)$ for each θ near θ^* and with the following properties:

  (a) $[X_{i,h}, X_{j,l}] = 0$ for all vector fields in this set;
  (b) for each $1 \leq i \leq n$ the subset $\{X_{i,h} | 1 \leq h \leq d_i\}$ spans $\mathcal{D}_i(\theta)$ for θ near θ^*.

Selecting the basis of $\mathcal{D}$ in this way insures that (3.70) holds in the Frobenius Theorem for Mechanism Design, i.e., for $w \equiv (w_i)_{1 \leq i \leq n}$ with $w_i \in \mathbb{R}^{d_i}$, the coordinates w_i number the points within an integral manifold of $\mathcal{D}_i$.

(ii) Let P_i denote the c_i-dimensional plane in Θ_i defined by

$$P_i \equiv \{(\theta^*_{(i,d_i)}, \theta_{(i,c_i)})\} | \theta_{(i,c_i)} \in \mathbb{R}^{c_i}\}. \tag{3.101}$$

After reindexing the standard coordinates in each $\Theta_i \subset \mathbb{R}^{d_i}$, it can be assumed without loss of generality that near θ^* the plane $P_i \times \{\theta^*_{-i}\}$ transversally intersects the integral manifolds of $\mathcal{D}_i$ that lie in $\Theta_i \times \theta^*_{-i}$. The c-dimensional plane P is then defined as $P \equiv \oplus_{i=1}^n P_i$.

As in the proof of the standard Frobenius Theorem, near θ^* the plane P transversally intersects the integral manifolds of $\mathcal{D}$. Selecting P in this way insures that (3.68) holds in the Frobenius Theorem for Mechanism Design.

The notation used here is complicated, and so the proof of the Frobenius Theorem for Mechanism Design will first be discussed informally in the simple case of $n = 2$ and $c_1 = d_1 = c_2 = d_2 = 1$. The purpose of this special case is to illustrate the issues that arise in adapting the proof of the standard Frobenius Theorem and to show how these issues are resolved.

3.5.1 Example: $n = 2$ and $c_1 = d_1 = c_2 = d_2 = 1$

The theorem is proven in this special case by defining nonzero vector fields X_1, X_2 near θ^* with the following properties:

$$X_1(\theta) \in \mathcal{D}_1(\theta) \text{ and } X_2(\theta) \in \mathcal{D}_2(\theta); \tag{3.102}$$

$$[X_1, X_2](\theta) = 0. \tag{3.103}$$

How such vector fields can be found is discussed below. I assume their existence for now and discuss their use in constructing the local coordinate system u. Represent X_1 and X_2 as

$$X_1(\theta) \equiv x_{11}(\theta)\frac{\partial}{\partial\theta_{1,1}} + x_{12}(\theta)\frac{\partial}{\partial\theta_{1,2}} \tag{3.104}$$

and

$$X_2(\theta) \equiv x_{21}\frac{\partial}{\partial\theta_{2,1}} + x_{22}(\theta)\frac{\partial}{\partial\theta_{2,2}}. \tag{3.105}$$

After renumbering the coordinates of Θ_1 and (separately) the coordinates of Θ_2, it can be assumed without loss of generality that

$$\frac{\partial}{\partial\theta_{1,2}}(\theta^*) \notin \mathcal{D}_1(\theta^*) \text{ and } \frac{\partial}{\partial\theta_{2,2}}(\theta^*) \notin \mathcal{D}_2(\theta^*) \tag{3.106}$$

for θ near θ^*. This means that $x_{11}(\theta)$ and $x_{21}(\theta)$ are both nonzero near θ^*. It also implies that the line

$$P_1 \equiv \{(\theta_{1,1}^*, \theta_{1,2})\}|\theta_{1,2} \in \mathbb{R}\} \tag{3.107}$$

transversally intersects the integral manifolds of $\mathcal{D}_1$ in $\Theta_1 \times \{\theta_2^*\}$ and the line

$$P_2 \equiv \{(\theta_{2,1}^*, \theta_{2,2})|\theta_{2,2} \in \mathbb{R}\} \tag{3.108}$$

transversally intersects the integral manifolds of $\mathcal{D}_2$ in $\Theta_2 \times \{\theta_1^*\}$. This is depicted in Figure 3.2. The plane

$$P = P_1 \oplus P_2 = \{\theta|\theta_{1,1} = \theta_{1,1}^*, \theta_{2,1} = \theta_{2,1}^*\} \tag{3.109}$$

thus transversally intersects the integral manifolds of $\mathcal{D}$ near θ^*.

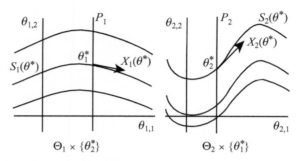

Figure 3.2. For $i = 1, 2$, the line $P_i = \{(\theta^*_{i,1}, \theta_{i,2}) \,\big|\, \theta_{i,2} \in \mathbb{R}\}$ transversally intersects the integral manifolds of $\mathcal{D}_i$ in $\Theta_i \times \{\theta^*_{-i}\}$.

Let $w = (w_1, w_2)$ and $m = (m_1, m_2) \in \mathbb{R}^2$. The local coordinate system $u \equiv (u_{(d)}, u_{(c)})$ is defined near θ^* as follows:

$$u(\theta) = (w, m)$$
$$\Leftrightarrow u_{(d)}(\theta) = w, \, u_{(c)}(\theta) = m \qquad\qquad (3.110)$$
$$\Leftrightarrow \theta = \rho(X_2, \rho(X_1, (\theta^*_{1,1}, m_1 + \theta^*_{1,2}, \theta^*_{2,1}, m_2 + \theta^*_{2,2}), w_1), w_2).$$

In words, $u(\theta) = (w, m)$ if and only if θ is reached by starting at

$$(\theta^*_{1,1}, m_1 + \theta^*_{1,2}, \theta^*_{2,1}, m_2 + \theta^*_{2,2}),$$

following the integral curve of X_1 through this point from $t = 0$ to $t = w_1$, and then following the integral curve of X_2 through

$$\rho(X_1, (\theta^*_{1,1}, m_1 + \theta^*_{1,2}, \theta^*_{2,1}, m_2 + \theta^*_{2,2}), w_1) \qquad\qquad (3.111)$$

from $t = 0$ to $t = w_2$. The proof of the standard Frobenius Theorem insures that this defines a local coordinate system on a neighborhood $O(\theta^*)$ of θ^*. The only difference here is the extra care that has been taken in selecting the transverse plane P.

It remains to be shown that u has the properties given in the Frobenius Theorem for Mechanism Design. By shrinking $O(\theta^*)$, it can be assumed without loss of generality that $u(O(\theta^*)) = (-\varepsilon, \varepsilon)^d$ for a sufficiently small value of ε. As in the statement of the Frobenius Theorem for Mechanism Design, represent u as a four-tuple of real-valued functions,

$$u \equiv (u_{(1,d_1)}, u_{(2,d_2)}, u_{(1,c_1)}, u_{(2,c_2)}) \equiv (w_1, w_2, m_1, m_2). \qquad (3.112)$$

Consider first statement (iii) in the theorem, which in this example requires that $D_{\theta_i} u_{(i,c_i)}$ is nonzero on $O(\theta^*)$. It is sufficient to show $D_{\theta_i} u_{(i,c_i)}(\theta^*) \neq 0$, for $D_{\theta_i} u_{(i,c_i)}$ would then be nonzero near θ^*, and $O(\theta^*)$ and ε can, if necessary, be reduced further in size. The function $u_{(i,c_i)}$ has a very simple form on the line $P_i \times \{\theta^*_{-i}\}$: for $\theta_{i,2}$ near $\theta^*_{i,2}$,

$$u_{(i,c_i)}((\theta^*_{i,1}, \theta_{i,2}), \theta^*_{-i}) = \theta_{1,2} - \theta^*_{1,2}, \tag{3.113}$$

from which it follows immediately that $D_{\theta_i} u_{(i,c_i)}(\theta^*) \neq 0$.

I turn next to the integral manifolds of $(\mathcal{D}_i)_{1 \leq i \leq n}$ and $\mathcal{D}$ near θ^*, which are addressed in (i) and (ii) of the theorem. Let $v \equiv u^{-1}$ and for $\theta' \in O(\theta^*)$ let $u(\theta') \equiv (w'_1, m'_1, w'_2, m'_2)$. The proof of the Frobenius Theorem implies that the maximal integral manifold $S(\theta')$ of $\mathcal{D}$ in $O(\theta^*)$ through θ' is

$$S(\theta') = \{\theta \in O(\theta^*) | u_{(c)}(\theta) = m'\} \equiv \{v(w, m') | w \in (-\varepsilon, \varepsilon)^2\}. \tag{3.114}$$

The proof of the Frobenius Theorem characterizes $S_i(\theta')$ as the set of points that are reached by following the integral curve of X_i through θ' for small t. This implies that

$$S_i(\theta') = \{\theta | u_{(c)}(\theta) = m', u_{(j,d_j)}(\theta) = w'_j \text{ for } j \neq i\} \tag{3.115}$$

$$= \{v((w_i, w'_{-i}), m') | w_i \in (-\varepsilon, \varepsilon)\}. \tag{3.116}$$

Because $D_{\theta_i} u_{(i,c_i)} \neq 0$ on $O(\theta^*)$, it follows from (3.115) that

$$S_i(\theta') = \{(\theta_i, \theta'_{-i}) \in O(\theta^*) | u_{(i,c_i)}(\theta_i, \theta'_{-i}) = m'_i\}. \tag{3.117}$$

The local coordinate system u thus satisfies conclusions (3.66)–(3.70) of the Frobenius Theorem for Mechanism Design.

To complete the argument that u has all properties listed in the Frobenius Theorem for Mechanism Design, it remains to be shown that u satisfies Property (iv) in the statement of the theorem, i.e., for $i = 1, 2$, the mapping $\theta_i = v_i(w, m)$ does not depend on w_{-i}. Again let $u(\theta') = (w', m')$. Consider the mapping $v(w'_i, \cdot, m') : (-\varepsilon, \varepsilon) \to O(\theta^*)$. The definition of the coordinate system u implies

$$v(w'_i, w_{-i}, m') = \rho(X_{-i}, \theta', w_{-i} - w'_{-i}), \tag{3.118}$$

i.e., changing the value of w_{-i} corresponds to movement along the integral curve $\rho(X_{-i}, \theta', t)$ of X_{-i} through θ' from $t = 0$ to $t = w_{-i} - w'_{-i}$. Because $X_{-i}(\theta) \in \mathcal{D}_{-i}(\theta)$, the value of θ_i does not vary away from θ'_i as one moves along this integral curve, i.e., $v_i(w'_i, w_{-i}, m') = \theta'_i$ for all $w_{-i} \in (-\varepsilon, \varepsilon)$. The mapping v_i thus does not depend on the value of w_{-i}.

The proof is now completed by constructing vector fields X_1, X_2 that satisfy (3.102) and (3.103). Given a d-dimensional integrable distribution $\mathcal{D}$ and a point $\theta^* \in \Theta$, the proof of the standard Frobenius Theorem constructs a set of vector fields $\{X_j\}_{1 \leq j \leq d}$ that span $\mathcal{D}(\theta)$ at every point θ near θ^* and

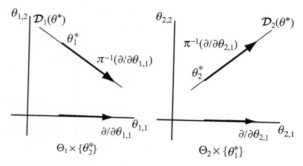

Figure 3.3. The figure illustrates the construction of nonzero vector fields X_1 and X_2 such that $X_1 \in \mathcal{D}_1$, $X_2 \in \mathcal{D}_2$, and $[X_1, X_2] = 0$.

such that $[X_j, X_l] = 0$ also holds for all $1 \le j, l \le d$. This construction is discussed in the proof of Theorem 5 in Section 2.5. Vector fields X_1, X_2 with these properties are needed here that also have the additional feature that $X_1 \in \mathcal{D}_1$ and $X_2 \in \mathcal{D}_2$. The construction in Theorem 5 is now modified to insure that X_1 and X_2 can be chosen with this additional property. Consider the projection mapping $\pi : \Theta \to \mathbb{R}^2$ onto the first coordinates of Θ_1 and Θ_2,

$$\pi(\theta) \equiv (\theta_{1,1}, \theta_{2,1}). \tag{3.119}$$

Statement (3.106) implies that the restriction of the derivative mapping $D_\theta \pi(\theta)$ to $\mathcal{D}(\theta)$ is an isomorphism onto $T_{\pi(\theta)} \mathbb{R}^2$ for θ near θ^*. For $i = 1, 2$, a smooth vector field X_i is thus well defined for θ near θ^* by the formula

$$X_i \equiv \left\{ D_\theta \pi^{-1} \left(\frac{\partial}{\partial \theta_{i,1}} \right) \right\} \cap \mathcal{D}. \tag{3.120}$$

This is illustrated at $\theta = \theta^*$ in Figure 3.3. The definition of π together with the properties of $\mathcal{D}_1$ and $\mathcal{D}_2$ given in (i) of *Direct Sum* imply that $X_i(\theta) \in \mathcal{D}_i(\theta)$ for $i = 1, 2$. The definition of these vectors in (3.120) implies

$$D_\theta \pi \cdot [X_1, X_2] = [D_\theta \pi \cdot X_1, D_\theta \pi \cdot X_2] \tag{3.121}$$

$$= \left[\frac{\partial}{\partial \theta_{1,1}}, \frac{\partial}{\partial \theta_{2,1}} \right] = 0.$$

The distribution $\mathcal{D}$ is integrable and hence $[X_1, X_2] \in \mathcal{D}$. Because $D_\theta \pi(\theta)$ is an isomorphism on $\mathcal{D}(\theta)$ for all θ near θ^*, (3.121) thus implies that $[X_1, X_2] = 0$, which is the desired result.

3.5.2 The General Case

The example of Subsection 3.5.1 is notable because while it makes the geometry, the calculations, and the notation of the proof of the Frobenius Theorem for Mechanism Design as simple as possible, it also illustrates every step of the general proof. As suggested by this example, the proof of the general result requires the following theorem.

Theorem 7: *Suppose that the distributions* $\mathcal{D}_1, \ldots, \mathcal{D}_n$ *and* $\mathcal{D}$ *on* Θ *have the properties given in* Direct Sum. *Let* θ^* *denote a point in* Θ. *There exists a set of d vector fields*

$$\{X_{i,h} | 1 \leq i \leq n, 1 \leq h \leq d_i\}$$

defined near θ^* *such that*

(i) $[X_{i,h}, X_{j,l}] = 0$ *for all pairs of vectors* $X_{i,h}$, $X_{j,l}$ *in this set;*
(ii) *for each* $1 \leq i \leq n$, *the subset* $\{X_{i,h} | 1 \leq h \leq d_i\}$ *defines a basis of* $\mathcal{D}_i(\theta)$ *for all* θ *near* θ^*.

Proof: As suggested in Subsection 3.5.1, the theorem is proven by modifying the construction in the proof of Theorem 5 in Section 2.5. After renumbering the coordinates separately in each of the parameter spaces $\Theta_1, \ldots, \Theta_n$, it can be assumed without loss of generality that

$$\frac{\partial}{\partial \theta_{i,h}}(\theta^*) \notin \mathcal{D}_i(\theta^*) \tag{3.122}$$

for $1 \leq i \leq n$ and $c_i + 1 < h \leq d_i + c_i$. Let $\pi : \Theta \to \mathbb{R}^d$ denote the projection mapping

$$\pi(\theta) \equiv (\theta_{(i,d_i)})_{1 \leq i \leq n}. \tag{3.123}$$

Statement (3.122) implies that the restriction of the derivative mapping $D_\theta \pi(\theta) : T_\theta \Theta \to T_{\pi(\theta)} \mathbb{R}^d$ to $\mathcal{D}(\theta)$ is an isomorphism for values of θ near θ^*. For $1 \leq i \leq n$ and $1 \leq h \leq d_i$, a smooth vector field $X_{i,h}$ is thus well defined for θ near θ^* by the formula

$$X_{i,h} \equiv \left(D_\theta \pi^{-1} \cdot \frac{\partial}{\partial \theta_{i,h}} \right) \cap \mathcal{D}. \tag{3.124}$$

The definition of π in (3.123) and the properties of $\mathcal{D}$ and $(\mathcal{D}_i)_{1 \leq i \leq n}$ in *Direct Sum* together imply that $X_{i,h}(\theta) \in \mathcal{D}_i(\theta)$ for all θ near θ^*. Notice also that

$$D_\theta \pi \cdot [X_{i,h}, X_{j,l}] = [D_\theta \pi \cdot (X_{i,h}), D_\theta \pi \cdot (X_{j,l})] \qquad (3.125)$$

$$= \left[\frac{\partial}{\partial \theta_{i,h}}, \frac{\partial}{\partial \theta_{ij,l}} \right] = 0$$

for all $1 \leq i, j \leq n$, $1 \leq h \leq d_i$, and $1 \leq l \leq d_j$. The distribution $\mathcal{D}$ is integrable and hence $[X_{i,h}, X_{j,l}] \in \mathcal{D}$. Because $D_\theta \pi(\theta)$ is an isomorphism on $\mathcal{D}(\theta)$ for all θ near θ^*, (3.125) implies that $[X_{i,h}, X_{j,l}] = 0$, which is the desired result.   ∎

Proof of the Frobenius Theorem for Mechanism Design: As in the proof of Theorem 7, it is assumed here that the coordinates have been renumbered so that (3.122) holds. The set of vector fields

$$\{X_{i,h} | 1 \leq i \leq n, 1 \leq h \leq d_i\} \qquad (3.126)$$

has also been selected to satisfy the conclusions of this theorem. For $1 \leq i \leq n$, define the c_i-dimensional plane P_i in Θ_i as

$$P_i \equiv \{\theta_i | \theta_{(i,d_i)} = \theta^*_{(i,d_i)}\}. \qquad (3.127)$$

Statement (3.122) implies that $\oplus_{i=1}^n P_i$ transversally intersects the integral manifolds of $\mathcal{D}$ near θ^*.

The local coordinate system u is now defined using $\oplus_{i=1}^n P_i$ and the set of vector fields $\{X_{i,h} | 1 \leq i \leq n, 1 \leq h \leq d_i\}$ in the manner in which the locally coordinate system is constructed in the proof of the standard Frobenius Theorem and in Subsection 3.5.1. Some notation is needed. Given any C^∞ vector field X and a real number t', the mapping $\rho_{X,t'} : \Theta \to \Theta$ is defined by the formula

$$\rho_{X,t'}(\theta) = \rho(X, \theta, t'). \qquad (3.128)$$

The point $\rho_{X,t'}(\theta)$ is thus reached by following the integral curve of X through θ from $t = 0$ to $t = t'$. For $w \equiv (w_{i,h})_{1 \leq i \leq n, 1 \leq h \leq d_i} \in \mathbb{R}^d$, define the mapping $\mathcal{X}_w : \Theta \to \Theta$ as

$$\mathcal{X}_w(\theta) \equiv \left(\bigodot_{1 \leq i \leq n, 1 \leq h \leq d_i} \rho_{X_{i,h}, w_{i,h}} \right)(\theta), \qquad (3.129)$$

where the right side of (3.129) represents the composition of the mappings $(\rho_{X_{i,h}, w_{i,h}})_{1 \le i \le n, 1 \le h \le d_i}$ evaluated at θ.[10] Define u as follows:

$$u(\theta) = (w, m) \Leftrightarrow \theta = X_w((\theta^*_{(i,d_i)}, \theta^*_{(i,c_i)} + m_i)_{1 \le i \le n}). \qquad (3.130)$$

In words, $u(\theta) = (w, m)$ if and only if θ is reached by starting at

$$(\theta^*_{(i,d_i)}, \theta^*_{(i,c_i)} + m_i)_{1 \le i \le n} \in \bigoplus_{i=1}^{n} P_i \qquad (3.131)$$

and following the integral curve of $X_{1,1}$ from $t = 0$ to $t = w_{1,1}$, then following the integral curve of $X_{1,2}$ from $t = 0$ to $t = w_{1,2}, \ldots,$ and finally following the integral curve of X_{n,d_n} from $t = 0$ to $t = w_{n,d_n}$. The proof of the standard Frobenius Theorem implies that u is a local coordinate system on an open neighborhood $O(\theta^*)$ of θ^*. By choosing $O(\theta^*)$ and ε sufficiently small, it can be assumed that $u(O(\theta^*)) = (-\varepsilon, \varepsilon)^d$.

As in the statement of the theorem, let $u(\theta') \equiv (w', m')$ and let $v \equiv u^{-1}$. The proof of the standard Frobenius Theorem also implies that

$$S(\theta') = \{\theta \,|\, u_{(c)}(\theta) = m'\} \qquad (3.132)$$

$$\equiv \{\theta \,|\, \theta = v(w, m'), w \in (-\varepsilon, \varepsilon)^d\},$$

i.e., u satisfies (3.66) and (3.67). The local characterization of maximal integral manifolds in the proof of the standard Frobenius Theorem implies that for each $1 \le i \le n$,

$$S_i(\theta') = \{\theta \,|\, u_{(c)}(\theta) = m', u_{(j,d_j)}(\theta) = w'_j \text{ for } j \ne i\} \qquad (3.133)$$

$$= \{\theta \,|\, \theta = v((w_i, w'_{-i}), m') \text{ for } w_i \in (-\varepsilon, \varepsilon)^{d_i}\}. \qquad (3.134)$$

Statements (3.69) and (3.70) thus hold. Once (iii) in the statement of Theorem 6 is established (i.e., rank $D_{\theta_i} u_{(i,c_i)} = c_i$ on $O(\theta^*)$), it follows from (3.133) that

$$S_i(\theta') = \{(\theta_i, \theta'_{-i}) \in O(\theta^*) \,|\, u_{(i,c_i)}(\theta_i, \theta'_{-i}) = m'_i\}, \qquad (3.135)$$

i.e., u satisfies (3.68). That rank $D_{\theta_i} u_{(i,c_i)} = c_i$ near θ^* is obvious from the simple form of $u_{(i,c_i)}$ on $\bigoplus_{i=1}^{n} P_i$:

$$u_{(i,c_i)}(\theta) = \theta_{(i,c_i)} - \theta^*_{(i,c_i)} \text{ if } \theta \in \bigoplus_{i=1}^{n} P_i. \qquad (3.136)$$

---

[10] Recall from Section 2.5 that the order of composition in (3.129) is irrelevant because $[X_{i,h}, X_{j,l}] = 0$ for all $X_{i,h}$ and $X_{j,l}$.

It remains to be shown that the mapping $v_{(i)}$ depends only on the values of w_i and m and not on the value of w_{-i}. Consider the mapping $\theta = v(w, m)$. For some $j \neq i$ and some choice of $1 \leq h \leq d_j$, fix all the variables in this mapping at the values determined by the point (w', m') except the value of $w'_{j,h}$, which will be allowed to vary away from $w'_{j,h}$. The definition of the coordinate system implies that changing the value of $w_{j,h}$ corresponds to a movement along the integral curve $\rho(X_{j,h}, \theta', t)$ of $X_{j,h}$ through θ' from $t = 0$ to $t = w_{j,h} - w'_{j,h}$. Because $X_{j,h}(\theta) \in \mathcal{D}_j(\theta)$, the value of θ_i does not vary away from θ'_i as one moves along this integral curve, i.e., the value of $v_i(w, m)$ does not change as $w_{j,h}$ is varied.   ∎

3.6 *Global Product Structure*

The bottleneck in Figure 3.1 to establishing the global equivalence of *Message Process*, *Product Structure*, and *Direct Sum* is *Direct Sum*⇒*Message Process*. The arguments and the examples of Sections 2.6 and 2.7 that showed why *Distribution*⇒*Mapping* in general only holds locally also imply that *Direct Sum*⇒*Message Process* only holds locally.

Combining the implications *Direct Sum*⇒*Message Process* locally and *Message Process*⇒*Product Structure* globally in Figure 3.1 implies that *Direct Sum*⇒*Product Structure* holds locally.[11] This implication holds globally if one of the requirements of *Product Structure* is relaxed. Recall the discussion of *Distribution*⇒*Foliation* in Subsections 2.6.2 and 2.6.3: an integral manifold of a distribution is a submanifold of Θ, and a submanifold of Θ in this text satisfies (2.1), i.e., it is an *imbedded* submanifold of Θ. The maximal integral manifold of a distribution may only be an *immersed* submanifold of Θ.[12] The implication *Direct Sum*⇒*Product Structure* does not hold globally because *Product Structure* requires that the integral manifolds $S_i(\theta)$ and $S(\theta)$ be imbedded submanifolds of Θ.

A global result can be obtained by relaxing the concept of a submanifold in *Product Structure*. Some notation is useful in this section for proving this result. Suppose that distributions $\mathcal{D}_1, \ldots, \mathcal{D}_n$ and $\mathcal{D}$ satisfy *Direct Sum*. For an arbitrary open set $O \subset \Theta$ that contains θ^*, let $S(\theta^*, O)$ and $S_i(\theta^*, O)$

---

[11] This is also proven directly in Section 3.4 by an application of the Frobenius Theorem for Mechanism Design.

[12] I use the stronger notion of an imbedded submanifold in this text because one of my goals is to shed light on message rules; the solution set in Θ_i determined by an equilibrium state of a message rule $\alpha_i(\cdot, m) = 0$ is (with appropriate regularity assumptions) an imbedded submanifold of Θ_i. See the discussion of *Message Process*⇒*Product Structure* globally in Section 3.3 for details.

denote the maximal integral manifolds of $\mathcal{D}$ and $\mathcal{D}_i$ through θ^* in O. Let $S_i^*(\theta^*, O)$ denote the projection of $S_i(\theta^*, O)$ into Θ_i. *Local Product Structure* and *Global Product Structure* are now defined using this new notation.

> **Local Product Structure:** For every $\theta^* \in \Theta$, there exists an open neighborhood $O(\theta^*) \subset \Theta$ of θ^* in which the following statements hold for every $1 \leq i \leq n$ and $\theta \in O(\theta^*)$:
>
> (i) $S(\theta, O(\theta^*))$ and $S_i(\theta, O(\theta^*))$ are imbedded submanifolds of $O(\theta^*)$;
>
> (ii) $S(\theta, O(\theta^*)) = \Pi_{i=1}^n S_i^*(\theta, O(\theta^*))$.

> **Global Product Structure:** For all $\theta^* \in \Theta$ and $1 \leq i \leq n$,
>
> (i) $S(\theta, \Theta)$ and $S_i(\theta, \Theta)$ are immersed submanifolds of Θ;
>
> (ii) $S(\theta^*, \Theta) = \Pi_{i=1}^n S_i^*(\theta^*, \Theta)$.

The implication *Direct Sum⇒Local Product Structure* has been established. The discussion in Subsection 2.6.2 implies that Property (i) of *Global Product Structure* follows from *Direct Sum*. The implication *Direct Sum⇒Global Product Structure* thus requires only a proof that

$$S(\theta^*, \Theta) = \prod_{i=1}^n S_i^*(\theta^*, \Theta) \tag{3.137}$$

for all $\theta^* \in \Theta$. Establishing (3.137) is the main purpose of this section.[13]

3.6.1 Example: Defining a Message Process Using Partitions

While the implication *Direct Sum⇒Equation* (3.137) may seem obvious, its proof is quite complicated, as is typical of global results. The value of this result must therefore be justified. Although it may always be worthwhile to determine the extent to which a local result also holds globally, this subsection justifies this result in terms of the broader aims of mechanism design.

The objective of this text is to develop a first-order approach to the construction of mechanisms. The global result *Direct Sum⇒Global Product*

---

[13] In the language of Hurwicz et al. (1978), it is shown in this section that while *Direct Sum* is not sufficient to guarantee the existence of a "message-indexed product structure" in Θ, it does define a "parameter-indexed product structure" in Θ. A preliminary effort to establish a global version of *Direct Sum⇒Product Structure* can be found in Section 3.2.G (p. 90) of their manuscript.

Structure is valuable in a more abstract approach to mechanism design in which the message process is not necessarily C^∞ and the messages themselves are not necessarily even vectors of real numbers. As demonstrated below, *Direct Sum* is sufficient in this abstract approach for the construction globally of a message process on Θ. This is rather striking, for first-order conditions are typically necessary but not sufficient in mathematical problems. The implication *Direct Sum*$\Rightarrow$*Global Product Structure* in particular insures uniqueness of the equilibrium message in the constructed message process for each $\theta \in \Theta$. While uniqueness of the equilibrium message may not be a necessary feature in every message process, it is at times quite useful. The implication *Direct Sum*$\Rightarrow$*Global Product Structure* thus reveals how this property is guaranteed in a first-order approach.

The essential ingredients of this abstract approach to message processes are the $n + 1$ partitions

$$\{S_i(\theta)|\theta \in \Theta\}_{1 \le i \le n} \tag{3.138}$$

and

$$\left\{ \prod_{i=1}^{n} S_i^*(\theta) \,|\, \theta \in \Theta \right\} \tag{3.139}$$

of Θ. *Product Structure* postulates these partitions; in a more abstract approach to mechanism design, however, each set $S_i(\theta)$ need not be a submanifold of Θ (either imbedded or immersed). From this more abstract perspective, the regularity conditions of *Product Structure* concerning the geometric structure of the sets $S_i(\theta)$ are nonessential but perhaps helpful ingredients for constructing the desired partitions.

Direct Sum implies that the integral manifolds of the distributions $\mathcal{D}_1, \ldots, \mathcal{D}_n$ define partitions of the form (3.138). Also, the assumption in *Direct Sum* that $\mathcal{D}$ is integrable implies that $\{S(\theta)|\theta \in \Theta\}$ is a partition of Θ. As will be seen below, however, (3.139) must partition Θ if uniqueness of the equilibrium message is to hold. Given *Direct Sum*$\Rightarrow$*Global Product Structure*, however, Equation (3.137) together with the fact that $\{S(\theta)|\theta \in \Theta\}$ is a partition of Θ implies that (3.139) is also a partition of this space.[14]

---

[14] Equation (3.137) of course also implies that each maximal integral manifold $S(\theta)$ of D is the Cartesian product of the maximal integral manifolds $S_1(\theta), \ldots, S_n(\theta)$ of $D_1, \ldots, D_n$. Equation (3.137) is thus more than a statement that the set (3.139) is a partition of Θ, which is all that is drawn from this equation in this discussion.

In the abstract approach to mechanism design, the partitions in (3.138) and (3.139) define a message process as follows: for each $1 \leq i \leq n$,[15]

$$M_i \equiv \{S_i^*(\theta) | \theta \in \Theta\} \tag{3.140}$$

and

$$\mu_i(\theta_i) = \{S_i^*(\theta') | \theta_i \in S_i^*(\theta')\} \times M_{-i}. \tag{3.141}$$

The messages selected by the ith agent are the sets $S_i^*(\theta')$ that contain his parameter θ_i. This models a basic feature of a language, which is that a word or a term (such as $S_i^*(\theta')$) may represent a variety of different instances (any $\theta_i \in S_i^*(\theta')$). A message profile $m = (S_i^*(\theta))_{1 \leq i \leq n}$ is an equilibrium message for θ' in this mechanism ($m \in \mu(\theta')$) if and only if $\theta_i' \in S_i^*(\theta)$ for each $1 \leq i \leq n$. This can be stated equivalently as

$$m = (S_i^*(\theta))_{1 \leq i \leq n} \in \mu(\theta') \Leftrightarrow \theta' \in \prod_{i=1}^{n} S_i^*(\theta). \tag{3.142}$$

It is obvious that $(S_i^*(\theta'))_{1 \leq i \leq n} \in \mu(\theta')$ and so $\mu(\theta')$ is nonempty for all $\theta' \in \Theta$. Applying (3.142), the assumption that (3.139) is a partition of Θ insures that $(S_i^*(\theta'))_{1 \leq i \leq n}$ is the unique equilibrium message for θ'. Starting from *Direct Sum* and constructing the partitions by integrating the distributions, the implication *Direct Sum* $\Rightarrow$ *Global Product Structure* thus implies uniqueness of the equilibrium message for each $\theta' \in \Theta$.

3.6.2 A Test for *Product Structure*

All that remains to be shown is that (3.137) of *Global Product Structure* follows from *Direct Sum*. I thus begin with a necessary and sufficient condition for verifying (3.137) in the case of $n = 2$. This condition will prove useful in the analysis that follows.

Let $O = O_1 \times O_2$ be an open subset of Θ such that $O_1 \subset \Theta_1$ and $O_2 \subset \Theta_2$. The condition in Lemma 8 for verifying that (3.137) holds within O is set theoretic in nature.[16] It concerns the sets

$$\{S_1(\theta, O)\}_{\theta \in O}, \{S_2(\theta, O)\}_{\theta \in O}, \text{ and } \{S(\theta, O)\}_{\theta \in O} \tag{3.143}$$

purely as partitions of O, without reference to the geometric structure of the sets $S_1(\theta, O)$, $S_2(\theta, O)$, and $S(\theta, O)$. With an eye toward the abstract

---

[15] In the language of Hurwicz et al. (1978), a "parameter-indexed product structure" as given by the partitions in (3.138) and (3.139) is used here to define a "message-indexed product structure" in which the messages consist of the sets in the partitions.

[16] Lemma 8 generalizes Lemma 2 of Williams (1981).

approach to constructing mechanisms that is discussed in Subsection 3.6.1, it is assumed in this lemma that partitions of O as in (3.143) are given such that for $i = 1, 2$ and all $\theta \in O,$[17]

$$S_i(\theta, O) \subset S(\theta, O) \tag{3.144}$$

and

$$S_i(\theta, O) \subset O_i \times \{\theta_{-i}\}. \tag{3.145}$$

Lemma 8: *Let $O = O_1 \times O_2$ be an open subset of Θ such that $O_1 \subset \Theta_1$ and $O_2 \subset \Theta_2$. Let*

$$\{S_1(\theta, O)\}_{\theta \in O}, \quad \{S_2(\theta, O)\}_{\theta \in O}, \quad \text{and} \quad \{S(\theta, O)\}_{\theta \in O} \tag{3.146}$$

be partitions of O that satisfy (3.144) and (3.145). The equation

$$S(\theta', O) = S_1^*(\theta', O) \times S_2^*(\theta', O) \tag{3.147}$$

holds for all $\theta' \in O$ if and only if

$$S_i(\theta', O) \cap S_j(\theta'', O) = \{(\theta_i'', \theta_j')\} \tag{3.148}$$

holds for all $\theta' \in O$, $i \neq j$, and $\theta'' \in S(\theta', O)$.

It is important to notice that the issue in (3.148) is the nonemptiness of the intersection and not the uniqueness of the point of intersection: if $S_i(\theta', O) \cap S_j(\theta'', O) \neq \phi$, then it clearly satisfies (3.148) because $S_i(\theta', O) \subset O_i \times \{\theta_j'\}$ and $S_j(\theta'', O) \subset O_j \times \{\theta_i''\}$.

Proof: **(3.148)$\Rightarrow$(3.147).** This implication is proven by showing that a point in the set on one side of (3.147) also lies in the set on the other side. For $\theta'' \in S(\theta', O)$, (3.148) implies in the case of $i = 1$ and $j = 2$ that

$$S_1(\theta', O) \cap S_2(\theta'', O) = \{(\theta_1'', \theta_2')\}, \tag{3.149}$$

and so $\theta_1'' \in S_1^*(\theta', O)$. Setting $i = 2$ and $j = 1$ in (3.148) implies

$$S_2(\theta', O) \cap S_1(\theta'', O) = \{(\theta_1', \theta_2'')\}, \tag{3.150}$$

and so $\theta_2'' \in S_2^*(\theta', O)$. Therefore,

$$\theta'' \in S_1^*(\theta', O) \times S_2^*(\theta', O). \tag{3.151}$$

---

[17] It may be helpful at this point to remind the reader that superscripts in this text distinguish points in Θ while subscripts distinguish the coordinates of a particular point.

Consider next

$$\theta'' = (\theta_1'', \theta_2'') \in S_1^* (\theta', O) \times S_2^* (\theta', O).$$ (3.152)

Clearly,

$$\theta_1'' \in S_1^* (\theta', O) \Rightarrow (\theta_1'', \theta_2') \in S_1 (\theta', O) \subset S (\theta', O)$$ (3.153)

and

$$\theta_2'' \in S_2^* (\theta', O) \Rightarrow (\theta_1', \theta_2'') \in S_2 (\theta', O) \subset S (\theta', O).$$ (3.154)

Because $\{S(\theta, O)\}_{\theta \in O}$ partitions O, it follows that

$$S \left((\theta_1'', \theta_2'), O \right) = S \left((\theta_1', \theta_2''), O \right) = S (\theta', O).$$ (3.155)

Replace θ' and θ'' in (3.148) with (θ_1'', θ_2') and (θ_1', θ_2''). It implies in the case of $i = 2$ and $j = 1$ that

$$S_2 \left((\theta_1'', \theta_2'), O \right) \cap S_1 \left((\theta_1', \theta_2''), O \right) = \{\theta''\},$$ (3.156)

and therefore

$$\theta'' \in S_1 \left((\theta_1', \theta_2''), O \right) \subset S \left((\theta_1', \theta_2''), O \right) = S (\theta' O).$$ (3.157)

(3.147)$\Rightarrow$(3.148). Because $S(\theta'', O) = S(\theta', O)$, (3.147) implies that

$$S_i^* (\theta'', O) = S_i^* (\theta', O)$$ (3.158)

for $i = 1, 2$. Therefore,

$$\theta_i'' \in S_i^* (\theta'', O) = S_i^* (\theta', O) \Rightarrow (\theta_i'', \theta_j') \in S_i (\theta', O)$$ (3.159)

and

$$\theta_j' \in S_j^* (\theta', O) = S_j^* (\theta'', O) \Rightarrow (\theta_i'', \theta_j') \in S_j (\theta'', O),$$ (3.160)

which together imply (3.148). ∎

3.6.3 *Global Product Structure* in the Case of $n = 2$

The implication *Direct Sum$\Rightarrow$Global Product Structure* is established in this subsection for the case of $n = 2$. This special case is then used to establish the result for arbitrary n in Subsection 3.6.4.[18]

[18] The following proof originates in Williams (1982c).

Theorem 9 (*Direct Sum⇒Global Product Structure* for $n = 2$): *Let O = $O_1 \times O_2$ be an open subset of Θ. If $\mathcal{D}_1$, $\mathcal{D}_2$ and $\mathcal{D} = \mathcal{D}_1 \oplus \mathcal{D}_2$ satisfy Direct Sum, then*

$$S(\theta, O) = S_1^*(\theta, O) \times S_2^*(\theta, O)$$

for all $\theta \in O$. In particular, setting $O = \Theta$ completes the proof that Direct Sum⇒Global Product Structure.

Proof: The result is proven by showing that (3.148) holds for $\theta' \in O$ and $\theta'' \in S(\theta', O)$. It is assumed without loss of generality that $i = 1$ and $j = 2$. The objective is thus to prove

$$(\theta_1'', \theta_2') \in S_1(\theta', O) \cap S_2(\theta'', O). \tag{3.161}$$

The proof begins with a construction. The connectedness of $S(\theta', O)$ implies that there exists a simple, rectifiable curve $\gamma : [0, 1] \to O$ such that $\gamma(0) = \theta'$, $\gamma(1) = \theta''$, and $C = \gamma([0, 1]) \subset S(\theta', O)$. Write $\gamma = (\gamma_1, \gamma_2)$, where $\gamma_i : [0, 1] \to O_i$, and let $C_i = \gamma_i([0, 1])$. Because C is compact, the sets C_1, C_2 and $C_1 \times C_2$ are also compact.

The next step is the construction of an open cover of $C_1 \times C_2$ with particular properties. There exists at each point $\theta \in C_1 \times C_2$ an open set $O(\theta) = O(\theta_1) \times O(\theta_2)$ in which *Local Product Structure* holds. Selecting an open set of this form at each $\theta \in C_1 \times C_2$ defines an open cover of this set. Consider the metric $\langle \cdot \rangle$ defined on Θ by the formula

$$\langle \theta \rangle = \langle (\theta_1, \theta_2) \rangle = \sup \{ \|\theta_1\|, \|\theta_2\| \}, \tag{3.162}$$

where $\|\cdot\|$ denotes the standard Euclidean metric on O_1 and O_2. Let ℓ denote a Lebesgue number for the cover relative to the metric $\langle \cdot \rangle$. The significance of the number ℓ is as follows. For $\theta^* \in C_1 \times C_2$ and $0 < \delta \leq \ell$, the ball $\mathcal{B}(\theta^*, \delta)$ relative to the metric (3.162) centered at θ^* has the form $B_1(\theta_1^*, \delta) \times B_2(\theta_2^*, \delta)$, where $B_i(\theta_i^*, \delta)$ is a ball centered at θ_i^* relative to the standard Euclidean metric $\|\cdot\|$. By the definition of a Lebesgue number for a cover, $\mathcal{B}(\theta^*, \delta)$ is a subset of some set $O(\theta)$ in the cover of $C_1 \times C_2$ selected above. *Local Product Structure* thus holds within $\mathcal{B}(\theta^*, \delta)$.

The final step in the construction is to divide C into pieces, each of which has length less than ℓ. Specifically, select

$$0 = t_1 < t_2 < \cdots < t_m = 1 \tag{3.163}$$

and corresponding points

$$\theta' = \theta^1 = \gamma(t_1), \theta^2 = \gamma(t_2), \cdots, \theta'' = \theta^m = \gamma(t_m) \tag{3.164}$$

such that

$$\langle \gamma(t) - \theta^s \rangle, \langle \gamma(t) - \theta^{s+1} \rangle < \ell \qquad (3.165)$$

for $1 \leq s \leq m - 1$ and $t \in [t_s, t_{s+1}]$. In words, each point $\gamma(t)$ along the curve C between consecutive points θ^s and θ^{s+1} lies within ℓ of each of these points in the metric $\langle \cdot \rangle$.

All the elements that are needed for the proof have now been constructed. It is shown below that for $1 \leq s \leq r \leq m - 1$,

$$\gamma_1([t_r, t_{r+1}]) \subset S_1^* \left(\left(\theta_1^r, \theta_2^s \right), O \right) \qquad (3.166)$$

and

$$\gamma_2([t_s, t_{s+1}]) \subset S_2^* \left(\left(\theta_1^{r+1}, \theta_2^s \right), O \right). \qquad (3.167)$$

The desired result (3.161) follows from (3.166) and (3.167) by the following argument. Applying (3.166) in the case of $s = 1$ implies

$$\gamma_1(t_{r+1}) = \theta_1^{r+1} \in S_1^* \left(\left(\theta_1^r, \theta_2^1 \right), O \right). \qquad (3.168)$$

Because $\{ S_1^*((\theta_1, \theta_2^1), O) \}_{\theta_1 \in O_1}$ is a partition of O_1, (3.168) implies

$$S_1^* \left(\left(\theta_1^r, \theta_2^1 \right), O \right) = S_1^* \left(\left(\theta_1^{r+1}, \theta_2^1 \right), O \right) \qquad (3.169)$$

for $1 \leq r \leq m - 1$. Consequently,

$$S_1^* \left(\left(\theta_1^1, \theta_2^1 \right), O \right) = S_1^* \left(\left(\theta_1^2, \theta_2^1 \right), O \right) = \cdots = S_1^* \left(\left(\theta_1^m, \theta_2^1 \right), O \right), \qquad (3.170)$$

and so

$$\theta_1^m \in S_1^* \left(\left(\theta_1^1, \theta_2^1 \right), O \right). \qquad (3.171)$$

Because $\theta^1 = \theta'$ and $\theta^m = \theta''$, it follows that

$$\left(\theta_1'', \theta_2' \right) \in S_1 \left(\theta', O \right). \qquad (3.172)$$

A similar argument using (3.167) in the case of $r = m - 1$ implies

$$\left(\theta_1'', \theta_2' \right) \in S_2 \left(\theta'', O \right), \qquad (3.173)$$

which together with (3.172) establishes (3.161).

Statements (3.166) and (3.167) are now established by induction on $r - s$. Consider first $r - s = 0$ or $r = s$. Statements (3.166) and (3.167) in this case are

$$\gamma_1([t_s, t_{s+1}]) \subset S_1^* \left(\theta^s, O \right) \qquad (3.174)$$

and

$$\gamma_2 \left([t_s, t_{s+1}] \right) \subset S_2^* \left(\theta^s, O \right). \tag{3.175}$$

The construction at the beginning of the proof implies that (i) *Local Product Structure* holds within $\mathcal{B}(\theta^s, \ell)$ and (ii) $\gamma \left([t_s, t_{s+1}] \right) \subset S \left(\theta^s, \mathcal{B}(\theta^s, \ell) \right)$. *Local Product Structure* within $\mathcal{B}(\theta^s, \ell)$ implies

$$S \left(\theta^s, \mathcal{B}(\theta^s, \ell) \right) = S_1^* \left(\theta^s, \mathcal{B}(\theta^s, \ell) \right) \times S_2^* \left(\theta^s, \mathcal{B}(\theta^s, \ell) \right). \tag{3.176}$$

Property (ii) implies

$$\gamma_1 \left([t_s, t_{s+1}] \right) \subset S_1^* \left(\theta^s, \mathcal{B}(\theta^s, \ell) \right) \tag{3.177}$$

and

$$\gamma_2 \left([t_s, t_{s+1}] \right) \subset S_2^* \left(\theta^s, \mathcal{B}(\theta^s, \ell) \right). \tag{3.178}$$

Statements (3.177) and (3.178) imply (3.174) and (3.175), respectively, because

$$S_i^* \left(\theta, \mathcal{B}(\theta, \ell) \right) \subset S_i^* \left(\theta, O \right) \tag{3.179}$$

for $i = 1, 2$ and all $\theta \in O$.

The proof is now completed by showing that (3.166) and (3.167) hold for r and s such that $r - s = q > 0$ given the induction hypothesis that these statements hold for r and s such that $0 \leq r - s \leq q$. The induction hypothesis implies that (3.166) holds when s is replaced with $s + 1$:

$$\gamma_1 \left([t_r, t_{r+1}] \right) \subset S_1^* \left(\left(\theta_1^r, \theta_2^{s+1} \right), O \right). \tag{3.180}$$

It also implies that (3.167) holds when r is replaced with $r - 1$:

$$\gamma_2 \left([t_s, t_{s+1}] \right) \subset S_2^* \left(\left(\theta_1^r, \theta_2^s \right), O \right) = S_2^* \left(\left(\theta_1^r, \theta_2^{s+1} \right), O \right), \tag{3.181}$$

where the equality follows from $\gamma_2 \left(t_{s+1} \right) = \theta_2^{s+1}$. Let $\mathcal{B} = \mathcal{B}((\theta_1^r, \theta_2^{s+1}), \ell)$. The following statements are true by construction: (i) *Local Product Structure* holds within $\mathcal{B}$; (ii) $\left\| \gamma_1 (t) - \theta_1^r \right\|$, $\left\| \gamma_2 (t) - \theta_2^{s+1} \right\| \leq \ell$. *Local Product Structure* within $\mathcal{B}$ implies

$$S \left((\theta_1^r, \theta_2^{s+1}), \mathcal{B} \right) = S_1^* \left((\theta_1^r, \theta_2^{s+1}), \mathcal{B} \right) \times S_2^* \left((\theta_1^r, \theta_2^{s+1}), \mathcal{B} \right). \tag{3.182}$$

Property (ii) along with statements (3.180) and (3.181) then imply

$$\left(\gamma_1 (t_r), \gamma_2 (t_s) \right) = \left(\theta_1^r, \theta_2^s \right) \tag{3.183}$$

and

$$\left(\gamma_1 (t_{r+1}), \gamma_2 (t_s) \right) = \left(\theta_1^{r+1}, \theta_2^s \right) \tag{3.184}$$

are in $S((\theta_1^r, \theta_2^{s+1}), \mathcal{B})$. It follows that

$$S\left((\theta_1^r, \theta_2^{s+1}), \mathcal{B}\right) = S\left((\theta_1^r, \theta_2^s), \mathcal{B}\right) = S\left((\theta_1^{r+1}, \theta_2^s), \mathcal{B}\right). \tag{3.185}$$

Again applying *Local Product Structure*, (3.185) implies

$$S_1^*\left((\theta_1^r, \theta_2^{s+1}), \mathcal{B}\right) = S_1^*\left((\theta_1^r, \theta_2^s), \mathcal{B}\right) \text{ and} \tag{3.186}$$

$$S_2^*\left((\theta_1^r, \theta_2^{s+1}), \mathcal{B}\right) = S_1^*\left((\theta_1^{r+1}, \theta_2^s), \mathcal{B}\right). \tag{3.187}$$

Substitution into (3.180) and (3.181) followed by an application of (3.179) implies the desired results of (3.166) and (3.167). ∎

3.6.4 *Global Product Structure* for Arbitrary n

Assume that the distributions $\mathcal{D}_1, \ldots, \mathcal{D}_n$, and $\mathcal{D} = \oplus_{i=1}^n \mathcal{D}_i$ satisfy *Direct Sum*. For $1 \le i \le n$, define the distribution $\mathcal{D}_{-i}$ on Θ as

$$\mathcal{D}_{-i}(\theta) = \bigoplus_{j \ne i} \mathcal{D}_j(\theta). \tag{3.188}$$

Each of the distributions $\mathcal{D}_{-i}$ is integrable because $\mathcal{D}$ is integrable and

$$\mathcal{D}_{-i}(\theta) \subset T_\theta \left(\{\theta_i\} \times \prod_{j \ne i} \Theta_j \right) \tag{3.189}$$

for all $\theta \in \Theta$.[19] *Direct Sum* ⟹ *Global Product Structure* for arbitrary n will be proven below by applying this implication in the case of $n = 2$ (as proven in Theorem 9) to each pair of distributions $\mathcal{D}_i$ and $\mathcal{D}_{-i}$.

For an open set $O = \Pi_{i=1}^n O_i$, let $S_{-i}(\theta, O)$ denote the maximal integrable manifold of $\mathcal{D}_{-i}$ in O and let $S_{-i}^*(\theta, O)$ denote its projection into $\Pi_{j \ne i}^n O_j$. It is clear that

$$S_{-i}(\theta, O) = \{\theta_i\} \times S_{-i}^*(\theta, O) \subset \{\theta_i\} \times \prod_{j \ne i} O_j. \tag{3.190}$$

The distributions $\mathcal{D}_i, \mathcal{D}_{-i}$ and $\mathcal{D} = \mathcal{D}_i \oplus \mathcal{D}_{-i}$ thus satisfy *Direct Sum* in the case of $n = 2$. Theorem 9 therefore implies

$$S(\theta, O) = S_i^*(\theta, O) \times S_{-i}^*(\theta, O) \tag{3.191}$$

---

[19] The integrability of $\mathcal{D}_{-i}$ can be proven formally by following the steps of the proof that the integrability of the direct sum $\mathcal{D}$ implies the integrability of each distribution $\mathcal{D}_i$. This argument can be found in Section 3.2 immediately after the formal statements of *Direct Sum*, *Product Structure*, and *Message Process*.

for any $\theta \in O$. Lemma 8 then implies

$$S_i \left(\theta^*, O \right) \cap S_{-i} \left(\theta^{**}, O \right) = \left\{ \theta \mid \theta_i = \theta_i^{**}, \theta_{-i} = \theta_{-i}^* \right\} \tag{3.192}$$

for any $\theta^*, \theta^{**} \in S(\theta, O)$ and $\theta \in O$. Both (3.191) and (3.192) are used in the proof of the following result.

Theorem 10 (*Direct Sum$\Rightarrow$Global Product Structure*): *Let* $O = \Pi_{i=1}^n O_i$ *be an open subset of* $\Theta = \Pi_{i=1}^n \Theta_i$. *If* $\mathcal{D}_1, \ldots, \mathcal{D}_n$ *and* $\mathcal{D} = \oplus_{i=1}^n \mathcal{D}_i$ *satisfy* Direct Sum, *then*

$$S(\theta, O) = \prod_{i=1}^n S_i^* (\theta, O) \tag{3.193}$$

for all $\theta \in O$. *In particular, setting* $O = \Theta$ *completes the proof that* Direct Sum$\Rightarrow$Global Product Structure.

Proof: It is shown that a point in the set on either side of (3.193) must lie in the set on the other side. For $\theta' \in S(\theta, O)$, (3.191) implies

$$\theta' \in S(\theta, O) = S_i^* (\theta, O) \times S_{-i}^* (\theta, O), \tag{3.194}$$

and so $\theta_i' \in S_i^*(\theta, O)$. Because i is arbitrary, it follows that $\theta' \in \Pi_{i=1}^n S_i^* (\theta, O)$.

Now consider $\theta' \in \Pi_{i=1}^n S_i^* (\theta, O)$. Because $\theta_i' \in S_i^*(\theta, O)$ and $S_i(\theta, O) \subset S(\theta, O)$, it follows that

$$\left(\theta_1, \ldots, \theta_{i-1}, \theta_i', \theta_{i+1}, \ldots, \theta_n \right) \in S(\theta, O). \tag{3.195}$$

Statement (3.192) implies the following:

$$\theta^*, \theta^{**} \in S(\theta, O) \Rightarrow \tag{3.196}$$

$$\left(\theta_i^{**}, \theta_{-i}^* \right) = \left(\theta_1^*, \ldots \theta_{i-1}^*, \theta_i^{**}, \theta_{i+1}^*, \ldots, \theta_n^* \right)$$

$$\in S_i(\theta^*, O) \subset S(\theta^*, O) = S(\theta, O).$$

A sequence of $n - 1$ steps now proves that $\theta' \in S(\theta, O)$:

Step 1. Statement (3.195) implies

$$\left(\theta_1', \theta_2, \ldots, \theta_n \right), \left(\theta_1, \theta_2', \theta_3, \ldots, \theta_n \right) \in S(\theta, O). \tag{3.197}$$

Applying (3.196) in the case of $i = 2$ implies

$$\left(\theta_1', \theta_2', \theta_3, \ldots, \theta_n \right) \in S(\theta, O). \tag{3.198}$$

Step 2. Because

$$\left(\theta'_1, \theta'_2, \ldots, \theta_n\right), \left(\theta_1, \theta_2, \theta'_3, \theta_4, \ldots, \theta_n\right) \in S(\theta, O), \tag{3.199}$$

applying (3.196) in the case of $i = 3$ implies

$$\left(\theta'_1, \theta'_2, \theta'_3, \theta_4 \ldots, \theta_n\right) \in S(\theta, O). \tag{3.200}$$

$$\vdots$$

Step $n - 1$. Because

$$\left(\theta'_1, \theta'_2, \ldots, \theta'_{n-1}, \theta_n\right), \left(\theta_1, \ldots, \theta_{n-1}, \theta'_n\right) \in S(\theta, O), \tag{3.201}$$

applying (3.196) in the case of $i = n$ implies

$$\theta' \in S(\theta, O). \tag{3.202}$$

∎

3.7 Differential Ideal

This chapter concludes with a restatement of *Direct Sum* in terms of differential forms and ideals. This approach is dual to the approach of this text, which states the first-order conditions for the construction of a message process in terms of vector fields and distributions. A development of differential forms and ideals is beyond the scope of this text. The purpose of this section is to place in print a restatement of *Direct Sum* as *Differential Ideal* along with some references for the sake of the reader who is already familiar with differential forms and ideals. The use of this material in the remainder of the text is limited to Subsections 4.1.2, 4.6.5, and 4.6.6.[20, 21]

Differential Ideal: For each $1 \le i \le n$, a C^∞ differential ideal $\mathcal{I}_i$ exists on Θ with the following properties:

    (i) $\mathcal{I}_i$ is generated by $c_i + \Sigma_{j \ne i}(d_j + c_j)$ independent 1-forms;

---

[20] The statement of *Differential Ideal* that follows below originates in Part IV of Hurwicz et al. (1978). Its equivalence with *Direct Sum* is addressed in Theorem 7 of their manuscript. This approach is developed further in Saari (1984) (see in particular (pp. 257–259).

[21] All differential forms and ideals are assumed C^∞ in this section. The following terminology is used. The *span* of a set of 1-forms consists of all linear combinations of these forms with elements of $C^\infty(\Theta, \mathbb{R})$ as the scalars. *Independence* is linear independence relative to this kind of linear combination. An ideal is *generated* by a set of 1-forms $\{v_1, \ldots, v_t\}$ if every element ρ of the ideal can be expressed as $\rho = \Sigma_{i=1}^t \rho_i \wedge v_i$, where each ρ_i is a k_i-form (with a 0-form interpreted as an element of $C^\infty(\Theta, \mathbb{R})$).

(ii) $d\theta_{j,t} \in \mathcal{I}_i$ for each $j \neq i$ and $1 \leq t \leq d_j + c_j$;
(iii) $\mathcal{I} = \cap_{i=1}^{n} \mathcal{I}_i$ is generated by 1-forms.

The dual relationship between a distribution and an ideal that is generated by 1-forms is analogous to the relationship between a plane and the orthogonal plane that is determined by it. The distribution $\mathcal{D}_i$ in *Direct Sum* is d_i-dimensional and hence the ideal $\mathcal{I}_i$ that is its dual is $c_i + \Sigma_{j \neq i}(d_j + c_j)$-dimensional within Θ. This is captured in (i) of *Differential Ideal*. Property (ii) in *Direct Sum* is that $\mathcal{D}_i(\theta)$ lies in the span of

$$\left\{ \frac{\partial}{\partial \theta_{i,t}} \right\}_{1 \leq t \leq d_i + c_i}. \tag{3.203}$$

This property is dual to (ii) in *Differential Ideal*, which states that certain 1-forms are in $\mathcal{I}_i$. The integrability of each $\mathcal{D}_i$ is equivalent to the assumption that each ideal $\mathcal{I}_i$ is generated by 1-forms and is a differential ideal.[22]

The ideal $\mathcal{I} = \cap_{i=1}^{n} \mathcal{I}_i$ is dual to the $\Sigma_{i=1}^{n} d_i$-dimensional distribution $\mathcal{D} \equiv \oplus_{i=1}^{n} \mathcal{D}_i$. Several properties of $\mathcal{I}$ follow from (i) and (ii) of *Differential Ideal*:

1. The ideal $\mathcal{I}$ is a differential ideal because each $\mathcal{I}_i$ is differential. This follows immediately from the definition of a differential ideal.

2. Statements (i) and (ii) imply that there exists for each ideal $\mathcal{I}_i$ a set of c_i 1-forms

$$\left\{ \omega_{i,t} \,|\, 1 \leq t \leq c_i \right\}$$

with the following properties:

(a) $\mathcal{I}_i$ is generated by

$$\left\{ \omega_{i,t} \,|\, 1 \leq t \leq c_i \right\} \cup \left\{ d\theta_{j,t} \,|\, j \neq i, 1 \leq t \leq d_j + c_j \right\};$$

(b) each $\omega_{i,t}$ lies in the span of

$$\left\{ d\theta_{i,t} \,|\, 1 \leq t \leq d_i + c_i \right\}.$$

(c) It is straightforward to show that the $\Sigma_{i=1}^{n} c_i$ 1-forms

$$\left\{ \omega_{i,t} \,|\, 1 \leq i \leq n, 1 \leq t \leq c_i \right\} \tag{3.204}$$

are independent and span the set of 1-forms in $\mathcal{I}$.

---

[22] The term *differential ideal* is defined in Warner (1971, Def. 2.29, p. 74)). The duality between an ideal generated by 1-forms and a distribution is discussed in Spivak (1979, p. 292) and Warner (1971, Prop. 2.28, p. 73). The equivalence between the differentiability of an ideal generated by 1-forms and the integrability of the corresponding distribution is addressed in Theorem 2.30 of Warner (1971, p. 74) and Proposition 14 of Spivak (1979, p. 293).

As a consequence of Points 1 and 2, Property (iii) in *Differential Ideal* need not assert that $\mathcal{I}$ is differential nor that it contains $\Sigma_{i=1}^n c_i$ independent 1-forms.

Property (iii) of *Differential Ideal* is needed for the ideal $\mathcal{I}$ to be dual to the integrable distribution $\mathcal{D} \equiv \oplus_{i=1}^n \mathcal{D}_i$. This is true because duality holds between integrable distributions and differential ideals *generated by* 1-*forms*, not simply differential ideals. The role of Property (iii) has been obscured in the literature; it is sometimes replaced with the assumption that $\mathcal{I}$ satisfies some combination of Points 1 and 2 above.[23] As shown in the following example, Property (iii) is not implied by (i) and (ii) of *Differential Ideal* and it is distinct from Points 1 and 2. The marginal contribution of Property (iii) over Point 2 is that it insures that the 1-forms in (3.204) that span all 1-forms in $\mathcal{I}$ in fact also generate the ideal $\mathcal{I}$.

3.7.1 Example: Properties (iii) of *Differential Ideal* and of *Product Structure*

The example of Subsection 3.2.2 is now reworked in terms of differential forms and ideals. That example presents distributions $\mathcal{D}_1$ and $\mathcal{D}_2$ satisfying all the assumptions of *Direct Sum* except (ii), i.e., $\mathcal{D}_1 \oplus \mathcal{D}_2$ is not integrable. The corresponding integral manifolds $S_1(\theta)$ and $S_2(\theta)$ satisfy properties (i) and (ii) of *Product Structure* but not (iii), which is the requirement that the product sets in

$$\left\{ S_1^*(\theta) \times S_2^*(\theta) \mid \theta \in \Theta \right\}$$

partition Θ. It is now shown that the differential ideals $\mathcal{I}_1$ and $\mathcal{I}_2$ defined by the distributions $\mathcal{D}_1$ and $\mathcal{D}_2$ satisfy Assumptions (i) and (ii) of *Differential Ideal* but not (iii). As noted above, the significance of Property (iii) of *Differential Ideal* has been overlooked in the literature. This example highlights the importance of this property by identifying its role in insuring that the product sets partition Θ.

---

[23] This point was first brought to my attention by John Eisenberg and Fabio Rojas. To my knowledge, it has not caused any errors in the literature because (i) the assumption that $\mathcal{I}$ satisfies Point 1 or 2 is redundant but not wrong, and (ii) authors have typically used the assumption that $\mathcal{I}$ is generated by 1-forms even if they fail to state it. Note in particular that Saari (1984, p. 257) adds to the standard definition of an ideal the requirement that it be generated by 1-forms, while Hurwicz et al. (1978, Eq. (2.1), p. 99) explicitly identify a set of 1-forms that generate the ideal $\mathcal{I}$. It should be stated explicitly in Theorem 2.1(b) of Saari (1984) that the c linearly independent 1-forms in $\mathcal{I}$ generate this ideal.

Recall that $\Theta_1 = \Theta_2 = \mathbb{R}^2_{++}$. The distribution $\mathcal{D}_1$ is spanned by

$$X_1(\theta) \equiv \frac{\partial}{\partial \theta_{1,1}} + \theta_{2,1} \frac{\partial}{\partial \theta_{1,2}},$$

and hence the differential ideal $\mathcal{I}_1$ that is dual to $\mathcal{D}_1$ is spanned by

$$\left\{ -\theta_{2,1} d\theta_{1,1} + d\theta_{1,2}, \, d\theta_{2,1}, \, d\theta_{2,2} \right\}.$$

Similarly, the distribution $\mathcal{D}_2$ is spanned by

$$X_2(\theta) \equiv \frac{\partial}{\partial \theta_{2,1}} + \theta_{1,1} \frac{\partial}{\partial \theta_{2,2}},$$

and hence the corresponding differential ideal $\mathcal{I}_2$ is spanned by

$$\left\{ d\theta_{1,1}, \, d\theta_{1,2}, \, -\theta_{1,1} d\theta_{2,1} + d\theta_{2,2} \right\}.$$

The integrability of $\mathcal{I}_1$ is verified by

$$d\left[-\theta_{2,1} d\theta_{1,1} + d\theta_{1,2} \right] = -d\theta_{2,1} \wedge d\theta_{1,1} \in \mathcal{I}_1,$$

and the integrability of $\mathcal{I}_2$ is verified by

$$d\left[-\theta_{1,1} d\theta_{2,1} + d\theta_{2,2} \right] = -d\theta_{1,1} \wedge d\theta_{2,1} \in \mathcal{I}_2.$$

The differential ideals $\mathcal{I}_1$ and $\mathcal{I}_2$ thus satisfy Assumptions (i) and (ii) of *Differential Ideal.*

It is now shown by contradiction that Assumption (iii) of *Differential Ideal* does not hold. If $\mathcal{I}_1 \cap \mathcal{I}_2$ is generated by 1-forms, then it must be generated by $-\theta_{2,1} d\theta_{1,1} + d\theta_{1,2}$ and $-\theta_{1,1} d\theta_{2,1} + d\theta_{2,2}$ because these 1-forms span all the 1-forms in $\mathcal{I}_1 \cap \mathcal{I}_2$. Consider the 2-form

$$d[-\theta_{2,1} d\theta_{1,1} + d\theta_{1,2}] = -d\theta_{2,1} \wedge d\theta_{1,1},$$

which is in $\mathcal{I}_1 \cap \mathcal{I}_2$ because this intersection is a differential ideal. There must exists 1-forms

$$\rho = \rho_{1,1} d\theta_{1,1} + \rho_{1,2} d\theta_{1,2} + \rho_{2,1} d\theta_{2,1} + \rho_{2,2} d\theta_{2,2}$$

and

$$\nu = \nu_{1,1} d\theta_{1,1} + \nu_{1,2} d\theta_{1,2} + \nu_{2,1} d\theta_{2,1} + \nu_{2,2} d\theta_{2,2}$$

such that

$$-d\theta_{2,1} \wedge d\theta_{1,1} = \rho \wedge \left(-\theta_{2,1}d\theta_{1,1} + d\theta_{1,2}\right) + \nu \wedge \left(-\theta_{1,1}d\theta_{2,1} + d\theta_{2,2}\right),$$
$$(3.205)$$

where each $\rho_{i,t}$ and $\nu_{i,t}$ is a C^∞ real-valued function on Θ. The right side of (3.205) expands as follows:

$$\left[\rho_{1,1} + \theta_{2,1}\rho_{1,2}\right] d\theta_{1,1} \wedge d\theta_{1,2} + \left[\theta_{2,1}\rho_{2,1} - \theta_{1,1}\nu_{1,1}\right] d\theta_{1,1} \wedge d\theta_{2,1}$$
$$+ \left[\theta_{2,1}\rho_{2,2} + \nu_{1,1}\right] d\theta_{1,1} \wedge d\theta_{2,2} - \left[\rho_{2,1} + \theta_{1,1}\nu_{1,2}\right] d\theta_{1,2} \wedge d\theta_{2,1} \quad (3.206)$$
$$+ \left[-\rho_{2,2} + \nu_{1,2}\right] d\theta_{1,2} \wedge d\theta_{2,2} + \left[\theta_{1,1}\nu_{2,2} + \nu_{2,1}\right] d\theta_{2,1} \wedge d\theta_{2,2}.$$

Equating coefficients of the left side of (3.205) with (3.206) implies

$$0 = \rho_{1,1} + \theta_{2,1}\rho_{1,2}, \qquad (3.207)$$
$$-1 = \theta_{2,1}\rho_{2,1} - \theta_{1,1}\nu_{1,1}, \qquad (3.208)$$
$$0 = \theta_{2,1}\rho_{2,2} + \nu_{1,1}, \qquad (3.209)$$
$$0 = \rho_{2,1} + \theta_{1,1}\nu_{1,2}, \qquad (3.210)$$
$$0 = -\rho_{2,2} + \nu_{1,2}, \text{ and} \qquad (3.211)$$
$$0 = \theta_{1,1}\nu_{2,2} + \nu_{2,1}. \qquad (3.212)$$

The last step of the argument shows that this system of six equations in the eight variables

$$\rho_{1,1}, \, \rho_{1,2}, \, \rho_{2,1}, \, \rho_{2,2}, \, \nu_{1,1}, \, \nu_{1,2}, \, \nu_{2,1}, \, \nu_{2,2}$$

is unsolvable. Equation (3.211) implies

$$\rho_{2,2} = \nu_{1,2}. \qquad (3.213)$$

If $\rho_{2,2} \equiv \nu_{1,2} \equiv 0$, then (3.209)–(3.210) imply $\nu_{1,1} \equiv \rho_{2,1} \equiv 0$, which contradicts (3.208). Suppose instead that these functions are not identically zero on Θ. At points where they are nonzero, Equations (3.210) and (3.209) imply

$$\theta_{1,1} = \frac{-\rho_{2,1}}{\nu_{1,2}} \text{ and } \theta_{2,1} = \frac{-\nu_{1,1}}{\rho_{2,2}}.$$

Substitution of $\theta_{2,1} = -v_{1,1}/\rho_{2,2}$ into (3.208) implies

$$-1 = -\left(\frac{v_{1,1}}{\rho_{2,2}}\right)\rho_{2,1} - \theta_{1,1}v_{1,1}$$

$$= v_{1,1}\left(\theta_{1,1} + \frac{\rho_{2,1}}{\rho_{2,2}}\right)$$

$$= v_{1,1}\left(\theta_{1,1} + \frac{\rho_{2,1}}{v_{1,2}}\right),$$

where the replacement of $\rho_{2,2}$ with $v_{1,2}$ in the last line follows from (3.213). The desired contradiction is now obtained by substituting $-\rho_{2,1}/v_{1,2}$ for $\theta_{1,1}$.

4

Realizing a C^∞ Mapping

Recall from Section 1.1 that a mechanism $\mathcal{M}$ realizes a mapping $F : \Theta \to \mathbb{R}^k$ if $\zeta(\mu(\theta)) = F(\theta)$ for all $\theta \in \Theta$, where $\mu(\theta)$ is the set of equilibrium messages for $\theta \in \Theta$ and ζ is the outcome mapping of $\mathcal{M}$. The revelation mechanism and the parameter transfer mechanisms discussed in Section 1.1 demonstrate that there always exist mechanisms that realize a given mapping F. These mechanisms, however, require all but at most one of the n agents to transfer their private information to the message space. Given these rather coarse solutions to the problem of realization, the question becomes the following: Is it possible to exploit the particular features of a given mapping F in order to construct a mechanism that economizes on the amount of information that the agents transfer to the message space in order to realize F?

This question originates in the case in which the mapping F specifies a Pareto optimal allocation of private goods for n agents in an economy. The private information of any single agent (e.g., a consumer's preferences, or the cost function of a firm) can be quite complicated, and yet the agents manage to achieve a Pareto optimal allocation by communicating in a market using the relatively small set of signals consisting of prices and proposed trades. One objective of the theory of realization is to understand what distinguishes those mappings F (such as the net trade of some agent in some commodity in a Pareto optimal allocation) that can be realized using a relatively small set of signals.[1] The prevalence of decentralization in economic life suggests that many mappings of interest in economics either have this property or

---

[1] This objective is analogous to the central problem of implementation theory, which is to identify the properties that an objective F must satisfy if it can be implemented in the sense of a given solution concept. Maskin monotonicity (Maskin, 1999), for instance, is a necessary condition on F for implementation in the sense of Nash equilibrium. The emphasis here, however, is on the properties of F that permit economy in communication and not on the properties that permit incentive compatibility.

else can be approximated in some sense by mappings that have it. A second objective of the theory is to explore the existence of alternatives to familiar mechanisms (e.g., the price mechanism) that realize a given mapping F. The theory of realization in this sense provides a basis for objectively evaluating familiar mechanisms by comparing them with all conceivable alternatives that realize the same mapping F.

To be more precise, assumption (i) of *Message Process* is that agent i's equilibrium message set $\mu_i(\theta_i)$ is the solution set in M of an equation $\alpha_i(\theta_i, m) = 0$, where $\alpha_i : \Theta_i \times M \to \mathbb{R}^{c_i}$ is a C^∞ mapping. Regularity condition (iii) of *Message Process* implies that c_i measures of the number of variables that agent i communicates to the message space M in equilibrium.[2] A value of c_i that is less than dim Θ_i means that agent i is able to encode information in choosing his message m_i (i.e., $\alpha_i(\theta_i^*, m) = \alpha_i(\theta_i, m) = m_i$ for distinct values of θ_i^* and θ_i' in Θ_i). A large difference between c_i and dim Θ_i means that agent i communicates using a set of signals M_i that is small relative to his parameter space Θ_i. This motivates the following definition.[3]

Definition 11: *The **profile** of the mechanism $\mathcal{M}$ is the vector $(c_i)_{1 \leq i \leq n}$, where c_i is the dimension of the range M_i of agent i's message adjustment rule $\alpha_i(\theta_i, m)$.*

The number c_i can be any nonnegative natural number at or below dim Θ_i. The profile of the revelation mechanism satisfies $c_i = \dim \Theta_i$ for all values of i, while the profile of a parameter transfer mechanism has this property for all but the one value of i for which $c_i = 1$. It is therefore of particular interest whether or not a mechanism exists that can be used to realize F in which $c_i < \dim \Theta_i$ for more than one value of i. It may be true that decreasing the value of c_i by switching from one mechanism to another comes only at the expense of increasing the value of c_j for some other $j \neq i$. The sum

$$c \equiv \sum_{i=1}^{n} c_i \equiv \dim M \tag{4.1}$$

---

[2] I take for granted here the meaningfulness of the dimension of the message space as a measure of information. Dimension and other measures of information in mechanism design are discussed at length in Mount and Reiter (1974, Sec. II.2) and in Hurwicz (1986, Sec. II).

[3] The vector $(c_i)_{1 \leq i \leq n}$ is referred to as the *type* of the mechanism $\mathcal{M}$ in Williams (1982a, 1984). I switch here to the term "profile" to avoid confusion with the use of "type" to describe an agent's private information in Bayesian mechanism design and game theory. The related notation $\{\underset{\sim}{k}; \underset{\sim}{d}\}$, where $\underset{\sim}{k} = (\dim \Theta_i)_{1 \leq i \leq n}$ and $\underset{\sim}{d} = (d_i)_{1 \leq i \leq n}$, is used in Hurwicz et al. (1978) in reference to the product structure defined by a mechanism.

is thus also of interest, for it measures the total communication from the agents to the message space.

The first-order approach to the construction of message processes that is outlined in Chapter 3 provides a general method for addressing the mechanisms that realize a given mapping F. Consistent with the differential approach of this text, it is assumed in this chapter that the mapping F is C^∞. It is also assumed that

$$\mathcal{M} \text{ satisfies Message Process and its outcome mapping } \zeta \text{ is } C^\infty. \quad (4.2)$$

I begin this chapter by discussing the relationship between the realization problem and the local equivalence of *Direct Sum, Product Structure,* and *Message Process.* This relationship is summarized in Theorem 12. For each possible profile $(c_i)_{1 \le i \le n}$ of mechanism, Corollaries 13 and 14 to Theorem 12 present a system of algebraic equations whose coefficients are determined by the derivatives of F and with the property that the mechanisms of profile $(c_i)_{1 \le i \le n}$ that realize F are determined by the solutions of this system. These corollaries reduces the existence of a mechanism of a particular profile that realizes F to the solvability of a specific algebraic system. While any such system may be very difficult to solve, there are well-developed algebraic methods for investigating its solvability and for searching for solutions.

Section 4.2 presents a bound on the minimal dimension of a message space M that can be used to realize a given real-valued function f. This bound has been derived by considering the solvability of the systems in Corollaries 13 and 14 for the various possible profiles of mechanisms. It is stated in terms of the first and second derivatives of f. Section 4.4 concerns a result that shows that a generic mapping F can only be realized by variants of the revelation mechanism and the parameter transfer mechanisms. It is therefore necessary that all but at most one of the n agents must transfer all their private information to the message space in order to realize a generic mapping. This result is also derived by considering the solvability of the systems in Corollaries 13 and 14. Subsection 4.3 and Sections 4.5–4.8 then apply the results of this chapter to several economic models. Finally, the genericity result poses some serious questions concerning the usefulness of the first-order approach to the construction of mechanisms. These questions are addressed in Section 4.9.

4.1 Necessary and Sufficient Conditions

Recall from Figure 3.1 that *Message Process* ⟹ *Product Structure* ⟹ *Direct Sum* holds globally in Θ while *Direct Sum* ⟹ *Message Process* only holds locally.

Theorem 12 concerns the first-order approach to the construction of a mechanism that realizes a given mapping F. *Necessity* in this theorem means starting with a given mechanism $\mathcal{M}$ that realizes F and that satisfies the regularity conditions of (4.2) and then deriving a necessary condition that must be satisfied by $D_\theta F$ together with the distributions $(\mathcal{D}_i)_{1 \le i \le n}$ and $\mathcal{D}$ in *Direct Sum* defined by the message process of $\mathcal{M}$. This necessary condition holds globally because *Message Process* $\Rightarrow$ *Product Structure* $\Rightarrow$ *Direct Sum* holds globally. *Sufficiency* in this theorem means starting with distributions $(\mathcal{D}_i)_{1 \le i \le n}$ and $\mathcal{D}$ that satisfy *Direct Sum* and this condition involving $D_\theta F$ and then constructing a mechanism $\mathcal{M}$ that realizes F. Because *Direct Sum* $\Rightarrow$ *Message Process* holds locally, the mechanism $\mathcal{M}$ is only constructed locally.[4]

Theorem 12 (*Necessary and Sufficient Conditions for Realizing a* **C^∞** *Mapping*):

> **Necessity:** *Suppose that the mechanism $\mathcal{M}$ of profile $(c_i)_{1 \le i \le n}$ realizes the C^∞ mapping $F : \Theta \to \mathbb{R}^k$ and satisfies the regularity conditions of (4.2). The following two equivalent statements hold for the partition $\{ S(\theta) | \theta \in \Theta \}$ of* Product Structure *and the distribution $\mathcal{D}$ of* Direct Sum *that are defined by $\mathcal{M}$:*
>
> *(i) F is constant on $S(\theta)$ for every $\theta \in \Theta$;*
> *(ii) for every vector field $X \in \mathcal{D}$, $D_\theta F(\theta) \cdot X(\theta) = 0$ at every $\theta \in \Theta$.*
>
> **Sufficiency:** *Suppose that distributions $(\mathcal{D}_i)_{1 \le i \le n}$ and $\mathcal{D}$ are given that satisfy* Direct Sum *and such that Statement (ii) above holds. Let $(\Theta, M, (\mu_i)_{1 \le i \le n})$ denote a message process on a neighborhood $O(\theta^*)$ of $\theta^* \in \Theta$ defined by these distributions as in* Message Process. *There exists a C^∞ mapping $\zeta : M \to \mathbb{R}^k$ such that the mechanism $(O(\theta^*), M, (\mu_i)_{1 \le i \le n}, \zeta)$ of profile $(c_i)_{1 \le i \le n}$ realizes F on $O(\theta^*)$.*

Proof of Necessity: The defining equation $\zeta(u_{(c)}(\theta)) = F(\theta)$ of a realization implies that if $u_{(c)}(\theta^*) = u_{(c)}(\theta')$ for θ^* and $\theta' \in \Theta$, then $F(\theta^*) = F(\theta')$. It follows that

$$u_{(c)}^{-1}(u_{(c)}(\theta)) \subset F^{-1}(F(\theta)) \text{ for all } \theta \in \Theta. \tag{4.3}$$

---

[4] The essential content of Theorem 12 is presented in Theorem 6 of Hurwicz et al. (1978, p. 64). Statement (ii) of *Necessity* in Theorem 12 is presented in Lemma 1 (p. 35) of this manuscript.

Statement (i) then follows from the equality $u_{(c)}^{-1}(u_{(c)}(\theta)) = S(\theta)$, which is a consequence of how the message process $(\Theta, M, (\mu_i)_{1 \le i \le n})$ defines the partition $\{S(\theta) | \theta \in \Theta\}$. Because $\mathcal{D}(\theta)$ is the tangent plane to $S(\theta)$ at every $\theta \in \Theta$ and because $S(\theta)$ is connected, Statement (ii) is equivalent to (i). ∎

Proof of Sufficiency: The proof that *Direct Sum* ⇒ *Product Structure* locally starts with the local coordinate system u defined at θ^* with the properties given in the Frobenius Theorem for Mechanism Design. The message process $(\Theta, M, (\mu_i)_{1 \le i \le n})$ is constructed from u so that $M = (-\varepsilon', \varepsilon')^c$ for some $0 < \varepsilon' < \varepsilon$, where $(-\varepsilon, \varepsilon)^{d+c}$ is the range of u. Recall that $u(\theta^*) \equiv (w^*, m^*) \equiv 0$ and that $v \equiv u^{-1}$. For the purposes of this proof, define the open neighborhood $O(\theta^*)$ of θ^* as $O(\theta^*) \equiv v((-\varepsilon', \varepsilon')^{d+c})$. The desired outcome mapping $\zeta : M \to \mathbb{R}^k$ is defined by the formula

$$\zeta(m) \equiv F(v(w^*, m)). \tag{4.4}$$

The mapping ζ is C^∞ because F and v are C^∞. Formula (4.4) implies that

$$\zeta(u_{(c)}(\theta)) = F(v(w^*, u_{(c)}(\theta))). \tag{4.5}$$

Property (3.67) of the Frobenius Theorem for Mechanism Design implies

$$v(w^*, u_{(c)}(\theta)) \in S(\theta). \tag{4.6}$$

Statement (ii) (or equivalently, (i)) then implies that $\zeta(u_{(c)}(\theta)) = F(\theta)$. ∎

The necessary and sufficient conditions of Theorem 12 for the local realization of a given mapping F are restated in the following corollary as a set of conditions on vector fields that form bases of the distributions $(\mathcal{D}_i)_{1 \le i \le n}$ defined by $\mathcal{M}$.

Corollary 13: *Statements I and II below are equivalent. Each presents a set of necessary and sufficient conditions for the existence of a mechanism $\mathcal{M}$ with profile $(c_i)_{1 \le i \le n}$ that realizes F on some neighborhood $O(\theta^*)$ of θ^* and that satisfies the regularity conditions of (4.2).*

I. *There exists C^∞ vector fields $\{X_{i,h} \,|\, 1 \le h \le d_i, 1 \le i \le n\}$ near θ^* that have the following properties for all $1 \le i, j \le n, 1 \le h \le d_i$, and $1 \le l \le d_j$:*

   (a) *$X_{i,h}$ lies in the span of $\{\partial/\partial\theta_{i,t}\}_{1 \le t \le d_i + c_i}$;*
   (b) *$[X_{i,h}, X_{j,l}] = 0$;*
   (c) *$D_\theta F(\theta) \cdot X_{i,h}(\theta) = 0$.*

II. *There exists a local coordinate system* $u : O(\theta^*) \to (-\varepsilon, \varepsilon)^{d+c} \subset W \times$
   M with inverse mapping $v \equiv u^{-1}$ *such that*
   (a) for each $1 \leq i \leq n$,
      (i) $rank\, D_{\theta_i} u_{(i,c_i)} = c_i$ *on* $O(\theta^*)$ *and*
      (ii) $v_{(i)} : (-\varepsilon, \varepsilon)^{d+c} \to \Theta_i$ *depends only on* $w_i \in \mathbb{R}^{d_i}$ *and* $m \in \mathbb{R}^c$;
   (b) $F \circ v$ *does not depend on* w.

Statement I follows from Theorem 12 together with Theorem 7, which asserts the existence locally of a basis of vector fields of the distribution $\mathcal{D} = \oplus_{i=1}^{n} \mathcal{D}_i$ defined by the message process of $\mathcal{M}$ that satisfies (a) and (b). Statement II restates I using a local coordinate system u that is defined from the vector fields in I. A local coordinate system u with the desired properties is constructed from these vector fields in the proof of the Frobenius Theorem for Mechanism Design.

4.1.1 Equations for Realization on the Objective F

Given the goal of realizing the mapping F, each possible profile $(c_i)_{1 \leq i \leq n}$ of mechanism defines a distinct system of equations of the form in Statement I of Corollary 13. Represent each vector field $X_{i,h}(\theta)$ as

$$X_{i,h}(\theta) = \sum_{t=1}^{d_i+c_i} a_{i,h,t}(\theta) \frac{\partial}{\partial \theta_{i,t}}(\theta). \qquad (4.7)$$

The system of equations defined by (b) and (c) of Statement I can be regarded as a system whose variables are the coordinate functions

$$\{a_{i,h,t} \,|\, 1 \leq i \leq n, 1 \leq h \leq d_i, 1 \leq t \leq d_i + c_i\}. \qquad (4.8)$$

Repeated differentiation of the equations in (b) and (c) produces polynomial equations on the derivatives of these coordinate functions with coefficients determined by the derivatives of F.[5] For each upper bound m on the order of derivatives considered, a finite system of polynomial equations is in this way derived that must be solved at each θ near θ^* for the existence of a mechanism of the given profile that realizes F near θ^*.

The remainder of this chapter concerns results that are proven by considering the systems of equations obtained in this way. Given the system determined by the profile $(c_i)_{1 \leq i \leq n}$ and the upper bound m on the order

---

[5] These equations are in fact homogeneous, which is a valuable algebraic property. It is not needed, however, for the discussion here.

of derivatives considered, it is desirable to eliminate the variables corresponding to the derivatives of the functions in (4.8) from this system. A set of necessary conditions on the derivatives of F would in this way be obtained for the existence of a mechanism of profile $(c_i)_{1 \leq i \leq n}$ that realizes F. Tarski's generalization of Sturm's theorem states the existence of a finite set of systems of polynomial equalities and inequalities on the derivatives of F for the solvability of the system determined by $(c_i)_{1 \leq i \leq n}$ and m.[6] The Tarski–Seidenberg algorithm[7] in principle provides a method for eliminating the variables from the original system to produce these systems on the derivatives of F alone. Equipped with these systems of equations, one could eliminate certain profiles as possibilities for realizing F and thereby narrow the search for mechanisms that realize this mapping.

There are $\sum_{i=1}^{n} d_i$ vector fields that are the variables in the system initially defined by Statement I of Corollary 13, which means that there are $\sum_{i=1}^{n} d_i(d_i + c_i)$ component functions $a_{i,h,t}(\theta)$ that form the variables once the initial system is rewritten in terms of these functions. Differentiation of the equations in this system m times produces equations whose variables include all lth order derivatives of the functions $a_{i,h,t}(\theta)$ for $l \leq m$. The system also depends on the desired profile of the mechanism, and so there are as many distinct systems to consider as there are profiles of interest. The point is that while it is possible in principle to derive equations on the derivatives of F by systematically applying the Tarski–Seidenberg algorithm to each of these systems, the task in practice seems overwhelming.

Alternative approaches are discussed in the next two sections. The first approach begins by deriving a necessary condition on the first and second derivatives of a real-valued function f for realization through a mechanism of profile $(1, 1)$ in the specific case of $n = 2$ agents and $\dim \Theta_1 = \dim \Theta_2 = 2$. The equation derived in this simple case is then generalized to richer settings. This is discussed in Section 4.2, with the resulting equations applied in several examples in Section 4.3. The second approach involves carefully counting the number of independent equations in the systems described above and then comparing the number of equations to the number of variables (i.e., the derivatives of F and the component functions $a_{i,h,t}$ of appropriate order). Statement II. of Corollary 13 is especially helpful at this point in calculating the number of variables relative to the number of

---

[6] Tarski's generalization of Sturm's theorem is stated in Jacobson (1975, Thm. 16, p. 312). A familiar illustration of this theorem concerns the quadratic equation $ax^2 + bx + c = 0$: a necessary and sufficient condition on a, b, and c for the existence of a solution $x \in \mathbb{R}$ is the polynomial inequality $b^2 - 4ac \geq 0$.

[7] See, for instance, Jacobson (1975, pp. 295–316).

equations. It is possible in this way to characterize the solvability of such systems in the case of a generic mapping F. This in turn characterizes the profiles of mechanisms that realize a generic mapping. This is discussed in Section 4.4.

4.1.2 Necessary and Sufficient Conditions Using *Differential Ideal*

For the sake of completeness of this text and for the derivations in Subsections 4.6.5 and 4.6.6, the necessary and sufficient conditions of Theorem 12 and Corollary 13 are restated in this subsection using *Differential Ideal*.[8] The following notation is needed. Represent the mapping $F : \Theta \to \mathbb{R}^k$ as

$$F = (f_l)_{1 \leq l \leq k}, \tag{4.9}$$

where $f_l : \Theta \to \mathbb{R}$. For each $1 \leq l \leq k$ and each agent i, define the 1-form $d_i f_l$ as

$$d_i f_l \equiv \sum_{t=1}^{\dim \Theta_i} \frac{\partial f_l}{\partial \theta_{i,t}} d\theta_{i,t}. \tag{4.10}$$

This implies the formula

$$df_l = \sum_{i=1}^{n} \sum_{t=1}^{\dim \Theta_i} \frac{\partial f_l}{\partial \theta_{i,t}} d\theta_{i,t} = \sum_{i=1}^{n} d_i f_l. \tag{4.11}$$

Corollary 14: *A mechanism $\mathcal{M}$ with profile $(c_i)_{1 \leq i \leq n}$ exists that realizes $F = (f_l)_{1 \leq l \leq k}$ on some neighborhood $O(\theta^*)$ of θ^* and that satisfies the regularity conditions of (4.2) if and only if there exists C^∞ differential ideals $\mathcal{I}_1, \ldots, \mathcal{I}_n$ satisfying the properties of* Differential Ideal *such that*

$$d_i f_l \in \mathcal{I}_i \tag{4.12}$$

for each agent i and each component function f_l of F.

---

[8] Theorem 7 of Hurwicz et al. (1978, p. 99) addresses the equivalence between the necessary and sufficient conditions for realization of Theorem 12 that use the theory of distributions with the conditions of Corollary 14 below that use the theory of differential ideals. Corollary 14 is also established in Theorems 2.1 and 2.2 of Saari (1984, p. 258). Finally, Saari (1984, Thm. 2.3) extends Corollary 14 to the case in which each agent i may observe some but not all of the parameters θ_{-i} of the other agents, while Saari (1988, Thm. 4.2) extends it to the case in which there is a constraint $K(\theta) = 0$ on the elements of Θ.

Realization of F requires that each function f_l be constant on every set $S_i(\theta) \subset S(\theta)$. This is equivalent to

$$df_l \in \mathcal{I}_i \tag{4.13}$$

for all i. Property (ii) of *Differential Ideal* states that $d\theta_{j,t} \in \mathcal{I}_i$ for all $j \neq i$ and $1 \leq t \leq \dim \Theta_j$, and so $d_j f_l \in \mathcal{I}_i$ for $j \neq i$. Closure of an ideal under addition of forms implies

$$df_l - \sum_{j \neq i} d_j f_l = d_i f_l \in \mathcal{I}_i, \tag{4.14}$$

which is (4.12). The condition (4.12) is thus a reduced form of (4.13), which expresses from a first-order perspective the requirement that F is constant on the sets $S(\theta)$ defined by the mechanism that realizes F.

4.1.3 The Multiplicity of Mechanisms

Before continuing the study of the realization problem, it is worthwhile to first recognize that there exists many different mechanisms of each profile. This is true except in the case of $c_i = \dim \Theta_i$ for each agent i, which corresponds to complete revelation. The realization problem in this case is trivial. The purpose of this subsection is to explore the variety of mechanisms that exists for each nontrivial profile and the senses in which they may differ. The point is that there exists a priori many possible solutions to the realization problem, which makes it a worthwhile exercise.

Given a mechanism $\mathcal{M} = (\Theta, M, (\mu_i)_{1 \leq i \leq n}, \zeta)$ that realizes the mapping F, different mechanisms can easily be constructed that also realize F simply by changing the coordinates in M. Let $\varphi : M \to \mathbb{R}^c$ be any C^∞, one-to-one nonsingular mapping. The mechanism

$$\mathcal{M}' = \left(\Theta, \varphi(M), (\varphi \circ \mu_i)_{1 \leq i \leq n}, \zeta \circ \varphi^{-1}\right) \tag{4.15}$$

realizes F. The message adjustment rules $(\alpha_i)_{1 \leq i \leq n}$ of $\mathcal{M}$ can also be changed without affecting the message correspondences $(\mu_i)_{1 \leq i \leq n}$, thereby preserving the realization of F. The alternative mechanisms that are generated by these methods are of interest if the goal is to interpret the messages of M or to study the mechanism out of equilibrium (e.g., in consideration of incentives, adjustment to equilibrium, or the complexity of the message adjustment rules).

Notice that these methods do not affect the underlying product structure of the mechanism $\mathcal{M}$. Theorem 12 identifies product structure (or its corresponding direct sum) as the fundamental solution variable in the realization problem. An exploration of the range of possible solutions to the realization problem for a given profile thus requires a study of the different product structures that exist for this profile. This is the topic in the remainder of the subsection.

What makes two product structures different from one another? Going beyond simply checking whether or not the partitions of the product structures are distinct, it can instead be asked whether or not they have geometric properties that fundamentally distinguish them from one another. Modern geometry adopts a coordinate-free approach in the sense that it seeks properties of sets that do not depend on the choices of coordinates for labeling their points. It is only with this approach that geometric properties intrinsic to a set are identified. It is thus reasonable to consider whether or not one product structure can be transformed into the other by changing the coordinates in Θ. A *local change of coordinates at* θ^* is a C^∞, nonsingular, one-to-one mapping

$$\varsigma : O'(\theta^*) \to O''(\theta^*) \qquad (4.16)$$

such that $\varsigma(\theta^*) = \theta^*$ and $\varsigma(O'(\theta^*)) = O''(\theta^*)$, where $O'(\theta^*)$ and $O''(\theta^*)$ denote open neighborhoods of θ^*. For partitions $\{S'(\theta)\}_{\theta \in \Theta}$ and $\{S''(\theta)\}_{\theta \in \Theta}$ of Θ that satisfy *Product Structure* and share a common profile, there exists a local change of coordinates $\varsigma : O'(\theta^*) \to O''(\theta^*)$ at θ^* such that

$$\varsigma\left(S'(\theta) \cap O'(\theta^*)\right) = S'(\varsigma(\theta)) \cap O''(\theta^*) \qquad (4.17)$$

for $\theta \in O'(\theta^*)$. The individual sets of the two partitions are thus identified by ς. The existence of ς follows from the Frobenius Theorem by setting

$$\varsigma = \left(u''\right)^{-1} \circ u', \qquad (4.18)$$

where u' and u'' are the local coordinate systems for $\{S'(\theta)\}_{\theta \in \Theta}$ and $\{S''(\theta)\}_{\theta \in \Theta}$ whose existence is guaranteed by this theorem. Product structures of the same profile are thus indistinguishable locally, given the freedom to change coordinates. Arbitrary coordinate changes on Θ fundamentally destroy the separation of parameters among the agents that is the focus of this text, and so identifying product structures in this manner is simply too crude of an approach.

It is reasonable, however, to consider changes of coordinates within each agent's parameter space. A coordinate-free approach with respect to an agent's parameters is appropriate in many economic problems; if the points in Θ_i index distinct preferences of agent i over a set of choices for the agents, for instance, then the issue of interest is the range of agent i's preferences over Θ_i and not the manner in which those preferences are indexed. This motivates the following equivalence of product structures of a given profile near $\theta^* \in \Theta$. Consider local changes of coordinates $\varsigma : O'(\theta^*) \to O''(\theta^*)$ at θ^* such that

(i) $O'(\theta^*) = \prod_{i=1}^{n} O'_i(\theta_i^*)$ and $O''(\theta^*) = \prod_{i=1}^{n} O''_i(\theta_i^*)$, where $O'_i(\theta_i^*)$ and $O''_i(\theta_i^*)$ are open neighborhoods of θ_i^* in Θ_i;

(ii) $\varsigma = (\varsigma_1, \ldots, \varsigma_n)$, where $\varsigma_i : O'_i(\theta_i^*) \to O''_i(\theta_i^*)$ is a local change of coordinates at θ_i^*.

Define product structures $\{S'(\theta)\}_{\theta \in \Theta}$ and $\{S''(\theta)\}_{\theta \in \Theta}$ as *equivalent at θ^** if there exists a local change of coordinates ς at θ^* that satisfies (i), (ii), and (4.17) above for all $\theta \in O'(\theta^*)$. In words, two product structures are equivalent at θ^* if, sufficiently near θ^*, the sets of one can be mapped to the sets of the other through a separate change of coordinates in each agent's parameter space. Product structures that are not equivalent in this sense fundamentally model distinct modes of communication among the agents. Notice that while the Frobenius Theorem for Mechanism Design reduces all product structures of a given profile near θ^* to the same canonical form through the choice of a local coordinate system, it does not imply that all product structures with the same profile are equivalent in this sense. The local change of coordinates ς defined by (4.18) using this theorem typically does not satisfy (ii) above (i.e., the mapping ς_i depends upon θ_{-i}).

This equivalence meshes with the realization problem because it respects the separation of parameters among the agents. Suppose again that $\mathcal{M} = (\Theta, M, (\mu_i)_{1 \le i \le n}, \zeta)$ realizes the mapping F. For any local change of coordinates $\varsigma : O'(\theta^*) \to O''(\theta^*)$ at θ^* that satisfies (i)–(ii) above, the mechanism

$$\mathcal{M}'' = (O'(\theta^*), M, (\mu_i \circ \varsigma_i)_{1 \le i \le n}, \zeta) \qquad (4.19)$$

realizes $F \circ \varsigma$ on $O'(\theta^*)$. Locally, a mechanism $\mathcal{M}$ that realizes a mapping F is easily adapted to realize $F \circ \varsigma$, and F can be realized by a mechanism of a particular profile if and only if $F \circ \varsigma$ can also be realized by such a mechanism. Considering the realization of $F \circ \varsigma$ for arbitrary local changes of coordinates ς satisfying (i)–(ii) can therefore be a useful technique for reducing F so as to simplify its realization without changing the profiles of solution mechanisms.

Relative to this notion of equivalence, Williams (1982a, Thm. 18) showed that there exists a continuum of different equivalence classes of product structures near θ^* of each profile $(c_i)_{1 \le i \le n}$ whenever $c_i < \dim \Theta_i$ for at least one i. Product structure is uniquely determined if $c_i = \dim \Theta_i$ for each i; except for this degenerate case, there are many messages processes of each profile near any given θ^* and hence many candidate solutions to the realization problem. This is true even when using a notion of equivalence that identifies mechanisms that may differ in their message adjustment rules, the choice of coordinates in the message space or in each agent's parameter space, or away from the selected point θ^*. While each of these issues may be meaningful in a particular economic problem, they only serve to expand the senses in which there are many distinct mechanisms of each nontrivial profile.

4.2 A Lower Bound on Message Space Dimension

This section concerns equations on the first and second derivatives of a function f that provide information about the profiles of mechanisms that realize this function. The discussion is limited to the case of $n = 2$ agents. The process of eliminating the variables from the systems of equations in Corollary 13 to obtain the desired equations on f is illustrated first in Subsection 4.2.1 in the case of dim $\Theta_1 = $ dim $\Theta_2 = 2$. A generalization of the equation derived in this special case is then discussed in Subsection 4.2.2.

It is first worthwhile to address the significance of the case in which there are $n = 2$ agents and the objective is a real-valued function f. Turning first to the objective, consider a mapping $F : \Theta \to \mathbb{R}^k$ and a mechanism $\mathcal{M}$ that realizes F. Represent F and the outcome mapping ζ of $\mathcal{M}$ in terms of their component functions,

$$F = (f_1, \ldots, f_k) \text{ and } \zeta = (\zeta_1, \ldots, \zeta_k).$$

Realizing F necessitates realizing each component function f_j in the sense that f_j is realized by the mechanism $\mathcal{M}_j$ defined from $\mathcal{M}$ by restricting ζ to its jth component function ζ_j. The profile $(c_i)_{1 \leq i \leq n}$ of any mechanism that realizes F is therefore at least as large in each of its n components as the profile of some mechanism that realizes f_j. This suggests some obvious bounds, e.g., if $\underline{c}^j$ denotes the smallest dimension of message space that is needed to realize f_j and $\underline{c}$ denotes the smallest dimension needed to realize F, then $\underline{c} \geq \max_j \underline{c}_j$. As mentioned above, Theorem 16 in Section 4.4 states that a generic f_j can only be realized by a mechanism whose profile $(c_i)_{1 \leq i \leq n}$ satisfies $c_i = $ dim Θ_i for all but at most one value of i. Verifying that at least one of the component functions f_j is generic in this sense is therefore sufficient to verify that F is also generic in this sense. Useful information concerning the possible realizations of a mapping F may therefore be obtained by addressing the possible realizations of each of its component functions f_j.

The restriction to the case of $n = 2$ in this section, however, seems in practice to be more limiting. Given the goal of realizing a mapping $F : \prod_{i=1}^{n} \Theta_i \to \mathbb{R}^k$, one could of course either (i) partition the agents into two sets or (ii) fix the parameters of all but two of the agents. Both of these approaches produce realization problems in the case of $n = 2$ agents that are necessarily solved in realizing F. Unlike the method above of restricting attention to realizing a component function of F, however, neither of these techniques in practice tends to provide much insight into the possibilities for realizing F. This is perhaps because each of these techniques fails to address the compounding of the information required for realization that commonly occurs as the number of agents increases.[9]

Some new notation is helpful for the remainder of this chapter. For $1 \leq i \neq j \leq n$, $D^2_{\theta_i, \theta_j} f$ denotes the dim $\Theta_i \times$ dim Θ_j matrix of mixed partials

$$D^2_{\theta_i, \theta_j} f \equiv \left(\frac{\partial^2 f}{\partial \theta_{i,l} \partial \theta_{j,k}} \right)_{1 \leq l \leq \dim \Theta_i, 1 \leq k \leq \dim \Theta_j}, \tag{4.20}$$

and $BMH_{\theta_i, \theta_j}(f)$ (for "bordered mixed Hessian") denotes the (dim $\Theta_i +$ 1) $\times$ (dim $\Theta_j + 1$) matrix

$$BMH_{\theta_i, \theta_j}(f) \equiv \begin{pmatrix} 0 & D_{\theta_j} f \\ \left(D_{\theta_i} f \right)^T & D^2_{\theta_i, \theta_j} f \end{pmatrix}. \tag{4.21}$$

4.2.1 Example: Existence of a Mechanism of Profile (1, 1) That Realizes f in the Case of $n = 2$ and dim $\Theta_1 = $ dim $\Theta_2 = 2$

A necessary and sufficient condition on the function f will be derived in this case for the existence of a mechanism of profile (1, 1) that realizes

---

[9] This is illustrated in the following example. Consider a C^∞ function $f : \Theta \to \mathbb{R}$ where $\Theta \subset \mathbb{R}^m$. Assume the regularity condition $\partial f / \partial \theta_i \neq 0$ holds in Θ for $1 \leq i \leq m$. If $n = 1$ agent observes $\theta \in \Theta$, then f can be realized with a message space of dimension 1 by having the agent report $f(\theta)$. If one agent observes $\theta_1 \in \mathbb{R}$ and a second agent observes $\theta_{-1} \in \mathbb{R}^{m-1}$, then f requires a message space of dimension at least 2 for realization. This is easily generalized to the case of $n = j + 1$ agents for some $j < m$: if for $1 \leq i \leq j$ agent i observes $\theta_i \in \mathbb{R}$ and agent $j + 1$ observes $(\theta_{j+1}, \ldots, \theta_m)$, then f requires a message space of dimension at least $j + 1$ for realization. The function f to be realized does not change in each of these $m - 1$ cases and yet the dimension of the message space increases in the number n of agents who privately observe components of $\theta \in \Theta$.

f near a point θ^*. It is assumed throughout this subsection that f satisfies the regularity condition

$$\left(\frac{\partial f}{\partial \theta_{1,1}}, \frac{\partial f}{\partial \theta_{1,2}} \right), \left(\frac{\partial f}{\partial \theta_{2,1}}, \frac{\partial f}{\partial \theta_{2,2}} \right) \neq (0, 0) \tag{4.22}$$

near θ^*.

Applying Theorem 12, the existence of such a mechanism is equivalent to the existence of 1-dimensional distributions $\mathcal{D}_1$ and $\mathcal{D}_2$ satisfying *Direct Sum* and with the property that Statement (ii) of *Necessity* in Theorem 12 holds. Specifically, (ii) requires here that

$$D_\theta f(\theta) \cdot X(\theta) = 0 \tag{4.23}$$

for every vector field $X \in \mathcal{D}_1 \oplus \mathcal{D}_2$ and for θ near θ^*. Because each $\mathcal{D}_i$ is 1-dimensional, (4.23) along with the regularity condition (4.22) implies that $\mathcal{D}_1$ is the span of

$$X_1 \equiv \left(\frac{\partial f}{\partial \theta_{1,2}} \right) \frac{\partial}{\partial \theta_{1,1}} - \left(\frac{\partial f}{\partial \theta_{1,1}} \right) \frac{\partial}{\partial \theta_{1,2}}, \tag{4.24}$$

and $\mathcal{D}_2$ is the span of

$$X_2 \equiv \left(\frac{\partial f}{\partial \theta_{2,2}} \right) \frac{\partial}{\partial \theta_{2,1}} - \left(\frac{\partial f}{\partial \theta_{2,1}} \right) \frac{\partial}{\partial \theta_{2,2}}. \tag{4.25}$$

Each of these distributions is integrable because it is 1-dimensional. The distributions $\mathcal{D}_1$ and $\mathcal{D}_2$ thus satisfy *Direct Sum* if and only if

$$[X_1, X_2](\theta) \in \mathcal{D}(\theta). \tag{4.26}$$

Theorem 12 thus implies that (4.26) is necessary and sufficient for the existence of a mechanism of profile $(1, 1)$ that realizes f near θ^*.

Condition (4.26) can be reduced as follows. Applying formula (2.6) for the Lie bracket, $[X_1, X_2]$ equals

$$\left(\frac{\partial f}{\partial \theta_{2,1}} \frac{\partial^2 f}{\partial \theta_{1,2} \partial \theta_{2,2}} - \frac{\partial f}{\partial \theta_{2,2}} \frac{\partial^2 f}{\partial \theta_{1,2} \partial \theta_{2,1}} \right) \frac{\partial}{\partial \theta_{1,1}}$$

$$+ \left(\frac{\partial f}{\partial \theta_{2,2}} \frac{\partial^2 f}{\partial \theta_{1,1} \partial \theta_{2,1}} - \frac{\partial f}{\partial \theta_{2,1}} \frac{\partial^2 f}{\partial \theta_{1,1} \partial \theta_{2,2}} \right) \frac{\partial}{\partial \theta_{1,2}} \tag{4.27}$$

$$+ \left(\frac{\partial f}{\partial \theta_{1,2}} \frac{\partial^2 f}{\partial \theta_{1,1} \partial \theta_{2,2}} - \frac{\partial f}{\partial \theta_{1,1}} \frac{\partial^2 f}{\partial \theta_{1,2} \partial \theta_{2,2}} \right) \frac{\partial}{\partial \theta_{2,1}}$$

$$+ \left(\frac{\partial f}{\partial \theta_{1,1}} \frac{\partial^2 f}{\partial \theta_{1,2} \partial \theta_{2,1}} - \frac{\partial f}{\partial \theta_{1,2}} \frac{\partial^2 f}{\partial \theta_{1,2} \partial \theta_{2,1}} \right) \frac{\partial}{\partial \theta_{2,2}}.$$

Condition (4.26) is equivalent to

$$[X_1, X_2] = \lambda_1 X_1 + \lambda_2 X_2 \tag{4.28}$$

for some real-valued functions λ_1 and λ_2. Because $X_1 \in \mathcal{D}_1$ and $X_2 \in \mathcal{D}_2$, it is clear from (4.27) that (4.28) holds if and only if

$$
\begin{aligned}
&\left(\frac{\partial f}{\partial \theta_{2,1}} \frac{\partial^2 f}{\partial \theta_{1,2} \partial \theta_{2,2}} - \frac{\partial f}{\partial \theta_{2,2}} \frac{\partial^2 f}{\partial \theta_{1,2} \partial \theta_{2,1}} \right) \frac{\partial}{\partial \theta_{1,1}} \\
&+ \left(\frac{\partial f}{\partial \theta_{2,2}} \frac{\partial^2 f}{\partial \theta_{1,1} \partial \theta_{2,1}} - \frac{\partial f}{\partial \theta_{2,1}} \frac{\partial^2 f}{\partial \theta_{1,1} \partial \theta_{2,2}} \right) \frac{\partial}{\partial \theta_{1,2}} \\
&= \lambda_1 X_1 = \lambda_1 \left(\frac{\partial f}{\partial \theta_{1,2}} \frac{\partial}{\partial \theta_{1,1}} - \frac{\partial f}{\partial \theta_{1,1}} \frac{\partial}{\partial \theta_{1,2}} \right),
\end{aligned}
\tag{4.29}
$$

and

$$
\begin{aligned}
&\left(\frac{\partial f}{\partial \theta_{1,2}} \frac{\partial^2 f}{\partial \theta_{1,1} \partial \theta_{2,2}} - \frac{\partial f}{\partial \theta_{1,1}} \frac{\partial^2 f}{\partial \theta_{1,2} \partial \theta_{2,2}} \right) \frac{\partial}{\partial \theta_{2,1}} \\
&+ \left(\frac{\partial f}{\partial \theta_{1,1}} \frac{\partial^2 f}{\partial \theta_{1,2} \partial \theta_{2,1}} - \frac{\partial f}{\partial \theta_{1,2}} \frac{\partial^2 f}{\partial \theta_{1,2} \partial \theta_{2,1}} \right) \frac{\partial}{\partial \theta_{2,2}} \\
&= \lambda_2 X_2 = \lambda_2 \left(\frac{\partial f}{\partial \theta_{2,2}} \frac{\partial}{\partial \theta_{2,1}} - \frac{\partial f}{\partial \theta_{2,1}} \frac{\partial}{\partial \theta_{2,2}} \right).
\end{aligned}
\tag{4.30}
$$

A function λ_1 exists that solves (4.29) if and only if

$$
\begin{aligned}
&\frac{\partial f}{\partial \theta_{1,2}} \left(\frac{\partial f}{\partial \theta_{2,2}} \frac{\partial^2 f}{\partial \theta_{1,1} \partial \theta_{2,1}} - \frac{\partial f}{\partial \theta_{2,1}} \frac{\partial^2 f}{\partial \theta_{1,1} \partial \theta_{2,2}} \right) \\
&= -\frac{\partial f}{\partial \theta_{1,1}} \left(\frac{\partial f}{\partial \theta_{2,1}} \frac{\partial^2 f}{\partial \theta_{1,2} \partial \theta_{2,2}} - \frac{\partial f}{\partial \theta_{2,2}} \frac{\partial^2 f}{\partial \theta_{1,2} \partial \theta_{2,1}} \right).
\end{aligned}
\tag{4.31}
$$

This equation is also necessary and sufficient for the solvability of (4.30) for λ_2. Equation (4.31) is thus a necessary and sufficient condition on f for the existence of a mechanism of profile $(1, 1)$ that realizes f near θ^*. This equation can be written more conveniently as

$$
0 = \det \begin{pmatrix}
0 & \frac{\partial f}{\partial \theta_{2,1}} & \frac{\partial f}{\partial \theta_{2,2}} \\
\frac{\partial f}{\partial \theta_{1,1}} & \frac{\partial^2 f}{\partial \theta_{1,1} \partial \theta_{2,1}} & \frac{\partial^2 f}{\partial \theta_{1,1} \partial \theta_{2,2}} \\
\frac{\partial f}{\partial \theta_{1,2}} & \frac{\partial^2 f}{\partial \theta_{1,2} \partial \theta_{2,1}} & \frac{\partial^2 f}{\partial \theta_{1,2} \partial \theta_{2,2}}
\end{pmatrix},
\tag{4.32}
$$

or, using the notation introduced in (4.20) and (4.21), as

$$0 = \det \begin{pmatrix} 0 & D_{\theta_2} f \\ \left(D_{\theta_1} f \right)^T & D^2_{\theta_1,\theta_2} f \end{pmatrix} = \det BMH_{\theta_1,\theta_2}(f). \qquad (4.33)$$

4.2.2 Chen's Bound on Minimal Message Space Dimension

Equation (4.33) was first derived by Hurwicz in 1979 in the case of $n = 2$ agents and $\dim \Theta_1 = \dim \Theta_2 = 3$. It was derived in this case as a necessary condition on f for the existence of a mechanism $\mathcal{M}$ that realizes f whose message space M has dimension less than 4 (the dimension required by parameter transfer in this case). In the case of arbitrary values of $\dim \Theta_1$ and $\dim \Theta_2$, the smallest dimension required by a parameter transfer mechanism is $\min(\dim \Theta_1, \dim \Theta_2) + 1$. I generalized Hurwicz's result in Williams (1982a, Ch. 2; 1984, p. 294) to the case of arbitrary values of $\dim \Theta_1$ and $\dim \Theta_2$ in the following sense: a function f can be realized by a mechanism $\mathcal{M}$ on the open set Θ whose message space has dimension less than $\min(\dim \Theta_1, \dim \Theta_2) + 1$ only if $BMH_{\theta_1,\theta_2}(f)$ is singular at every point in Θ, i.e.,

$$\text{rank } BMH_{\theta_1,\theta_2}(f) < \min(\dim \Theta_1, \dim \Theta_2) + 1. \qquad (4.34)$$

It is useful at this point to note the dimension of the message space required for realizing a generic function f in the case of $n = 2$ agents. Let $C^\infty(\Theta, \mathbb{R})$ denote the set of C^∞ real-valued functions on Θ equipped with the Whitney C^∞ topology.[10] For all functions f in some open, dense subset of $C^\infty(\Theta, \mathbb{R})$, the set of points in Θ at which (4.34) holds has Lebesgue measure zero. A generic smooth function f can therefore be realized on the open set Θ only by mechanisms in which the dimension of the message space is at least as large as that required by a parameter transfer mechanism. This result is generalized below in Theorem 16.

The finest result relating the dimension of a message space M needed to realize a function f to the derivatives of this function was obtained by Chen (1989; 1992, Thm. 1, p. 259). His result supersedes these earlier results by

---

[10] More generally, for $k \geq 1$ let $C^\infty(\Theta, \mathbb{R}^k)$ denote the set of C^∞ mappings from Θ to $\mathbb{R}^k$ equipped with the Whitney C^∞ topology. This space will be needed in the following sections. Golubitsky and Guillemin (1973, Ch. II, Sec. 3) is one of many references for this topology.

bounding below the dimension of the message space of any mechanism that realizes the function f.[11]

Theorem 15: *If the mechanism $\mathcal{M}$ realizes the function $f : \Theta_1 \times \Theta_2 \to \mathbb{R}$ and satisfies the regularity conditions of (4.2), then*

$$\dim M \geq \operatorname{rank} BMH_{\theta_1, \theta_2}(f), \qquad (4.35)$$

where M is the message space of $\mathcal{M}$.

Chen's theorem provides a lower bound on the dimension of the message space needed to realize a given function f. It does not guarantee the existence of a mechanism $\mathcal{M}$ that realizes f whose message space M has dimension equal to rank $BMH_{\theta_1, \theta_2}(f)$. In practice, however, Chen's theorem typically provides a tight bound[12] on the dimension of the message space that is needed to realize f. His result is thus an important step toward the goal of deriving conditions directly on f that reveal the profiles of mechanisms that realize this function.

Chen (1992) also bounds below the dimension of the message space needed to realize a mapping $F : \prod_{i=1}^{n} \Theta_i \to \mathbb{R}^k$, first in the case of $n = 2$ (Thm. 2, p. 263) and then in the case of $n \geq 2$ (Thm. 3, p. 265). The bounds in these cases are not nearly so easy to state and apply as (4.35). Unfortunately, the complexity of his solution may simply mirror the inherent complexity of the problem. Chen's analysis suggests that his bound for a mapping F is likely to be tight in the case of $n = 2$ but not in the case of $n > 2$. Finally, while his bounds for mappings are complicated, they can be coded in a computer program that computes a lower bound on

---

[11] A similar result has been proven in the computer science literature by Abelson (1980). The goal in his paper is to compute the value of a C^2 function $f(\theta_1, \theta_2)$ using two processors, the ith of which has access only to the value of θ_i. A dynamic exchange of information between the processors is considered. In each stage, processor i computes the values of some functions using θ_i and values that have sent in past stages to it from the other processor. Abelson shows that the total number of values that must be exchanged between the two processors is at least rank $D^2_{\theta_1, \theta_2} f$. The two bounds differ by at least one because a final message in which $f(\theta)$ is recorded is not counted by Abelson, as it is here (in the sense that $f(\theta)$ can be computed from the message variables). Chen's bound (4.35) can also be tighter by virtue of incorporating the additional information contained in $D_{\theta_1} f$ and $D_{\theta_2} f$ into the bound.

[12] Chen (1992, pp. 267–270) discusses in some detail the reasons why this bound is likely to be tight.

message space dimension for realizing whatever mapping F is entered into the program (Chen, 1992, Sec. 6).[13]

4.3 Example: Realizing an Implicitly Defined Function

This section applies Theorem 15 to the problem of realizing locally a function $x = f(\theta_1, \theta_2)$ that is defined as the solution of an equation

$$\psi(x, \theta_1, \theta_2) = 0, \tag{4.36}$$

where $\psi : \mathbb{R}^{1+n_1+n_2} \to \mathbb{R}$ is a C^∞ function. It is assumed throughout this section that $\partial \psi / \partial x \neq 0$ to insure the existence of f locally. A special case of interest is when $\psi(x, \theta_1, \theta_2)$ has the form

$$0 = \psi(x, \theta_1, \theta_2) = R_1(x, \theta_1) - R_2(x, \theta_2), \tag{4.37}$$

where each $R_i : \mathbb{R}^{n_i+1} \to \mathbb{R}$ is C^∞. This special case commonly arises in microeconomic theory as the first-order condition for optimally selecting x given θ_1 and θ_2.[14, 15] It is illustrated in Subsections 4.3.1 and 4.3.2 in the context of a Walrasian equilibrium in the trade of two goods between two agents.

---

[13] The reader should also note Theorem 4″ of Hurwicz et al. (1978, p. 60), which was the first lower bound on the dimension of the message space needed to realize a given function f. This bound is stated in terms of the first derivatives of f and the ranks of the matrices $D^2_{\theta_i, \theta_j} f$, and it applies to the case of $n \geq 2$ agents. The subsequent work that is cited above of Hurwicz, Williams, and then Chen builds on ideas and techniques that are evident in this preliminary result.

[14] Saari (1995, pp. 235–236) takes a general approach to the realization of an implicitly defined mapping. Note in particular his extension of Corollary 14 to this form of the objective.

[15] Two common examples are (i) the problem of selecting an optimal level x of a public good for two agents in the case of quasilinear utility and (ii) the task for a firm of optimally dividing production between two of its plants. In (i), let $V_i(x, \theta_i)$ denote the value that agent i receives from an amount x of the public good given his preference parameter vector θ_i. The optimal level x of the public good solves the equation

$$\frac{\partial V_1}{\partial x}(x, \theta_1) + \frac{\partial V_2}{\partial x}(x, \theta_2) = 0,$$

which has the form of (4.37). In (ii), let $C_i(x_i, \theta_i)$ denote the cost of producing an amount x_i of a good at plant i. To produce a given amount y, the firm should select production levels x_1 and x_2 for the two plants that equate the marginal costs of production:

$$\frac{\partial C_1}{\partial x_1}(x_1, \theta_1) - \frac{\partial C_2}{\partial x_2}(x_2, \theta_2) = 0.$$

Setting $x_2 = y - x_1$ and replacing x_1 with x produces an equation of the form (4.37). These are two examples of the team decision problem that is discussed in Section 4.7.

The objective in this section is to compare the informational requirements of realizing a function f^* that arises from a system of the form (4.37) as compared to the informational requirements of realizing a function f that is defined implicitly by a generic function ψ. In particular, the informational requirements of realizing the Walrasian allocation f^* in the bilateral trading problem is compared below to the informational requirements of realizing a non-Walrasian Pareto optimal allocation. Several economic issues that are illustrated by this example are discussed at the end of this section.

Chen's Bound for Generic Ψ (x, θ_1, θ_2) *and for the Special Case of (4.37)*
Implicit differentiation of (4.36) implies

$$0 = \frac{\partial \psi}{\partial x} \cdot D_{\theta_i} f + D_{\theta_i} \psi \tag{4.38}$$

$$\Leftrightarrow D_{\theta_i} f = -\left(\frac{\partial \psi}{\partial x}\right)^{-1} D_{\theta_i} \psi. \tag{4.39}$$

Setting $i = 1$ and differentiating (4.38) with respect to θ_2 implies

$$0 = \frac{\partial \psi}{\partial x} \cdot D^2_{\theta_1,\theta_2} f + A + D^2_{\theta_1,\theta_2} \psi \tag{4.40}$$

$$\Leftrightarrow D^2_{\theta_1,\theta_2} f = -\left(\frac{\partial \psi}{\partial x}\right)^{-1} \left(A + D^2_{\theta_1,\theta_2} \psi\right), \tag{4.41}$$

where A is the $n_1 \times n_2$ matrix whose entry in row t and column s is

$$a_{t,s} = \frac{\partial^2 \psi}{\partial \theta_{2,s} \partial x} \cdot \frac{\partial f}{\partial \theta_{1,t}} \tag{4.42}$$

The matrix in the bound (4.35) on minimal message space dimension for realizing f is thus

$$BMH_{\theta_1,\theta_2}(f) \equiv -\left(\frac{\partial \psi}{\partial x}\right)^{-1} \begin{pmatrix} 0 & D_{\theta_2} \psi \\ \left(D_{\theta_1} \psi\right)^T & A + D^2_{\theta_1,\theta_2} \psi \end{pmatrix}. \tag{4.43}$$

Formulas (4.39) and (4.42) imply that

$$a_{t,s} = -\frac{\partial^2 \psi}{\partial \theta_{2,s} \partial x} \left(\frac{\partial \psi}{\partial x}\right)^{-1} \frac{\partial \psi}{\partial \theta_{1,t}}, \tag{4.44}$$

and so column s in A is

$$-\frac{\partial^2 \psi}{\partial \theta_{2,s} \partial x} \left(\frac{\partial \psi}{\partial x}\right)^{-1} \left(D_{\theta_1} \psi\right)^T. \tag{4.45}$$

The rank of $BMH_{\theta_1,\theta_2}(f)$ is therefore the same as the rank of the matrix

$$
\begin{pmatrix}
0 & D_{\theta_2}\psi \\
\left(D_{\theta_1}\psi\right)^T & D^2_{\theta_1,\theta_2}\psi
\end{pmatrix}
\tag{4.46}
$$

evaluated at points (x, θ_1, θ_2) at which $x = f(\theta_1, \theta_2)$.

The matrix (4.46) has rank equal to $\min\{n_1, n_2\} + 1$ for a generic function $\psi(x, \theta_1, \theta_2)$, which is the minimal dimension of a message space required to realize a generic function f. In the special case of a solution $x = f^*(\theta_1, \theta_2)$ of an equation of the form (4.37), $D^2_{\theta_1,\theta_2}\psi$ is the $n_1 \times n_2$ zero matrix. The matrix (4.46) then has rank 2 as long as $\partial\psi/\partial\theta_{1,i} \neq 0$ for some i and $\partial\psi/\partial\theta_{2,j} \neq 0$ for some j.[16] The bound (4.35) implies that a message space of dimension at least 2 is needed to realize f^*.

Chen's bound in the case of a function f defined by a generic Ψ is tight, for a parameter transfer mechanism exists that realizes f with a message space of dimension $\min\{n_1, n_2\} + 1$. Chen's bound is also tight in the case of f^* defined by a equation of the form (4.37). The function f^* defined implicitly by (4.37) is realized as follows using a message space of dimension 2:

$$
\begin{aligned}
M &= \{(m_1, m_2, m_3) \,|\, m_1 = m_2\}, \\
\alpha_1(\theta_1, m) &= R_1(m_3, \theta_1) - m_2, \\
\alpha_2(\theta_2, m) &= R_2(m_3, \theta_2) - m_1, \\
\zeta(m) &= m_3.
\end{aligned}
\tag{4.47}
$$

This mechanism realizes f^* over any open set on which the solution x to (4.37) is uniquely determined, which is true locally because of the regularity condition $\partial\psi/\partial x \neq 0$.

[16] If $\partial\psi/\partial\theta_{i,k}(x, \theta_1, \theta_2) = 0$ for all (x, θ_1, θ_2) and $1 \leq k \leq n_i$, then ψ does not depend upon θ_i, i.e.,

$$
\psi(x, \theta_1, \theta_2) = (-1)^{j+1} R_j\left(x, \theta_j\right).
$$

The function f can then be realized locally using a message space of dimension 1:

$$
\begin{aligned}
M &= \mathbb{R}, \\
\alpha_j(\theta_j, m) &= R_j(m, \theta_j), \\
\zeta(m) &= m.
\end{aligned}
$$

If $\partial\psi/\partial\theta_{i,k}(x, \theta_1, \theta_2) = 0$ for $i = 1, 2$, all (x, θ_1, θ_2), and $1 \leq k \leq n_i$, then ψ does not depend upon (θ_1, θ_2) and so the problem of realization becomes trivial; a message space of dimension 0 is sufficient for realizing f^*. The bound (4.35) is thus tight even in these degenerate cases.

4.3.1 A Special Case of (4.37): Realizing a Walrasian Allocation

The model of bilateral trade is as follows. For $i = 1, 2$, agent i's utility function is $U_i(x_i, \theta_i)$, where $\theta_i \in \mathbb{R}^{n_i}$ determines his preferences and $x_i = (x_{i1}, x_{i2})$ is his bundle of the two goods. Agent 1's initial endowment is $w_1 = (1, 0)$ and agent 2's initial endowment is $w_2 = (0, 1)$. Let p denote the price of good 1 and let good 2 be a numèraire. Fixing the values of θ_1 and θ_2, an element (x_1^*, x_2^*, p) of $\mathbb{R}_{++}^5$ is a *Walrasian equilibrium* if it satisfies

$$x_1^* \in \arg\max \ U_1(x_1, \theta_1) \text{ s.t. } px_{11} + x_{12} = p, \tag{4.48}$$

$$x_2^* \in \arg\max \ U_2(x_2, \theta_2) \text{ s.t. } px_{21} + x_{22} = 1, \tag{4.49}$$

$$x_1^* + x_2^* = (1, 1). \tag{4.50}$$

As in Subsection 3.1.2, it is assumed that (θ_1, θ_2) is restricted to an open subset $\Theta_1 \times \Theta_2$ of $\mathbb{R}^{n_1+n_2}$ on which a Walrasian equilibrium (x_1^*, x_2^*, p) varies smoothly as a function of (θ_1, θ_2). For the purposes of this section, the focus here is on the realization locally of the function $x_{11}^* = f^*(\theta_1, \theta_2)$ that specifies agent 1's allocation of good 1 in equilibrium.

The first step is to show that f^* solves an equation of the form (4.37). The first-order conditions associated with (4.48) and (4.49) are

$$MRS_1(x_1, \theta_1) = p = MRS_2(x_2, \theta_2), \tag{4.51}$$

where MRS_i denotes agent i's marginal rate of substitution of good 2 for good 1,

$$MRS_i(x_i, \theta_i) \equiv \frac{\frac{\partial U_i}{\partial x_{i1}}(x_i, \theta_i)}{\frac{\partial U_i}{\partial x_{i2}}(x_i, \theta_i)}. \tag{4.52}$$

Subtracting the right side of (4.51) from its left side produces

$$MRS_1(x_1, \theta_1) - MRS_2(x_2, \theta_2) = 0. \tag{4.53}$$

An equation of the form (4.37) is obtained by substitution into (4.53). The feasibility condition $x_2 = (1, 1) - x_1$ eliminates x_2. Substituting $MRS_1(x_1, \theta_1)$ for p in agent 1's budget constraint produces

$$MRS_1(x_1, \theta_1)x_{11} + x_{12} = MRS_1(x_1, \theta_1). \tag{4.54}$$

With an appropriate regularity condition, (4.54) allows x_{12} to be expressed as a function of x_{11} and θ_1. Substitution of this function for x_{12} in (4.53) is the last step in reducing it to the form (4.37).

The *competitive mechanism* is an alternative to (4.47) as a mechanism for realizing f^* in this case. The presentation here generalizes the example of

Subsection 3.1.2 away from its dependence on specific functional forms of $U_1(x_1, \theta_1)$ and $U_2(x_2, \theta_2)$. Let $x_i^*(p)$ denote agent i's demand for goods 1 and 2 given his initial endowment and the price p for good 1. Consider $(x_1, x_2, p) \in \mathbb{R}_{++}^5$. The competitive mechanism has the following form when the outcome mapping $\zeta(\cdot)$ is limited to calculating $f^*(\theta_1, \theta_2)$:

$$M = \{(x_1, x_2, p) \mid px_{11} + x_{12} = p, \ px_{21} + x_{22} = 1, \ x_1 + x_2 = 1\},$$

$$\alpha_1(\theta_1, x_1, x_2, p) = x_1^*(p) - x_1, \tag{4.55}$$

$$\alpha_2(\theta_2, x_1, x_2, p) = x_2^*(p) - x_2,$$

$$\zeta(x_1, x_2, p) = x_{11}.$$

The budget equations and the equation of feasibility together imply that M has dimension 2. The bound (4.35) implies that the dimension of the competitive message space M is the smallest possible dimension of message space that can be used to realize f^*.

4.3.2 Realizing a Non-Walrasian Pareto Optimal Allocation

A slight modification of the objective in the above bilateral trading problem alters it to the generic case in which a message space of dimension $\min\{n_1, n_2\} + 1$ is required for realization. The task above is to realize the Walrasian allocation $x_{11}^* = f^*(\theta_1, \theta_2)$ of good 1 to agent 1. Consider now an allocation to the two agents that is Pareto optimal for every θ but not necessarily Walrasian. The problem of realizing the amount of good 1 given to agent 1 in this allocation is now considered.

Assume that Θ_1 and Θ_2 are restricted so that the utility functions of the agents are strictly concave. For fixed (θ_1, θ_2), the Pareto optimal allocations in this case are the solutions to the equation

$$0 = MRS_1(x_1, \theta_1) - MRS_2(x_2, \theta_2). \tag{4.56}$$

The feasibility condition $x_2 = (1, 1) - x_1$ can again be used to eliminate x_2 from this equation. In the case of the Walrasian allocation, (4.54) is solved to express x_{12} as a function of x_{11} and θ_1. Substitution into (4.56) then produces an equation of the form (4.37). Consider instead a perturbation $y(\theta_1, \theta_2)$ of the Walrasian allocation $x_{12}^*(\theta_1, \theta_2)$ of good 2 to agent 1,

$$y(\theta_1, \theta_2) = x_{12}^*(\theta_1, \theta_2) + \varepsilon(\theta_1, \theta_2), \tag{4.57}$$

where $\varepsilon(\theta_1, \theta_2)$ is a C^∞ function. Replace x_{12} in (4.56) with $y(\theta_1, \theta_2)$. For a sufficiently small $\varepsilon(\theta_1, \theta_2)$, it is possible to solve (4.56) for x_{11}^{**} implicitly to determine a Pareto optimal allocation.[17] Given the restrictions on the utility functions of the agents, $\varepsilon(\theta_1, \theta_2)$ can be chosen sufficiently small so that the allocation

$$x_1 = (x_{11}^{**}, y), \tag{4.58}$$

$$x_2 = (1, 1) - x_1 \tag{4.59}$$

is in the interior of the feasible set. If desired, Θ can be restricted and $\varepsilon(\theta_1, \theta_2)$ can be chosen sufficiently small so that this allocation is individually rational for each agent in addition to being Pareto optimal. It is the magnitude of $\varepsilon(\theta_1, \theta_2)$ that may need to be restricted to achieve these properties, however, not its derivatives at any single point. Equation (4.56) is in this way altered to the form

$$0 = \psi^{**}(x, \theta_1, \theta_2) \equiv R_1(x, y, \theta_1) - R_2(x, y, \theta_2), \tag{4.60}$$

where x_{11} has again been replaced by x and $y(\theta_1, \theta_2)$ is the C^∞ function in (4.57).

Of interest is realizing the function $x = f^{**}(\theta_1, \theta_2)$ that is defined implicitly by (4.60). Unlike the equation derived from (4.51) that implicitly defines the Walrasian allocation of good 1 to agent 1, the parameter vector θ_1 is not additively separated from the parameter vector θ_2 in (4.60) because of the dependence of y upon both vectors. To evaluate the bound (4.35) in the case of f^{**}, substitute into (4.46) to obtain

$$\begin{pmatrix} 0 & D_{\theta_2}\psi^{**} \\ \left(D_{\theta_1}\psi^{**}\right)^T & D_{\theta_1,\theta_2}^2\psi^{**} \end{pmatrix} \tag{4.61}$$

$$= \begin{pmatrix} 0 & -\left(D_{\theta_2}R_2 + \frac{\partial R_2}{\partial y}D_{\theta_2}y\right) \\ \left(D_{\theta_1}R_1 + \frac{\partial R_1}{\partial y}D_{\theta_1}y\right)^T & \left(\frac{\partial R_1}{\partial y} - \frac{\partial R_2}{\partial y}\right)D_{\theta_1,\theta_2}^2 y + B \end{pmatrix}, \tag{4.62}$$

---

[17] The regularity condition

$$\frac{\partial}{\partial x_{11}}[MRS_1(x_1, \theta_1) - MRS_2(x_2, \theta_2)] \neq 0$$

holding at the Walrasian equilibrium allocation $(x_{11}^*, x_{12}^*, 1 - x_{11}^*, 1 - x_{12}^*)$ is sufficient if $\varepsilon(\cdot)$ is chosen sufficiently small.

where B is the $n_1 \times n_2$ matrix whose entry in row t and column s is

$$b_{i,j} = -\frac{\partial y}{\partial \theta_{1,t}} \frac{\partial^2 R_2}{\partial \theta_{2,s} \partial y}. \tag{4.63}$$

The values of the terms

$$D_{\theta_1} R_1, \; D_{\theta_2} R_2, \; \frac{\partial R_1}{\partial y}, \; \frac{\partial R_2}{\partial y}, \; \text{and} \; \frac{\partial^2 R_2}{\partial \theta_{2,j} \partial y} \tag{4.64}$$

in the matrix (4.62) are determined by the choices of the agents' utility functions along with the values of x, y, θ_1, and θ_2 for which $x = f^{**}(y, \theta_1, \theta_2)$; the terms

$$D_{\theta_1} y, \; D_{\theta_2} y, \; D^2_{\theta_1, \theta_2} y, \; \text{and} \; \frac{\partial y}{\partial \theta_{1,t}} \tag{4.65}$$

in (4.62), however, can be specified arbitrarily at any such point $(x, y, \theta_1, \theta_2)$ through the choice of the perturbation $\varepsilon(\theta_1, \theta_2)$. If the terms

$$\frac{\partial R_1}{\partial y} - \frac{\partial R_2}{\partial y}, \; \frac{\partial R_1}{\partial y}, \; \text{and} \; \frac{\partial R_2}{\partial y} \tag{4.66}$$

are nonzero at the point $(x, y, \theta_1, \theta_2)$ in question, then the value of every entry of the matrix (4.62) except the row 1, column 1 entry of 0 can be freely varied by altering the values of the terms in (4.65) at the given point. Except in degenerate instances of the bilateral trading problem, it is clear that this matrix will have rank equal to $\min\{n_1, n_2\} + 1$ for a generic perturbation $\varepsilon(\theta_1, \theta_2)$. The bound (4.35) thus suggests that a generic smooth selection from the Pareto correspondence requires a message space of dimension at least $\min\{n_1, n_2\} + 1$ for realization, in contrast to the fixed dimension of 2 required by the Walrasian allocation.[18] Again, a parameter transfer mechanism indicates that Chen's bound is tight in this case.

4.3.3 Discussion

Recall that $f^*(\theta_1, \theta_2)$ denotes the Walrasian allocation of good 1 to agent 1 when preferences of the agents are determined by (θ_1, θ_2). An interesting aspect of the bilateral trading problem in Subsection 4.3.1 is that the dimension of the message space needed to realize $f^*(\theta_1, \theta_2)$ remains equal to 2 regardless of the dimensions n_1 and n_2 of the agents' parameter vectors.

---

[18] This result does not contradict the Second Fundamental Theorem of Welfare Economics, which asserts that any Pareto optimal allocation can be realized as an equilibrium of the competitive mechanism after appropriate monetary transfers among the agents. Rather, it suggests that realizing the appropriate transfers may require that a large amount of information be communicated by the agents concerning their preferences.

Despite the potentially large dimension of the agents' private information, the competitive mechanism realizes agent 1's allocation of good 1 using a relatively small set of signals; in fact, the competitive message space is of minimal dimension for realizing this component of the Walrasian allocation. This contrasts with the large amount of information that may be required to realize alternative Pareto optimal allocations, as suggested in Subsection 4.3.2. These results mirror the insight of Hayek (1945) concerning the informational efficiency of competitive equilibrium prices as a means of arranging trade. They are a special case of results concerning the informational efficiency of the competitive mechanism that have been proven for much more general informational environments and without the strong differentiability assumptions of this text.[19] An advantage here, however, is that the bound (4.35) is not limited to models of exchange.

It is also interesting that the mapping $f^*(\theta_1, \theta_2)$ is so strongly nongeneric that it lies in a nowhere dense subset of $C^\infty(\Theta_1 \times \Theta_2, \mathbb{R})$ consisting of those functions that can be realized with message spaces of dimension less than $\min\{n_1, n_2\} + 1$. This point is discussed in more depth in Section 4.5 below, where it is generalized to an exchange economy with n agents and k goods.

Two cautionary points concerning the above analysis should be noted. First, the statement that the competitive message space in (4.55) has dimension 2 reflects the fact that realization concerns the messages needed *in equilibrium* to realize an objective. If the goal is instead to study how agents find equilibrium or whether or not their messages are consistent with their self-interests, then it is appropriate to consider Cartesian products of the form $M_1 \times M_2$ without reduction through considerations of equilibrium. In the case of dynamic adjustment to equilibrium, M_i represents the messages adjusted by agent i. If the goal is to study the incentives of the agents, then M_i is the strategy space of agent i. In the trading model, the problem of finding competitive equilibrium is well studied and problematic. It is only made more difficult when the private information of individual agents is treated as a constraint and each agent chooses his messages according to his self-interest.[20]

---

[19] Results of this kind are proven in Hurwicz (1972), Mount and Reiter (1974), Osana (1978), and Walker (1977). The analysis of Subsections 4.3.1 and 4.3.2 illustrate in particular the result of Jordan (1982) that the competititve mechanism is *informationally efficient* among mechanisms that realize a Pareto efficient allocation.

[20] This has been studied by Reiter (1979), Jordan (1987), Mount and Reiter (1987), Saari and Williams (1986), and Williams (1985). Games whose Nash equilibria implement Walrasian allocations have been constructed by Hurwicz (1979) and by Schmeidler (1980). The general relationship between realization and Nash implementation is studied in Williams (1986).

Second, the above analysis of the competitive mechanism illustrates the limits on the insight provided by the bound (4.35) into the informational requirements for realizing a multivalued mapping F. Consider the problem of realizing $F = (f^*, g^*)$, where $f^*(\theta_1, \theta_2)$ is defined above and $g^*(\theta_1, \theta_2)$ is agent's 1's allocation of good 2 in a Walrasian equilibrium. The competitive mechanism collects enough information about (θ_1, θ_2) to compute the values of both $f^*(\theta_1, \theta_2)$ and $g^*(\theta_1, \theta_2)$. Starting from scratch with the two functions f^* and g^*, without knowing their origin in a model of bilateral trade, the bound (4.35) suggests that a message space of dimension 2 is needed to realize each of the functions f^* and g^*. This suggests that a message space of dimension 4 may be required to realize the mapping F. The bound (4.35) simply does not reveal that information used to compute one function f^* may assist in the computation of the other function g^*.

4.4 Genericity

It has been noted in the case of $n = 2$ agents that a generic smooth function f can only be realized by mechanisms whose message spaces are at least as large in their dimensions as some parameter transfer mechanism. The following result from Williams (1982a, 1984) is a stronger characterization of the mechanisms that realize a generic mapping F in that (i) it is not restricted to the special case of $n = 2$ agents and real-valued functions; (ii) it characterizes the profile $(c_i)_{1 \leq i \leq n}$ of any mechanism that realizes a generic mapping f, not just the total dimension $c \equiv \sum_{i=1}^{n} c_i$ of the message space of such a mechanism.

Theorem 16: *There exists an open, dense subset W of $C^\infty(\Theta, \mathbb{R}^k)$ in the Whitney C^∞ topology with the following property: if $F \in W$ and if $\mathcal{M}$ is a mechanism satisfying the regularity conditions of (4.2) that realizes F, then the profile $(c_i)_{1 \leq i \leq n}$ of $\mathcal{M}$ satisfies $c_i = \dim \Theta_i$ for all but at most one value of i.*

This theorem employs an especially strong notion of genericity. In some settings, "generic" means only that "almost all" elements of the topological space have the specified property, which admits the possibility that the set of elements that do not have the property can be locally dense. Here, each mapping in an open and dense subset W of $C^\infty(\Theta, \mathbb{R}^k)$ can only be realized by a mechanism whose profile satisfies $c_i = \dim \Theta_i$ for all but at most one value of i. This property of a mapping F is therefore robust to C^∞ perturbations of F.

Theorem 16 is proven by showing that if $c_i < \dim \Theta_i$ for more than one value of i, then a nontrivial algebraic equation exists that the derivatives of F at θ^* must satisfy if F can be realized near this point with a mechanism of profile $(c_i)_{1 \leq i \leq n}$. An equation of this kind is derived in Subsection 4.2.1 in the case of a real-valued function f, $n = 2$, and $\dim \Theta_1 = \dim \Theta_2 = 2$. Assuming that f satisfies the regularity condition (4.22) on $O \subset \Theta$, it can be realized by a mechanism of profile $(1, 1)$ near θ^* if and only if

$$\det BMH_{\theta_1, \theta_2}(f) = 0 \tag{4.67}$$

near this point. It is immediate that (4.67) is true wherever the regularity (4.22) fails to hold. Consequently, (4.67) is a necessary condition for the existence of a mechanism of profile $(1, 1)$ that realizes f near θ^*. If f can be realized near θ^* by a mechanism of profile $(0, 0)$, $(0, 1)$, or $(1, 0)$, then it is easily shown that it can be realized by a mechanism of profile $(1, 1)$. Equation (4.67) is therefore necessary for a function f to be nongeneric in the sense of Theorem 16. Conversely,

$$\det BMH_{\theta_1, \theta_2}(f) \neq 0 \tag{4.68}$$

holding at θ^* is sufficient to insure that f is generic in the sense of this theorem.

A weakness of the proof of Theorem 16 is that it does not produce an explicit test similar to (4.68) for verifying genericity in the sense of this theorem in the general case. At present, a comparably straightforward method for verifying that a given mapping F is generic has not yet been derived. This can make it difficult to formally establish that a particular objective is generic.

4.4.1 The Proof of the Genericity Result

The proof of Theorem 16 in Williams (1982a, 1984) goes beyond the scope of this text in formally addressing the topology on functions and local coordinate systems arbitrarily close to θ^*. It is possible here to outline the main ideas of the argument. A first step is to reduce the proof to the case of $k = 1$ in which F is a real-valued function.[21] Suppose that the mechanism $\mathcal{M}$ realizes the mapping $F = (f_j)_{1 \leq j \leq k}$. Let $\zeta = (\zeta_j)_{1 \leq j \leq k}$ denote the outcome mapping of $\mathcal{M}$. As shown in the introductory paragraphs of Section 4.2, the

---

[21] This observation is not made in Williams (1982a, 1984), which explains why the genericity results in these papers concern functions and not mappings. As shown here, however, the extension to mappings is immediate.

mechanism $\mathcal{M}_j$ obtained by restricting the outcome mapping of $\mathcal{M}$ to its jth component function ζ_j realizes f_j for each $1 \le j \le k$. Each mechanism $\mathcal{M}_j$ has the same profile as the original mechanism $\mathcal{M}$, and so Theorem 16 follows for all $k \in \mathbb{N}$ once it is proven for $k = 1$.

Fix a profile $(c_i)_{1 \le i \le n}$ such that $c_i < \dim \Theta_i$ for at least two values of i. Proving the result in the special case of real-valued functions is essentially a matter of showing that there exists a nontrivial algebraic equation on the derivatives of a function f that must be satisfied for the existence of a coordinate system u with the properties given in Statement II of Corollary 13. For $\ell \in \mathbb{N}$ let f^ℓ and u^ℓ denote the ℓth order Taylor polynomials of f and u at θ^*, respectively, with the constant terms $f(\theta^*)$ and $u(\theta^*)$ omitted. The coefficients of a polynomial of degree ℓ or less in p variables determine a vector of real numbers. All possible Taylor polynomials of degree ℓ in p variables with constant term equal to zero can be placed in a one-to-one correspondence with the points in $\mathbb{R}^{\delta(p,\ell)}$ for a particular number $\delta(p, \ell) \in \mathbb{N}$. The Taylor polynomial f^ℓ is thus identified with a point in $\mathbb{R}^{\delta(d+c,\ell)}$, where (as before) $d + c = \dim \Theta$. A local coordinate system u consists of $d + c$ functions; the Taylor polynomial u^ℓ is thus identified with a point in $\mathbb{R}^{(d+c)\delta(d+c,\ell)}$.[22] Let

$$U^\ell \subset \mathbb{R}^{\delta(d+c,\ell)} \times \mathbb{R}^{(d+c)\delta(d+c,\ell)} \tag{4.69}$$

denote the pairs (f^ℓ, u^ℓ) determined by pairs (f, u) that satisfy Statement II of Corollary 13. Of ultimate interest here is the projection $pr(f^\ell, u^\ell) = f^\ell \in \mathbb{R}^{\delta(d+c,\ell)}$ and the set

$$pr\left(U^\ell\right) \subset \mathbb{R}^{\delta(d+c,\ell)}, \tag{4.70}$$

which consists of the Taylor polynomials f^ℓ with constant term zero determined by those objectives f that can be realized near θ^* with a mechanism of profile $(c_i)_{1 \le i \le n}$. It will be argued below that if ℓ is sufficiently large[23] then $pr(U^\ell)$ is a subset of $\mathbb{R}^{\delta(d+c,\ell)}$ of dimension less than $\delta(d + c, \ell)$ determined by algebraic equations and inequalities.[24] Because its dimension

---

[22] The requirement of nonsingularity of u at θ^* identifies the Taylor polynomials of local coordinate systems with an open and dense subset of $\mathbb{R}^{(d+c)\delta(d+c,\ell)}$. This detail is ignored in this summary of the proof.

[23] This is a rare point in this text at which the assumption that functions, distributions, and vector fields are C^∞ as opposed to just C^2 explicitly used. Chen's theorem (Theorem 15 above) only assumes C^2. His theorem characterizes in the case of two agents the minimal dimension of the message space needed to realize a generic function. Although the proof of theorem 16 uses C^∞, Chen's theorem and the form of the system in Statement II of Corollary 13 clearly suggest that Theorem 16 should be provable using C^2 instead of C^∞.

[24] This step is proven in Theorem 3 of Williams (1984, pp. 282–283).

is strictly less than $\delta(d + c, \ell)$, there must exist at least one nontrivial algebraic equation that elements of $pr(U^\ell)$ must satisfy, which completes the argument.

The set U^ℓ must first be characterized. The mapping

$$\left(f^\ell, u^\ell\right) \longmapsto \left(\left(f \circ u^{-1}\right)^\ell, \left(u^{-1}\right)^\ell\right) = \left(\left(f \circ v\right)^\ell, v^\ell\right) \tag{4.71}$$

identifies each element of U^ℓ with a pair (g, v) that has the following properties in reference to Statement II of Corollary 13: (i) $(f \circ v)(w, m)$ depends only on $m \in \mathbb{R}^c$; (ii) for $v = (v_1, \ldots, v_n)$ and $1 \le i \le n$, the mapping

$$v_i : (-\varepsilon, \varepsilon)^{d+c} \to \Theta_i \subset \mathbb{R}^{d_i + c_i}$$

depends only on $w_i \in \mathbb{R}^{d_i}$ and $m \in M \subset \mathbb{R}^c$. Consequently, $(f \circ v)^\ell$ can be identified with a vector in $\mathbb{R}^{\delta(c, \ell)}$ and v^ℓ can be identified with a vector in $\mathbb{R}^\kappa$ where

$$\kappa = \sum_{i=1}^n (d_i + c_i)\, \delta\, (d + c_i, \ell)\,. \tag{4.72}$$

The $d_i + c_i = \dim \Theta_i$ term in this formula represents the $d_i + c_i$ component functions of v_i, each of which has a Taylor polynomial of degree ℓ in $d + c_i$ variables. The mapping (4.71) is algebraic and invertible; U^ℓ is thus isomorphic to a Euclidean space of dimension[25]

$$\delta\, (c, \ell) + \sum_{i=1}^n (d_i + c_i)\, \delta\, (d + c_i, \ell)\,.$$

Recall that $pr(U^\ell) \subset \mathbb{R}^{\delta(d+c, \ell)}$. It remains to be shown that

$$\delta(d + c, \ell) > \dim U^\ell = \delta\, (c, \ell) + \sum_{i=1}^n (d_i + c_i)\, \delta\, (d + c_i, \ell)$$

for ℓ sufficiently large. Notice that

$$\lim_{\ell \to \infty} \frac{\delta(s, \ell)}{\delta(t, \ell)} = \infty$$

if $s > t$. Because the number n of agents is fixed in this proof, it is sufficient to show that

$$d + c > c,\, d + c_i$$

---

[25] Specifically, as shown in Williams (1984, Thm. 2), this mapping proves that U^k is a C^∞ submanifold of the Euclidean space in (4.69) that is determined as a subset of this space by a system of algebraic equations and inequalities.

for all $1 \leq i \leq n$. Because $d = \Sigma_{j=1}^n d_j$, this holds if and only if

$$d_i \geq 1 \Leftrightarrow c_i < \dim \Theta_i$$

for at least two values of i, which is exactly the case addressed in the theorem.

4.4.2 The Information Collected in Realizing a Generic F

Theorem 16 implies that a generic smooth mapping F can only be realized by a mechanism that collects in equilibrium at least as much information in its message space as some parameter transfer mechanism. The purpose of this subsection is to give this statement a precise interpretation.

Let $\mathcal{M} = (\Theta, M, (\mu_i)_{1 \leq i \leq n}, \zeta)$ be a mechanism satisfying *Message Process* that realizes $F : \Theta \to \mathbb{R}^k$. Suppose that the profile of $\mathcal{M}$ satisfies $c_i = \dim \Theta_i$ for $i > 1$. As usual, let $u_{(c)} : \Theta \to M$ be the equilibrium mapping of $\mathcal{M}$. Let $\mathcal{M}^*$ be the parameter transfer mechanism whose profile also satisfies $c_i = \dim \Theta_i$ for $i > 1$:

for each agent $i > 1$, $M_i^* \equiv \Theta_i$ and $\alpha_i^*(\theta_i, m_i) \equiv m_i - \theta_i$,

$$M_1 \equiv \mathbb{R}^k \text{ and } \alpha_1^*(\theta_i, m) \equiv m_1 - F(\theta_1, m_2, \ldots, m_n), \qquad (4.73)$$

$$M^* \equiv \mathbb{R}^k \times \prod_{i>1} \Theta_i;$$

$$\zeta^*(m) \equiv m_1.$$

The equilibrium mapping $u_{(c)}^*$ of $\mathcal{M}^*$ is

$$u_{(c)}^*(\theta) \equiv (F(\theta), \theta_{-1}). \qquad (4.74)$$

Consider a specific point $\theta' \in \Theta$ and let $u_{(c)}(\theta') \equiv m'$. As illustrated in Figure 4.1, the idea that $\mathcal{M}$ collects as much information about the private parameters of the n agents as does the parameter transfer mechanism $\mathcal{M}^*$ is modeled here by proving the existence of a mapping $\xi : O(m') \to M^*$ defined on a neighborhood $O(m') \subset M$ of m' together with an open neighborhood $O(\theta')$ of θ' such that

$$\xi(u_{(c)}(\theta)) = u_{(c)}^*(\theta) \equiv (F(\theta), \theta_{-1}) \qquad (4.75)$$

for all $\theta \in O(\theta')$. Intuitively, the mapping ξ translates the messages in M into messages in M^*. The equality (4.75) states that the information about θ in the equilibrium messages $u_{(c)}^*(\theta)$ of the parameter transfer mechanism $\mathcal{M}^*$ can be extracted from the equilibrium messages $u_{(c)}(\theta)$ of $\mathcal{M}$.

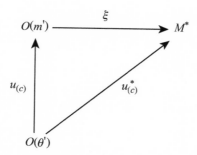

Figure 4.1. The mechanism $\mathcal{M}$ collects as much information about the private parameters θ of the n agents as does the parameter transfer mechanism $\mathcal{M}^*$ if the messages $u^*_{(c)}(\theta) \in M^*$ can be computed from the messages $u_{(c)}(\theta) \in O(m') \subset M$ by means of a mapping ξ.

The existence of the mapping ξ is a straightforward application of the Implicit Function Theorem applied to the system of equilibrium message equations $\alpha_i(\theta_i, m) = 0$ of the mechanism $\mathcal{M}$ for $i > 1$. Regard this system as $\sum_{i=2}^n \dim \Theta_i$ equations in the $\sum_{i=2}^n \dim \Theta_i$ parameters θ_{-1} of all agents except agent one. The regularity condition (iii) of *Message Process* implies that there exists a mapping φ from some open neighborhood $O(m')$ of m' into an open neighborhood $O(\theta'_{-1}) \subset \prod_{i=2}^n \Theta_i$ such that

$$\alpha_i(\theta_i, m) = 0 \text{ for all } i > 1 \text{ and } (\theta_{-1}, m) \in O(\theta'_{-1}) \times O(m') \Leftrightarrow \theta_{-1} = \varphi(m).$$
(4.76)

The mapping ξ is then defined on $O(m')$ by the equation

$$\xi(m) \equiv (\zeta(m), \varphi(m)),$$
(4.77)

and the open set $O(\theta')$ is defined as

$$O(\theta') \equiv \left\{ \theta \in u^{-1}_{(c)}\left(O(m')\right) | \theta_{-1} \in O(\theta'_{-1}) \right\}.$$
(4.78)

It is straightforward to verify that this definition of ξ makes Figure 4.1 commute. For $\theta \in O_{\theta'}$, $u_{(c)}(\theta) = m$ implies $\alpha_i(\theta_i, m) = 0$ for $i > 1$. Definition (4.78) implies $m \in O(m')$ and $\theta_{-1} \in O(\theta'_{-1})$; applying (4.76),

$$\varphi(m) = \theta_{-1}.$$
(4.79)

Because $\mathcal{M}$ realizes F, it follows that

$$\zeta(m) = F(\theta).$$
(4.80)

Combining (4.79) and (4.80) implies

$$\xi(m) \equiv (\zeta(m), \varphi(m)) = (F(\theta), \theta_{-1}) = u^*_{(c)}(\theta), \qquad (4.81)$$

which is the desired result.

4.5 Example: Realizing a Walrasian Allocation

An exchange economy with n agents and k goods is considered in this example, equipped with appropriate regularity assumptions so that the theory of this text applies. Let $x^*(\theta)$ be a mapping that selects a Walrasian allocation for each choice θ of the agents' preference parameters.[26] It is shown below that the competitive mechanism realizes $x^*(\theta)$ with a message space of dimension $n(k-1)$ in which each agent adjusts $k-1$ variables. The condition

$$\dim \Theta_i \geq k \text{ for all } 1 \leq i \leq n \qquad (4.82)$$

is sufficient to insure that the profile $(c_i)_{1 \leq i \leq n}$ of the competitive mechanism satisfies

$$c_i = k - 1 < \dim \Theta_i \qquad (4.83)$$

for each agent i. Relatively few restrictions are placed on an agent's preferences in general equilibrium theory; reflecting this generality, the space Θ_i that describes the range of agent i's preferences may be vast. It is thus plausible that $\dim \Theta_i$ is quite large for each agent i and so (4.82) holds. In this case, Theorem 16 together with (4.83) imply that $x^*(\theta)$ is nongeneric. The nongenericity of the Walrasian allocation mapping in the case of $n = 2$ agents and $k = 2$ goods that was noted near the end of Subsection 4.3 is thus generalized in this section to exchange economies with arbitrary numbers of agents and goods as long as (4.82) holds for each i.[27]

The model is as follows. The preferences of the ith agent are represented by the utility function $U_i(x_i, \theta_i)$, where $x_i \in \mathbb{R}^k_{++}$ denotes a bundle of k goods.

---

[26] Alternatively, the realization of the Walrasian net trades may be considered instead of the Walrasian allocation $x^*(\theta)$. This is an example of the *representation problem*, which concerns the ways in which a given objective can be reformulated while still respecting the distribution of information among the agents. Saari (1985) poses this problem and then addresses the relationship between representation and realization.

[27] As will be explained below, the bound (4.82) also insures that the competitive mechanism can satisfy a regularity condition of this text. This explains why $\dim \Theta_i \geq k$ is assumed in (4.82) to hold for all i instead of at least two values of i, which is all that is required to prove nongenericity of $x^*(\theta)$.

Let Δ denote the price simplex for k goods,

$$\Delta = \left\{ p = (p_j)_{1 \le j \le k} \in \mathbb{R}^k_+ \,\middle|\, \sum_{j=1}^{k} p_j = 1 \right\}. \tag{4.84}$$

Let $w_i \in \mathbb{R}^k_{++}$ denote agent i's initial allocation of the k goods. It is assumed that mappings $x_1^*, \ldots, x_n^*$ and p^* exist along with an open subset $O^\Delta \subset Int$ Δ with following two properties:

(i) For each agent i, $x_i^* : \Theta_i \times O^\Delta \to \mathbb{R}^k_{++}$ is a C^∞ selection from agent i's demand correspondence,

$$x_i^*(\theta_i, p) \in \arg\max_{x_i} U_i(x_i, \theta_i) \text{ s.t. } p \cdot x_i = p \cdot w_i. \tag{4.85}$$

(ii) The C^∞ mapping $p^* : \Theta \to O^\Delta$ determines the unique price vector $p^*(\theta)$ in O^Δ for θ for which the allocation $(x_i^*(\theta_i, p^*(\theta)))_{1 \le i \le n}$ is *feasible*,

$$\sum_{i=1}^{n} x_i^*\left(\theta_i, p^*(\theta)\right) = \sum_{i=1}^{n} w_i. \tag{4.86}$$

For each $\theta \in \Theta$,

$$\left(\left(x_i^*\left(\theta_i, p^*(\theta)\right) \right)_{1 \le i \le n}, p^*(\theta) \right) \tag{4.87}$$

is a *Walrasian equilibrium* for the exchange economy defined by θ.[28, 29]
Define $x^*(\theta)$ as the allocation in this Walrasian equilibrium,

$$x^*(\theta) \equiv \left(x_i^*\left(\theta_i, p^*(\theta)\right) \right)_{1 \le i \le n}. \tag{4.88}$$

Dependence among the component functions of $x^*(\theta)$ and $x_i^*(\theta_i, p)$ is now noted. This will be used below in characterizing the profile of the competitive mechanism. First, though $x^*(\theta) \in \mathbb{R}^{nk}$, it satisfies k equations of feasibility (4.86) along with the budget equations of each of the n agents. The budget

---

[28] I bypass here the issue of sufficient conditions on $U_1, \ldots, U_n$ for the existence of smooth mappings $(x_i^*)_{1 \le i \le n}$ and p^* with the above properties in order to keep the focus on realization.

[29] Restricting the price vector p to a sufficiently small open subset O^Δ of Int Δ so that the equilibrium price vector $p^*(\theta)$ is uniquely determined in the economy specified by θ reflects the local nature of the first-order approach of this text. Defining an open set O^Δ with this property may require that each agent i's parameter vector θ_i be restricted to an open subset of Θ_i, which also reflects the local perspective.

equation of the nth agent is implied by those of the other $n-1$ agents together with feasibility. There are thus $k+n-1$ independent equations that are satisfied by the components of $x^*(\theta)$, which can thus be regarded as an element of $C^\infty(\Theta, \mathbb{R}^{(n-1)(k-1)})$. Second, while $x_i^*(\theta_i, p) \in \mathbb{R}_{++}^k$, any one of its k component functions is determined by the other component functions and $p \in Int\, \Delta$ through the budget constraint $p \cdot x_i = p \cdot w_i$. The mapping $x_i^*(\cdot)$ can thus be regarded as an element of $C^\infty(\Theta \times O^\Delta, \mathbb{R}_{++}^{k-1})$.

Let $m = (m_i)_{1 \le i \le n}$, where $m_i \in \mathbb{R}^k$. The Walrasian allocation $x^*(\theta)$ is realized by the *competitive mechanism*, which is defined as follows:

$$M = \left\{ (m, p) \in \mathbb{R}_{++}^{kn} \times O^\Delta \;\middle|\; \begin{array}{l} \sum_{i=1}^n m_i = \sum_{i=1}^n w_i, \\[2mm] p \cdot m_i = p \cdot w_i,\ 1 \le i \le n \end{array} \right\},$$

$$\alpha_i(\theta_i, p) = x_i^*(\theta, p) - m_i = 0 \text{ for each agent } i, \qquad (4.89)$$

$$\zeta(m, p) \equiv m.$$

Realization of $x^*(\theta)$ is verified as follows:

$$\alpha_i(\theta_i, p) = 0 \text{ for each agent } i \Rightarrow$$

$$\sum_{i=1}^n x_i^*(\theta, p) = \sum_{i=1}^n m_i = \sum_{i=1}^n w_i \Rightarrow \qquad (4.90)$$

$$p = p^*(\theta) \text{ and } m = \left(x_i^*(\theta, p) \right)_{1 \le i \le n} = x^*(\theta).$$

Assumption (ii) above that $p^*(\theta)$ is the unique value of $p \in O^\Delta$ at which the market clears together with the constraint $\sum_{i=1}^n m_i = \sum_{i=1}^n w_i$ on messages support these implications. Assuming that (4.82) holds, the regularity condition

$$\text{rank } D_{\theta_i} x_i^*(\theta_i, p) = k - 1 \qquad (4.91)$$

can be imposed for each i. It insures that the competitive mechanism satisfies the regularity condition (iii) of *Message Process*.

The message space M is the solution set in a space of dimension $nk + k - 1$ of the k equations of feasibility along with n additional equations that represent each agent's budget constraint. As argued above concerning the range of x^*, the space M is the solution set of $n+k-1$ independent equations and its dimension is therefore $n(k-1)$. As in the two-agent, two-good case considered in Subsection 4.3, the dimension of the competitive message space is thus defined by the number n of agents and the number

k of goods independently of the dimensions of the parameter spaces of the agents. As argued above, the range of each $x_i^*(\cdot)$ can be regarded as $\mathbb{R}^{k-1}_{++}$ and not $\mathbb{R}^k_{++}$. Similar remarks apply to each mapping $\alpha_i(\theta_i, p)$, and hence the profile $(c_i)_{1 \le i \le n}$ of the competitive mechanism satisfies (4.83) for each agent i when (4.82) holds.

Given (4.82), Theorem 16 and the above mechanism thus together imply that a Walrasian allocation mapping $x^*(\theta)$ lies in a closed and nowhere dense subset of $C^\infty(\Theta, \mathbb{R}^{(n-1)(k-1)})$. As discussed at the beginning of Subsection 4.4.1, a mechanism that realizes a mapping is easily adapted to define a mechanism that realizes a given component function of the mapping. Consequently, for each agent i and each good j, the function that specifies agent i's allocation of good j in the Walrasian equilibrium for each $\theta \in \Theta$ lies in a closed and nowhere dense subset of $C^\infty(\Theta, \mathbb{R})$. The proof of Theorem 16 in fact shows that there exists a nontrivial polynomial equation that the derivatives of this function must satisfy.

The nongenericity of the allocation mapping $x^*(\theta)$ contrasts with a market excess demand mapping $\mathcal{E} : \Delta \to \mathbb{R}^k$, which specifies the aggregate excess demand for n agents in each of k goods for each price vector in Δ. The results of Debreu (1974), Mantel (1974), and Sonnenschein (1972, 1973) show that almost any mapping on the interior of the price simplex can represent excess demand for a well-behaved trading economy (as long as Walras' law holds near the boundary of Δ). A Walrasian allocation mapping of an exchange economy thus has special properties that distinguish it from arbitrary mappings while the excess demand mapping has almost no distinguishing characteristics. Beyond the statement that the Walrasian allocation mapping can be realized using a message space whose dimension is abnormally small relative to the dimension of the agents' private parameters, little else is known about the explicit mathematical properties that distinguish this mapping.[30]

4.6 Example: Prices in Terms of Endowments

Section 4.5 addressed the Walrasian allocation as a function of the agents' preferences. This section concerns Walrasian prices as functions of the

---

[30] Chen's bound (4.35) applies only in the case of $n = 2$. This bound also fails to provide any equations on the derivatives of the component functions of $x^*(\cdot)$ if the dimension $2(k-1)$ of the competitive message space in the case of $n = 2$ is at least as large as $\min\{\dim \Theta_1, \dim \Theta_2\} + 1$, which is the maximal dimension of the bordered mixed Hessian of a component function of $x^*(\cdot)$.

agents' initial endowments holding their preferences fixed. Explicit, non-trivial equations on the first and second derivatives of the price functions are derived that are independent of the preferences. These equations are analogous to the bordered mixed Hessian equation of Theorem 15.

The model of a mechanism that is the focus of this text originated in Hurwicz's effort to formalize Hayek's argument that competitive markets are informationally efficient. A crucial aspect of this problem is that the private information $\theta_i \in \Theta_i$ of agent i may be so vast in size that it cannot be communicated. Information concerning agent i's preferences is the motivating example. In the interest of obtaining results on observable parameters, this section assumes that $\theta_i \in \Theta_i \subset \mathbb{R}^k_{++}$ is agent i's endowment of the k goods. The dimension of each Θ_i need not be large in this discussion and the private knowledge of θ_i by agent i is not the issue. The mathematics of realizing a Walrasian price vector $p(\theta)$ remain applicable, however, and imply equations on $p(\theta)$. This is true despite any issues of interpretation concerning the competitive mechanism in this example.

This section is inspired by efforts in recent years to develop testable implications of general equilibrium theory. Properties of a mapping between observables in an exchange economy (e.g., initial allocations and prices) are derived in this section that may provide a theoretical basis for a comparative statics test of general equilibrium. Brown and Matzkin (1996) revived interest in the problem of deriving testable implications of general equilibrium theory by proving the existence of an algebraic system that n data points, each consisting of an initial allocation and an equilibrium price vector, necessarily satisfy. The following excerpt from their paper describes the objective of their work and the unsuccessful prior attempts to derive testable results concerning Walrasian equilibria:

Comparative statics is the primary source of testable restrictions in economic theory. This mode of analysis is most highly developed within the theory of the household and the theory of the firm, e.g., Slutsky's equation, Shephard's lemma, etc. As is well known from the Sonnenschein–Debreu–Mantel theorem, the Slutsky restrictions on individual excess demand functions do not extend to market excess demand functions. In particular, utility maximization subject to a budget constraint imposes no testable restrictions on the set of equilibrium prices, as shown by Mas-Colell (1977). The disappointing attempts of Walras, Hicks, and Samuelson to derive comparative statics for the general equilibrium model are chronicled in Ingrao and Israel (1990). Moreover, there has been no substantive progress in this field since Arrow and Hahn's discussion of monotone comparative statics for the Walrasian model (1971) (Brown and Matzkin, 1996, p. 1249).

This passage expresses the larger aims of this section. The equations on the derivatives of the Walrasian price mapping derived here depend fundamentally on the interaction of multiple agents in the competitive mechanism and are not derivable by considering the behavior of an individual agent. As in the rest of this text, the equations are derived using differential techniques and hence do not directly address finite observations of endowments and prices (as in Brown and Matzkin, 1996). It would thus be exaggerating to describe these equations as testable. They are, however, quite strong relative to other results in the literature on Walrasian equilibrium in terms of observable variables.[31, 32] Testability may depend on first achieving a deeper understanding of the relationship between Walrasian equilibrium and the endowment, and the results of this section clearly contribute in this sense.

I begin in Subsection 4.6.1 by discussing a modified version of the competitive mechanism that realizes a net trade vector for each agent and the price vector in a Walrasian equilibrium for each choice of the endowment. This modified competitive mechanism is discussed first in the most general form of a mechanism of Section 1.1 and then with the regularity conditions of this text. The remainder of this section then derives the equations that prices as functions of initial endowments must satisfy. Corresponding equations on the derivatives of the net trade mapping follow immediately from the equations on prices.

The equations on the derivatives of the price mapping are developed over four cases presented in Subsections 4.6.3–4.6.6. By following the same approach as in Subsection 4.2.1, the first case derives an equation for $k = 2$ goods and an arbitrary number n of agents. The second case then illustrates this equation in the case of Cobb–Douglas utility. The third case derives the

---

[31] The characterization of endowments as observable can be criticized on the grounds that agents may privately know their endowments and may choose to misreport or withold these quantities of goods. An agent's endowment, however, is both *physically demonstrable* and *communicable*, which is typically not true of preference information. It is also the case that endowments are easily assigned in an experimental setting while preferences of a subject are difficult to experimentally determine or control. All these points argue in favor of basing a comparative statics test of general equilibrium theory on endowments as the changing variables as opposed to agents' preferences.

[32] Chiappori et al. (2004) precedes the work of this section in addressing an endowment – competitive price mapping $p(\theta)$ using calculus (as opposed to the discrete methodology of Brown and Matzkin, 1996). Chiappori et al. derive an equation on the first derivatives of $p(\theta)$ (Eq. (6) in their paper) and variables that are interpreted as income effects; unlike this section, they do not succeed in deriving equations on $p(\theta)$ alone. It is worth noting that Equation (6) of their paper originates in a different aspect of Walrasian equilibrium (individual utility maximization) than the equations of this section (the informational decentralization of the competitive mechanism). It is thus likely that Equation (6) of Chiappori et al. complements the equations derived here. The relationship between the equations of this text and Equation (6) of Chiappori et al. remains to be fully clarified.

equations for $n = 2$ agents and $k = 3$ goods. This derivation illustrates the methodology of the general case, which is covered in Subsection 4.6.6. The simplest way of deriving the equations in the general case applies the methodology of *Differential Ideal*. This methodology is therefore used in the third and the fourth cases of this section.

4.6.1 The Competitive Mechanism with Net Trades as Messages

A C^∞, increasing, and strictly concave utility function $U_i(x_i)$ is fixed for each agent in this discussion, where $x_i \in \mathbb{R}^k_{++}$ denotes a bundle of $k \geq 2$ goods. The vector $\theta_i \in \Theta_i \subset \mathbb{R}^k_{++}$ is agent i's endowment. The price vector p is normalized in this section to lie in the $(k - 1)$-dimensional price simplex $\Delta \subset \mathbb{R}^k_+$. The competitive mechanism in terms of net trades is as follows:

$$M = \left\{ (m,\, p) \in \mathbb{R}^{kn} \times O^\Delta \;\middle|\; \begin{array}{c} \sum_{i=1}^n m_i = 0, \\ p \cdot m_i = 0,\, 1 \leq i \leq n \end{array} \right\};$$

for each agent i,

$$\mu_i(\theta_i) = \left\{ (m,\, p) \;\middle|\; m_i \in \arg\max_{m_i \in \mathbb{R}^k} U_i\,(m_i + \theta_i) \text{ s.t. } p \cdot m_i = 0 \right\}, \quad (4.92)$$

$$\zeta(m,\, p) \equiv (m,\, p).$$

The vector $m_i \in \mathbb{R}^k$ represents a net trade of agent i. Agent i's message correspondence $\mu_i(\cdot)$ specifies for each θ_i those pairs $(m,\, p)$ that are consistent with his excess demand correspondence given his endowment θ_i (i.e., the allocation $m_i + \theta_i$ maximizes agent i's utility given θ_i). An element $(m,\, p) \in M$ lies in $\mu(\theta) = \bigcap_{i=1}^n \mu_i(\theta_i)$ if and only if it is a Walrasian equilibrium for the economy determined by θ. It is clear that the mechanism (4.92) realizes the correspondence

$$F^* : \Theta \to \mathbb{R}^{nk} \times \Delta \qquad (4.93)$$

that specifies the set of Walrasian equilibria for each endowment θ.

This general version of the competitive mechanism is presented here to demonstrate that F^* has an unusual property.[33] For arbitrary initial allocations θ and θ', let θ'' denote any endowment for the trading economy that satisfies

$$\theta_i'' = \theta_i \text{ or } \theta_i' \text{ for each agent } i. \qquad (4.94)$$

---

[33] The following analysis applies a methodology that originates in Mount and Reiter (1974).

The correspondence F^* has the following property:

$$\text{if } (m, p) \in F^*(\theta) \cap F^*(\theta'), \text{ then } (m, p) \in F^* (\theta'') . \qquad (4.95)$$

Property (4.95) is true because

$$(m, p) \in F^*(\theta) \cap F^*(\theta') = \mu(\theta) \cap \mu(\theta')$$

$$= \left(\bigcap_{i=1}^{n} \mu_i(\theta_i) \right) \cap \left(\bigcap_{i=1}^{n} \mu_i(\theta_i') \right) \qquad (4.96)$$

$$\subset \bigcap_{i=1}^{n} \mu_i(\theta_i'') = \mu(\theta'') = F^*(\theta'').$$

The last inclusion holds because $\theta_i'' = \theta_i$ or θ_i'. Property (4.95) stems directly from the fact that F^* is realized by the competitive mechanism as given in (4.92). It is clearly a property that is not satisfied by an arbitrary correspondence F with the same domain and range as F^*. This property of F^* is noteworthy because it requires no additional assumptions on the economy besides those sufficient to insure existence of Walrasian equilibrium.

The regularity assumptions on mechanisms of this text are now imposed on the competitive mechanism. Assume that there exists C^∞ mappings $\chi_i(\cdot), \ldots, \chi_n(\cdot)$ and $p(\cdot)$ along with an open subset $O^\Delta \subset Int \ \Delta$ with the following properties:

(i) For each $1 \leq i \leq n$, $\chi_i : \Theta_i \times O^\Delta \to \mathbb{R}^k$ is agent i's excess demand mapping,

$$\chi_i (\theta_i, p) = \arg \max_{x_i} U_i (\Delta x_i + \theta_i) \text{ s.t. } p \cdot \Delta x_i = 0. \qquad (4.97)$$

(ii) The C^∞ mapping $p : \Theta \to O^\Delta$ determines the unique price vector $p(\theta) \in O^\Delta$ for θ for which the net trade vector $\chi_i((\theta_i, p(\theta)))_{1 \leq i \leq n}$ is *feasible*,

$$\sum_{i=1}^{n} \chi_i (\theta_i, p(\theta)) = 0.$$

(iii) The regularity condition

$$\text{rank } D_{\theta_i} \chi_i (\theta_i, p(\theta)) = k - 1 \qquad (4.98)$$

holds for $\theta \in \Theta$.

Conditions (i)–(ii) insure that

$$\left((\chi_i (\theta_i, p(\theta)))_{1 \leq i \leq n}, p(\theta) \right) \qquad (4.99)$$

is the only Walrasian equilibrium for the exchange economy defined by θ whose price vector lies in O^Δ. Notice that this is strictly weaker than assuming uniqueness of Walrasian equilibrium for θ.[34]

Let $\Lambda(\theta)$ denote the Walrasian equilibrium net trade mapping,

$$\Lambda(\theta) \equiv (\chi_i\,(\theta_i,\, p\,(\theta)))_{1\leq i\leq n}$$
$$\equiv \left(\Lambda_{q,t}\right)_{1\leq q\leq n,\, 1\leq t\leq k},$$

so that $\Lambda_{q,t}(\theta)$ is agent q's net trade of good t in the equilibrium determined by θ. At issue in the remainder of this section is the realization of $(\Lambda,\, p)$.

Using (i)–(iii), the competitive mechanism (4.92) is now modified to the form needed in this section:

$$M = \left\{ (m,\, p) \in \mathbb{R}^{kn} \times O^\Delta \,\middle|\, \begin{array}{c} \sum_{i=1}^{n} m_i = 0, \\ p \cdot m_i = 0,\, 1 \leq i \leq n \end{array} \right\},$$

$$\alpha_i(\theta_i,\, m,\, p) = \chi_i\,(\theta_i,\, p) - m_i = 0 \text{ for each agent } i, \qquad (4.100)$$

$$\zeta\,(m,\, p) \equiv (m,\, p).$$

The argument of Section 4.5 shows that the profile $(c_i)_{1\leq i\leq n}$ of the mechanism (4.100) satisfies $c_i = k - 1 < \dim \Theta_i$ for each i. Applying Theorem 16, this implies the nongenericity of both $p(\theta)$ and $\Lambda(\theta)$ and the existence of equations on their derivatives. The remainder of this section is devoted to deriving some of these equations.

4.6.2 *Product Structure, Direct Sum, and Differential Ideal* in Realizing Walrasian Prices

I begin in this subsection by discussing *Product Structure, Direct Sum,* and *Differential Ideal* as determined by the competitive mechanism (4.100). This is a suitable starting point because the equations on the derivatives of $p(\theta)$

---

[34] Results of Debreu (1970) imply that there exists for any endowment θ^* outside some closed null subset of $\mathbb{R}^{nk}_+$ an open neighborhood $O(\theta^*)$ and C^∞ mappings $p^1, \ldots, p^\ell$ from $O(\theta^*)$ into Δ that define the Walrasian equilibria for $\theta \in O(\theta^*)$: $p \in \Delta$ is a Walrasian equilibrium for $\theta \in O(\theta^*)$ if and only if $p = p^t(\theta)$ for some t. This is proven using assumption (i) above together with Debreu's assumption (A), which requires that the excess demand mapping $\chi_i(\theta_i, p)$ of at least one agent i has the property that $|\chi_i(\theta_i, p)|$ goes to infinity as the price of any good goes to zero. Walrasian equilibrium price vectors are thus isolated in Δ and vary smoothly with the endowment except at degenerate endowments. In this sense, (i) above implies (ii) and the price mapping p in (ii) is simply the selection of one of the mappings $p^1, \ldots, p^\ell$. Because Debreu (1970) assumes only that excess demand mappings are C^1, the price mappings $p^1, \ldots, p^\ell$ are C^1 in his paper. His results are easily altered to the C^∞ case discussed here.

that are derived in this section express the integrability of the distribution $\mathcal{D} = \oplus_{i=1}^{n}\mathcal{D}_i$ of *Direct Sum* and the differentiability of the ideal $\mathcal{I} = \cap_{i=1}^{n}\mathcal{I}_i$ of *Differential Ideal*. This subsection also identifies the dependence between the derivatives of the price mapping $p(\theta)$ and the net trade mapping $\Lambda(\theta)$. This dependence allows the following subsections to focus mainly on the derivatives of $p(\theta)$ alone and not $\Lambda(\theta)$.

Product Structure in the Competitive Mechanism
Let $\theta' \in \Theta$ and let (m', p') denote the equilibrium message for θ'. The set $S_i^*(\theta')$ is by definition the level set in Θ_i of agent i's excess demand mapping,

$$S_i^*(\theta') = \left\{\theta_i \,\middle|\, \alpha_i(\theta_i, m', p') = 0\right\}$$
$$= \left\{\theta_i \,\middle|\, \chi_i(\theta_i, p') - m_i' = 0\right\}. \tag{4.101}$$

The regularity condition (4.98) on excess demand insures that each $S_i^*(\theta')$ is a 1-dimensional submanifold of Θ_i.

An alternative characterization of $S_i^*(\theta')$ is now provided that will be useful in the derivations that follow in this section. It is now shown that

$$S_i^*(\theta') = \left\{\theta_i \,\middle|\, p\left(\theta_i, \theta'_{-i}\right) = p'\right\}. \tag{4.102}$$

It is clear that the set on the left side of (4.102) is contained in the set on the right side because the mechanism (4.100) realizes $p(\theta)$. Conversely, if θ_i lies in the set on the right side of (4.102), then

$$\chi_i(\theta_i, p') = -\sum_{j \neq i} \chi_j\left(\theta_j', p'\right) \tag{4.103}$$

because p' is a Walrasian equilibrium price vector for the endowment (θ_i, θ'_{-i}). The right side of (4.103) equals $\chi_i(\theta_i', p')$ because $p(\theta') = p'$. Consequently,

$$\chi_i(\theta_i, p') = \chi_i\left(\theta_i', p'\right) = m_i', \tag{4.104}$$

and so $\theta_i \in S_i^*(\theta')$.

The alternative formula (4.102) for $S_i^*(\theta')$ implies an alternative to the regularity condition (4.98) on excess demand. The matrix

$$D_{\theta_i} p = \left(\frac{\partial p_t}{\partial \theta_{i,s}}\right)_{1 \leq t \leq k, 1 \leq s \leq \dim \Theta_i} \tag{4.105}$$

has rank less than k because $p \in \Delta$. The regularity condition

$$\mathrm{rank}\ D_{\theta_i} p = k - 1 \tag{4.106}$$

on $p(\theta)$ is sufficient to insure that $S_i^*(\theta')$ is a 1-dimensional submanifold of Θ_i. Condition (4.106) is used below instead of (4.98) to insure that the competitive mechanism defines a *Product Structure* in the sense of this text.[35]

For notational simplicity, it is commonly assumed in the remainder of this section that the first $k-1$ rows of $D_{\theta_i} p$ are linearly independent. Let $p_{-k} : \Theta \to \mathbb{R}^{k-1}$ denote the mapping that consists of all prices in $p(\theta)$ except the price of the kth good,

$$p_{-k} = (p_1, p_2, \ldots, p_{k-1}). \tag{4.107}$$

For any agent i, the derivative $D_{\theta_i} p_{-k}$ is represented here by the $(k-1) \times \dim \Theta_i$ matrix

$$D_{\theta_i} p_{-k} \equiv \left(\frac{\partial p_t}{\partial \theta_{i,s}} \right)_{1 \le t \le k-1, 1 \le s \le \dim \Theta_i}. \tag{4.108}$$

The regularity assumption (4.106) is thus specified below to

$$\text{rank } D_{\theta_i} p_{-k} = k - 1 \quad \text{for each agent } i \tag{4.109}$$

as a matter of notational convenience.

Direct Sum, Differential Ideal, and Equations on the Net Trade Mapping $\Lambda(\theta)$

An interesting aspect of (4.102) and (4.109) for the purposes of this section is that they allow the distributions of *Direct Sum* and the differential ideals of *Differential Ideal* determined by the competitive mechanism (4.100) to be expressed purely in terms of the derivatives of $p(\theta)$ and not $\Lambda(\theta)$. Equations on the derivatives of $\Lambda(\theta)$ can then be derived using the derivatives of $p(\theta)$ as coefficients.[36] This explains why the rest of this section mostly concerns $p(\theta)$.

The equations on $\Lambda(\theta)$ are as follows. Given the regularity condition (4.109), and reflecting the fact that agent q's net trade $\Lambda_{q,t}$ in good t is

---

[35] The value of (4.106) over condition (4.98) on the excess demand functions lies in the exercise of examining a candidate mapping $p : \Theta \to \Delta$ to determine whether or not it is a Walrasian equilibrium price mapping for some exchange economy. One does not know in this exercise the preferences or the excess demand functions of the traders, for they are in fact the unknowns that are sought. Condition (4.106) allows one to apply the analysis that follows given only $p(\theta)$ and not $(\chi_i)_{1 \le i \le n}$.

[36] This is not surprising given the result of Chiappori et al. (2004, Thm. 6) that a generic price mapping $p(\theta)$ determines the agents' preferences and hence also their excess demand functions.

constant on each set $S_i^*(\theta) \times \{\theta_{-i}\}$, the vector

$$D_{\theta_i} \Lambda_{q,t} \equiv \left(\frac{\partial \Lambda_{q,t}}{\partial \theta_{i,s}} \right)_{1 \le s \le \dim \Theta_i} \tag{4.110}$$

must be expressible as a linear combination of the rows of the matrix $D_{\theta_i} p_{-k}$. This is equivalent to

$$\det \begin{pmatrix} D_{\theta_i} p_{-k} \\ D_{\theta_i} \Lambda_{q,t} \end{pmatrix} = 0 \tag{4.111}$$

holding for each agent q and each good t. Beyond (4.111), there will be no further need to address the derivatives of $\Lambda(\theta)$.

Turning next to *Direct Sum*, the 1-dimensional distribution $\mathcal{D}_i(\theta)$ is spanned by any nonzero vector field

$$X_i^*(\theta) \in T_\theta (\Theta_i \times \{\theta_{-i}\}) \tag{4.112}$$

that lies in the kernel of $D_{\theta_i} p_{-k}$ when this matrix is interpreted as a linear transformation on $T_\theta (\Theta_i \times \{\theta_{-i}\})$. The integrability of $\mathcal{D} = \oplus_{i=1}^n \mathcal{D}_i$ is equivalent to the $n(n-1)$ equations

$$\left[X_i^*, X_j^* \right] \in \mathcal{D} \tag{4.113}$$

for $1 \le i \ne j \le n$. These equations can be expressed in terms of the first and second derivatives of $p(\theta)$ by expressing each $X_i^*(\theta)$ in terms of the partial derivatives that define $D_{\theta_i} p_{-k}$. This is the approach taken in Subsection 4.6.3 below. Equations could also be derived in terms of $\Lambda(\theta)$ by expressing each $X_i^*(\theta)$ in terms of its derivatives. Given the regularity condition (4.109), however, all such equations are redundant to the system of equations given by (4.111) and the equations on $p(\theta)$ derived from (4.113), for they are simply alternative expressions of the integrability of the direct sum $\mathcal{D}$. Equations of this kind are illustrated, however, in the next subsection.

Turning to *Differential Ideal*, the regularity condition (4.109) implies that the 1-forms

$$d_i p_l = \sum_{t=1}^{\dim \Theta_i} \frac{\partial p_l}{\partial \theta_{i,t}} d\theta_{i,t} \tag{4.114}$$

for goods $1 \le l \le k - 1$ are independent. The ideal $\mathcal{I}_i$ is thus generated by the 1-forms in the set

$$\{d_i p_l \,|\, 1 \le l \le k - 1\} \cup \{d\theta_{j,t} \,|\, 1 \le j \ne i \le n, 1 \le t \le \dim \Theta_j\}. \tag{4.115}$$

The ideal $\mathcal{I} = \cap_{i=1}^{n} \mathcal{I}_i$ is therefore generated by the $n(k-1)$ 1-forms

$$\bigcup_{i=1}^{n} \{d_i \, p_l \, | \, 1 \leq l \leq k-1\}. \tag{4.116}$$

The differentiability of $\mathcal{I}$ is equivalent to the requirement that $d(d_j \, p_t)$ is in the set of 2-forms generated by (4.116) for each $1 \leq j \leq n$ and $1 \leq t \leq k-1$.[37] The objective of Subsections 4.6.5 and 4.6.6 below is to find a more convenient representation of this requirement.

4.6.3 $k = 2$ Goods and n Agents

The relevant equations are derived in this subsection in the case of $k = 2$ goods and n agents. Good 2 is a numèraire. Because only one price is considered, the superscript 1 is omitted and the price of good 1 is denoted simply as p. Define for each agent i the vector field

$$D_{\theta_i} \, p \equiv \frac{\partial p}{\partial \theta_{i,1}} \frac{\partial}{\partial \theta_{i,1}} + \frac{\partial p}{\partial \theta_{i,2}} \frac{\partial}{\partial \theta_{i,2}}. \tag{4.117}$$

Consistent with (4.109), assume for now that each of these n vector fields is nonzero.

Applying Theorem 12, the realization of $p(\theta)$ by the mechanism (4.100) implies the existence of 1-dimensional distributions $\mathcal{D}_1, \ldots, \mathcal{D}_n$ satisfying *Direct Sum* such that

$$D_\theta \, p \cdot X_i = 0 \tag{4.118}$$

for all $X_i \in \mathcal{D}_i$ and $1 \leq i \leq n$. Equation (4.118) is equivalent to

$$D_{\theta_i} \, p \cdot X_i = 0 \tag{4.119}$$

because $\mathcal{D}_i \subset T_\theta(\Theta_i \times \theta_{-i})$. Define for each agent i the vector field

$$X_i^* = \frac{\partial p}{\partial \theta_{i,2}} \frac{\partial}{\partial \theta_{i,1}} - \frac{\partial p}{\partial \theta_{i,1}} \frac{\partial}{\partial \theta_{i,2}}. \tag{4.120}$$

Because $D_{\theta_i} \, p \neq 0$, Equation (4.119) implies that the distribution $\mathcal{D}_i$ is spanned by X_i^*. The integrability of $\mathcal{D} = \oplus_{i=1}^{n} \mathcal{D}_i$ is therefore equivalent to

$$\left[X_i^*, X_j^* \right] \in \mathcal{D} \tag{4.121}$$

for all $1 \leq i \neq j \leq n$.

---

[37] The primary reason that the equations are derived below in the general case using the approach of *Differential Ideal* is that it directly implies the desired equations on the first and second derivatives of $p(\theta)$. In contrast, the approach using *Direct Sum* requires that one first select $X_i^*(\theta)$ orthogonal to each of the rows of $D_{\theta_i} \, p_{-k}$. This step is feasible but tedious, and so I follow the direct approach using *Differential Ideal*.

It is clear from formula (2.6) for the Lie bracket that $[X_i^*, X_j^*] \in \mathcal{D}_i \oplus \mathcal{D}_j$. Equation (4.121) therefore requires that $[X_i^*, X_j^*]$ is expressible as a linear combination of X_i^* and X_j^*. At this point, the analysis is identical to the reduction between Equations (4.25) and (4.33) in Subsection 4.2.1: $[X_i^*, X_j^*]$ can be written as a linear combination of X_i^* and X_j^* if and only if $p(\theta)$ satisfies the now familiar equation

$$\det \begin{pmatrix} 0 & \frac{\partial p}{\partial \theta_{j,1}} & \frac{\partial p}{\partial \theta_{j,2}} \\ \frac{\partial p}{\partial \theta_{i,1}} & \frac{\partial^2 p}{\partial \theta_{i,1} \partial \theta_{j,1}} & \frac{\partial^2 p}{\partial \theta_{i,1} \partial \theta_{j,2}} \\ \frac{\partial p}{\partial \theta_{i,2}} & \frac{\partial^2 p}{\partial \theta_{i,2} \partial \theta_{j,1}} & \frac{\partial^2 p}{\partial \theta_{i,2} \partial \theta_{j,2}} \end{pmatrix} = 0. \tag{4.122}$$

It was assumed in (4.109) that $D_{\theta_i} p \neq 0$; notice that (4.122) holds trivially if $D_{\theta_1} p$ or $D_{\theta_2} p$ is the zero vector. The mapping $p(\theta)$ therefore satisfies this equation for all $1 \le i \neq j \le n$ regardless of whether or not the regularity condition (4.109) holds.

The realization of agent q's equilibrium net trade $\Lambda_{q,t}(\theta)$ of good t is considered next. The same analysis that was applied to $p(\theta)$ above implies that

$$X_i^{**} \equiv \frac{\partial \Lambda_{q,t}}{\partial \theta_{i,2}} \frac{\partial}{\partial \theta_{i,1}} - \frac{\partial \Lambda_{q,t}}{\partial \theta_{i,1}} \frac{\partial}{\partial \theta_{i,2}} \in \mathcal{D}_i.$$

Alternatives to (4.122) include

$$\det \begin{pmatrix} 0 & \frac{\partial \Lambda_{q,t}}{\partial \theta_{j,1}} & \frac{\partial \Lambda_{q,t}}{\partial \theta_{j,2}} \\ \frac{\partial \Lambda_{q,t}}{\partial \theta_{i,1}} & \frac{\partial^2 p}{\partial \theta_{i,1} \partial \theta_{j,1}} & \frac{\partial^2 p}{\partial \theta_{i,1} \partial \theta_{j,2}} \\ \frac{\partial \Lambda_{q,t}}{\partial \theta_{i,2}} & \frac{\partial^2 p}{\partial \theta_{i,2} \partial \theta_{j,1}} & \frac{\partial^2 p}{\partial \theta_{i,2} \partial \theta_{j,2}} \end{pmatrix} = 0, \tag{4.123}$$

$$\det \begin{pmatrix} 0 & \frac{\partial p}{\partial \theta_{j,1}} & \frac{\partial p}{\partial \theta_{j,2}} \\ \frac{\partial p}{\partial \theta_{i,1}} & \frac{\partial^2 \Lambda_{q,t}}{\partial \theta_{i,1} \partial \theta_{j,1}} & \frac{\partial^2 \Lambda_{q,t}}{\partial \theta_{i,1} \partial \theta_{j,2}} \\ \frac{\partial p}{\partial \theta_{i,2}} & \frac{\partial^2 \Lambda_{q,t}}{\partial \theta_{i,2} \partial \theta_{j,1}} & \frac{\partial^2 \Lambda_{q,t}}{\partial \theta_{i,2} \partial \theta_{j,2}} \end{pmatrix} = 0, \tag{4.124}$$

or

$$\det \begin{pmatrix} 0 & \frac{\partial \Lambda_{q,t}}{\partial \theta_{j,1}} & \frac{\partial \Lambda_{q,t}}{\partial \theta_{j,2}} \\ \frac{\partial \Lambda_{q,t}}{\partial \theta_{i,1}} & \frac{\partial^2 \Lambda_{q,t}}{\partial \theta_{i,1} \partial \theta_{j,1}} & \frac{\partial^2 \Lambda_{q,t}}{\partial \theta_{i,1} \partial \theta_{j,2}} \\ \frac{\partial \Lambda_{q,t}}{\partial \theta_{i,2}} & \frac{\partial^2 \Lambda_{q,t}}{\partial \theta_{i,2} \partial \theta_{j,1}} & \frac{\partial^2 \Lambda_{q,t}}{\partial \theta_{i,2} \partial \theta_{j,2}} \end{pmatrix} = 0. \tag{4.125}$$

Equation (4.123) is derived from the requirement that $[X_i^*, X_j^*] \in \mathcal{D}_i \oplus \mathcal{D}_j$ by taking X_i^{**} as the basis of $\mathcal{D}_i$ and X_j^{**} as the basis of $\mathcal{D}_j$. Equation (4.124) is derived from the requirement that $[X_i^{**}, X_j^{**}] \in \mathcal{D}_i \oplus \mathcal{D}_j$ by taking X_i^* as the basis of $\mathcal{D}_i$ and X_j^* as the basis of $\mathcal{D}_j$. Finally, (4.125) is derived from the requirement that $[X_i^{**}, X_j^{**}] \in \mathcal{D}_i \oplus \mathcal{D}_j$ by taking X_i^{**} as the basis of $\mathcal{D}_i$ and X_j^{**} as the basis of $\mathcal{D}_j$. While perhaps interesting, Equations (4.123)–(4.125) and all others that may be derived in this way are redundant in the sense that they simply restate the integrability of $\mathcal{D} = \oplus_{i=1}^n \mathcal{D}_i$.

4.6.4 The Case of Cobb–Douglas Utility

The utility functions were not specified in the analysis of Subsection 4.6.3 and they do not appear in Equation (4.122). They are effectively variables that are eliminated in deriving (4.122). It can be reassuring, however, to verify that (4.122) holds in the case of particular utility functions for which $p(\theta)$ can be explicitly computed. This is accomplished here using a Cobb–Douglas utility function for each agent.

Let

$$U_1(x_{11}, x_{12}) = x_{11}^\delta x_{12}^{1-\delta}$$

and

$$U_2(x_{21}, x_{22}) = x_{21}^\gamma x_{22}^{1-\gamma},$$

for $\delta, \gamma \in (0, 1)$. A property of this utility function is that δ is the proportion of agent 1's income that he spends on good 1 and γ is the proportion that agent 2 spends on good 1. Consequently,

$$px_{11} = \delta(p\theta_{1,1} + \theta_{1,2}),$$
$$px_{21} = \gamma(p\theta_{2,1} + \theta_{2,2}),$$

where x_{i1} is agent i's demand for good 1 at the price p. Summing these two equations produces

$$p(x_{11} + x_{21}) = p(\delta\theta_{1,1} + \gamma\theta_{2,1}) + (\delta\theta_{1,2} + \partial\theta_{2,2}). \qquad (4.126)$$

The equation

$$x_{11} + x_{21} = \theta_{1,1} + \theta_{2,1}$$

is required for Walrasian equilibriuim. Substitution into (4.126) and simplifying implies

$$p\left[(1 - \delta)\theta_{1,1} + (1 - \gamma)\theta_{2,1}\right] = \delta\theta_{1,2} + \gamma\theta_{2,2},$$

and so

$$p(\theta) = \frac{\delta\theta_{1,2} + \gamma\theta_{2,2}}{(1 - \delta)\theta_{1,1} + (1 - \gamma)\theta_{2,1}}. \qquad (4.127)$$

It is now verified that (4.122) holds in the case of Cobb–Douglas utility. For notational convenience, let

$$B(\theta_{1,1}, \theta_{2,1}) \equiv (1 - \delta)\theta_{1,1} + (1 - \gamma)\theta_{2,1}.$$

Substitution into (4.122) produces

$$\frac{1}{B(\theta_{1,1}, \theta_{2,1})^2}$$

$$\times \begin{pmatrix} 0 & -(1 - \gamma)\left(\delta\theta_{1,2} + \gamma\theta_{2,2}\right) & \gamma B(\theta_{1,1}, \theta_{2,1}) \\ -(1 - \delta)\left(\delta\theta_{1,2} + \gamma\theta_{2,2}\right) & 2(1 - \delta)(1 - \gamma)p(\theta) & -\gamma(1 - \delta) \\ \delta B(\theta_{1,1}, \theta_{2,1}) & -\delta(1 - \gamma) & 0 \end{pmatrix}.$$

Consider the following sequence of operations on the above matrix: (i) multiply column 3 by $1/\gamma$; multiply column 2 by $1/(1 - \gamma)$; multiply row 2 by $1/(1 - \delta)$; multiply row 3 by $1/\delta$; add $1/B(\theta_{1,1}, \theta_{2,1})$ times column 1 to column 2; add $1/B(\theta_{1,1}, \theta_{2,1})$ times row 1 to row 2. This sequence of row and column operations produces the matrix

$$\begin{pmatrix} 0 & -\left(\delta\theta_{1,2} + \gamma\theta_{2,2}\right) & (1 - \delta)\theta_{1,1} + (1 - \gamma)\theta_{2,1} \\ -\left(\delta\theta_{1,2} + \gamma\theta_{2,2}\right) & 0 & 0 \\ (1 - \delta)\theta_{1,1} + (1 - \gamma)\theta_{2,1} & 0 & 0 \end{pmatrix},$$

which clearly has rank of 2 or less. Consequently, the price $p(\theta)$ as solved for in (4.127) satisfies (4.122).

4.6.5 $k = 3$ Goods and $n = 2$ Agents

The special case considered in this subsection illustrates the derivation in the general case. The first step is to specialize several observations that were made in Subsection 4.6.2. Let $p = (p_1, p_2, p_3)$. The regularity condition

(4.109) assumes that $d_i\, p_1$ and $d_i\, p_2$ are linearly independent for each agent i. The ideal $\mathcal{I}_i$ is generated by the 1-forms in

$$\{d_i\, p_1,\, d_i\, p_2\} \cup \{d\theta_{-i,t}\,|\,1 \le t \le 3\}, \tag{4.128}$$

which is a special case of (4.115). The ideal $\mathcal{I} = \mathcal{I}_1 \cap \mathcal{I}_2$ is generated by the 1-forms in

$$\{d_1\, p_1,\, d_1\, p_2,\, d_2\, p_1,\, d_2\, p_2\}, \tag{4.129}$$

which is a special case of (4.116). A necessary and sufficient condition for the differentiability of $\mathcal{I}$ is that

$$d\,(d_i\, p_l) \in \mathcal{I} \tag{4.130}$$

for $i, l = 1, 2$. For fixed l,

$$
\begin{aligned}
d\,(d_2\, p_l) &= -d\,(d_1\, p_l) \\
&= \frac{\partial^2 p_l}{\partial\theta_{1,1}\partial\theta_{2,1}}d\theta_{1,1} \wedge d\theta_{2,1} + \frac{\partial^2 p_l}{\partial\theta_{1,1}\partial\theta_{2,2}}d\theta_{1,1} \wedge d\theta_{2,2} + \frac{\partial^2 p_l}{\partial\theta_{1,1}\partial\theta_{2,3}}d\theta_{1,1} \wedge d\theta_{2,3} \\
&+ \frac{\partial^2 p_l}{\partial\theta_{1,2}\partial\theta_{2,1}}d\theta_{1,2} \wedge d\theta_{2,1} + \frac{\partial^2 p_l}{\partial\theta_{1,2}\partial\theta_{2,2}}d\theta_{1,2} \wedge d\theta_{2,2} + \frac{\partial^2 p_l}{\partial\theta_{1,2}\partial\theta_{2,3}}d\theta_{1,2} \wedge d\theta_{2,3} \\
&+ \frac{\partial^2 p_l}{\partial\theta_{1,3}\partial\theta_{2,1}}d\theta_{1,3} \wedge d\theta_{2,1} + \frac{\partial^2 p_l}{\partial\theta_{1,3}\partial\theta_{2,2}}d\theta_{1,3} \wedge d\theta_{2,2} + \frac{\partial^2 p_l}{\partial\theta_{1,3}\partial\theta_{2,3}}d\theta_{1,3} \wedge d\theta_{2,3}.
\end{aligned}
\tag{4.131}
$$

The differentiability of $\mathcal{I}$ is in this way reduced to the question of whether or not the 2-forms $d\,(d_2\, p_l)$ for $l = 1, 2$ lie in the set of 2-forms generated by (4.129).

A matrix is helpful in representing this spanning problem. Consider the matrix

$$
BMH_{1,2}(p,\, p_l)
$$

$$
= \begin{pmatrix}
0 & 0 & \dfrac{\partial p_1}{\partial\theta_{2,1}} & \dfrac{\partial p_1}{\partial\theta_{2,2}} & \dfrac{\partial p_1}{\partial\theta_{2,3}} \\[2ex]
0 & 0 & \dfrac{\partial p_2}{\partial\theta_{2,1}} & \dfrac{\partial p_2}{\partial\theta_{2,2}} & \dfrac{\partial p_2}{\partial\theta_{2,3}} \\[2ex]
\dfrac{\partial p_1}{\partial\theta_{1,1}} & \dfrac{\partial p_2}{\partial\theta_{1,1}} & \dfrac{\partial^2 p_l}{\partial\theta_{1,1}\partial\theta_{2,1}} & \dfrac{\partial^2 p_l}{\partial\theta_{1,1}\partial\theta_{2,2}} & \dfrac{\partial^2 p_l}{\partial\theta_{1,1}\partial\theta_{2,3}} \\[2ex]
\dfrac{\partial p_1}{\partial\theta_{1,2}} & \dfrac{\partial p_2}{\partial\theta_{1,2}} & \dfrac{\partial^2 p_l}{\partial\theta_{1,2}\partial\theta_{2,1}} & \dfrac{\partial^2 p_l}{\partial\theta_{1,2}\partial\theta_{2,2}} & \dfrac{\partial^2 p_l}{\partial\theta_{1,2}\partial\theta_{2,3}} \\[2ex]
\dfrac{\partial p_1}{\partial\theta_{1,3}} & \dfrac{\partial p_2}{\partial\theta_{1,3}} & \dfrac{\partial^2 p_l}{\partial\theta_{1,3}\partial\theta_{2,1}} & \dfrac{\partial^2 p_l}{\partial\theta_{1,3}\partial\theta_{2,2}} & \dfrac{\partial^2 p_l}{\partial\theta_{1,3}\partial\theta_{2,3}}
\end{pmatrix}, \tag{4.132}
$$

which generalizes the bordered mixed Hessian of Section 4.2. The issue of whether or not $d\,(d_2\,p_l)$ lies in the set of 2-forms generated by the 1-forms in (4.129) is equivalent to the question of whether or not the matrix (4.132) can be reduced through row and column operations to

$$\begin{pmatrix} 0 & 0 & \frac{\partial p_1}{\partial \theta_{2,1}} & \frac{\partial p_1}{\partial \theta_{2,2}} & \frac{\partial p_1}{\partial \theta_{2,3}} \\ 0 & 0 & \frac{\partial p_2}{\partial \theta_{2,1}} & \frac{\partial p_2}{\partial \theta_{2,2}} & \frac{\partial p_2}{\partial \theta_{2,3}} \\ \frac{\partial p_1}{\partial \theta_{1,1}} & \frac{\partial p_2}{\partial \theta_{1,1}} & 0 & 0 & 0 \\ \frac{\partial p_1}{\partial \theta_{1,2}} & \frac{\partial p_2}{\partial \theta_{1,2}} & 0 & 0 & 0 \\ \frac{\partial p_1}{\partial \theta_{1,3}} & \frac{\partial p_2}{\partial \theta_{1,3}} & 0 & 0 & 0 \end{pmatrix}. \tag{4.133}$$

Multiplying column 2 in (4.132) by a function $\lambda\,(\theta)$ and subtracting it from column 3, for instance, is equivalent to subtracting the 2-form $\lambda\,(\theta)\,d_1\,p_2 \wedge d\theta_{2,1}$ from the 2-form (4.131). Similarly, multiplying row 1 by $\tau\,(\theta)$ and subtracting it from row 5 is equivalent to subtracting the 2-form $\tau\,(\theta)\,d\theta_{1,3} \wedge d_2\,p_1$ from the 2-form (4.131). Given the regularity condition (4.109), the matrix in (4.133) has rank equal to 4. The differentiability of $\mathcal{I}$ is thus equivalent to

$$\det BMH_{1,2}(p,\,p_l) = 0 \tag{4.134}$$

holding for $l = 1, 2$.[38]

The differentiability of $\mathcal{I}$ is equivalent to the two polynomial equations given by (4.134) for $l = 1, 2$. Notice that (4.134) holds trivially if the regularity condition (4.109) does not hold and at least one of the pairs $\{d_1\,p_1, d_1\,p_2\}$ or $\{d_2\,p_1, d_2\,p_2\}$ is linearly dependent. The pair of equations given by (4.134) is thus satisfied wherever $p\,(\theta)$ is a C^∞ mapping, without the regularity condition (4.109) that is used in this derivation.

4.6.6 The General Case

Let Z_t denote the $t \times t$ zero matrix for any $t \in \mathbb{N}$. Recall from Subsection 4.6.2 that $D_{\theta_i}\,p_{-k}$ is defined for each agent i as the $(k - 1) \times \dim \Theta_i$ matrix

$$D_{\theta_i}\,p_{-k} = \left(\frac{\partial p_l}{\partial \theta_{i,t}}\right)_{1 \leq l \leq k-1, 1 \leq t \leq \dim \Theta_i}. \tag{4.135}$$

[38] This argument may suggest a proof of Theorem 15 to the reader.

The equations on $p(\theta)$ in the general case concern the *generalized bordered mixed Hessian* $BMH_{i,j}(p, p_l)$, which is the $(2k - 1) \times (2k - 1)$ matrix

$$BMH_{i,j}(p, p_l) = \begin{pmatrix} Z_{k-1} & D_{\theta_j} p_{-k} \\ \left(D_{\theta_i} p_{-k}\right)^T & D^2_{\theta_i,\theta_j} p_l \end{pmatrix}. \tag{4.136}$$

Theorem 17: *For fixed utility functions of the n agents over the k goods, suppose that the C^∞ mappings $p(\theta)$ and $\Lambda(\theta)$ select a Walrasian equilibrium price vector $p \in \Delta$ and net trade vector $\Lambda \in \mathbb{R}^{kn}$ for each choice $\theta \in \Theta \subset \mathbb{R}^{kn}_{++}$ of endowment for the economy. For any good l and for each pair of distinct agents i and j, the mapping $p(\theta)$ satisfies the equation*

$$\det BMH_{i,j}(p, p_l) = 0, \tag{4.137}$$

where $BMH_{i,j}(p, p_l)$ is defined in (4.136). The equations of the form (4.137) determines a system of $n(n - 1)(k - 1)$ independent equations on the first and second derivatives of $p(\theta)$.

Proof: Equation (4.137) holds trivially if either $D_{\theta_i} p_{-k}$ or $D_{\theta_j} p_{-k}$ has rank less than $k - 1$. Assuming instead that (4.109) holds for each agent so that each of these matrices has full rank equal to $k - 1$, the 1-forms in the set

$$\{d_t p_s \mid 1 \le t \le n, 1 \le s \le k - 1\} \tag{4.138}$$

generate $\mathcal{I} = \cap_{t=1}^n \mathcal{I}_t$. As suggested by the special case of $k = 3$ goods and $n = 2$ agents of Subsection 4.6.5, the equation for the given values of i, j, and l is derived from the requirement that

$$d(d_i p_l) \in \mathcal{I}. \tag{4.139}$$

This requires that

$$\sum_{1 \le s \le \dim \Theta_j} \sum_{1 \le t \le \dim \Theta_i} \frac{\partial^2 p_l}{\partial \theta_{j,s} \partial \theta_{i,t}} d\theta_{j,s} \wedge d\theta_{i,t} \tag{4.140}$$

is a linear combination of the 2-forms in the sets

$$\{d_j p_t \wedge d\theta_{i,s} \mid 1 \le t \le k - 1, 1 \le s \le \dim \Theta_i\}, \tag{4.141}$$

$$\{d_i p_t \wedge d\theta_{j,s} \mid 1 \le t \le k - 1, 1 \le s \le \dim \Theta_j\}. \tag{4.142}$$

Row operations on $BMH_{i,j}(p, p_l)$ involving the rows of $D_{\theta_j} p_{-k}$ and $D^2_{\theta_i,\theta_j} p_l$ correspond to reducing (4.140) using the 2-forms in the set (4.141), while column operations involving the columns of $(D_{\theta_i} p_{-k})^T$ and $D^2_{\theta_i,\theta_j} p_l$ correspond to reducing (4.140) using the 2-forms in the set (4.142). The requirement (4.139) thus implies that $BMH_{i,j}(p, p_l)$ can be reduced through row and column operations to

$$
\begin{pmatrix}
Z_{k-1} & D_{\theta_j} p_{-k} \\
\left(D_{\theta_i} p_{-k}\right)^T & Z_k
\end{pmatrix}.
\tag{4.143}
$$

This is equivalent to

$$
\text{rank } BMH_{i,j}(p, p_l) = 2k - 2,
\tag{4.144}
$$

which implies (4.137). ∎

4.7 Example: Team Decision Problems

Following Marshak and Radner (1972), a *team* is a group of n agents who share a common objective.[39] The agents may be impeded in their collective effort by the dispersal among themselves of information relevant to achieving the objective. The goal of team theory is to investigate the relationship among the distribution of information, the communication among the agents, and the objectives that they may collectively achieve. The assumption of a common objective puts aside the issue of individual incentives among the agents. With this qualification, team theory models a great variety of problems of organizations and society. Assuming that a mechanism models the equilibrium state of interaction among the agents, team theory from a broad perspective has much in common with the theory of realization.[40]

---

[39] I am grateful to Roy Radner for discussions concerning team theory that assisted me in writing this section.

[40] Team theory and the theory of realization share a common interest in modeling the connection between what agents know, what they may communicate, and what they may achieve. A major difference between the two theories is methodological: team theory commonly assumes that each agent has a Bayesian prior about all aspects of the state of the world that are unknown to him, which is not commonly assumed in the realization problem. The two theories also differ in their specifications of the variable to be optimized and the constraint in a collective decision problem. The objective of the agents is typically taken as given in the theory of realization. The issue is then the design of different *information structures* (as modeled by the product structure and the message process of a mechanism) that permit the agents to achieve the given objective. Team theory instead typically takes as given an information structure (based upon modeling considerations) and then addresses such issues as the optimal objective for the given information structure, or the value to the agents of information in addition to the given information structure.

Consistent with the approach of this text, it is assumed that the objective
F of the team is a C^∞ mapping from $\Pi_{i=1}^n \Theta_i$ to $\mathbb{R}^k$. The objective F of a
team could in principle be any mapping, and so Theorem 16 characterizes
the communication requirements of realizing a generic team objective. The
purpose of this section is to go beyond this cursory statement and apply
the results of this chapter to a central problem in team theory, namely the
realization of a Pareto optimal choice. This problem is investigated here
using a variety of common assumptions concerning the effect of an agent's
private information on the welfare of others.[41]

Private Values

Consider first the selection of a Pareto optimal choice when each agent's
utility satisfies a *private value* condition and is quasilinear in the team choice.
Agent i's utility $u_i(x, t_i, \theta_i)$ has the form

$$u_i(x, t_i, \theta_i) = V_i(x, \theta_i) - t_i, \qquad (4.145)$$

where $x \in \mathbb{R}^k$ is the team choice and t_i is a monetary transfer from agent i.
The assumption of private values is that each agent i's utility function is
determined solely by his own parameter vector θ_i and is therefore independent of the parameters of the other agents. The transfers $(t_i)_{1 \leq i \leq n}$ may be
used by the team to accomplish the team objective; they may provide the
proper incentives to elicit the private information of the agents, for instance,
or fund the choice x. The focus here, however, is on the objective itself and
the alternative ways in which it may be realized.

Because of the assumption that utility is transferable among the agents
through the monetary transfers, the Samuelson Criterion characterizes a

---

[41] Although the incentives of the agents are not explicitly addressed below, it is worth noting
that the construction of an optimal mechanism subject to Bayesian incentive compatibility
typically reduces to a team decision problem as discussed in the remainder of this section.
This follows from Myerson's principle that incentive compatibility can be incorporated
as a constraint into the design of an optimal mechanism by replacing the given utility
functions of the agents with their *virtual utility functions*. These functions are defined
from the given utility functions using the joint distribution of the agents' parameters. The
search for an optimal Bayesian mechanism is in this way reduced to selecting a Pareto
optimal choice for each determination of the agents' parameters relative to their virtual
utilities. See Wilson (1993, Sec. 2) for a formulation of Myerson's principle in a general
model. The revelation principle is invoked in the design of an optimal mechanism to
reduce the search to revelation mechanisms. The discussion in the rest of this subsection
relates to the question of whether or not an optimal objective that is constructed in this
way can be implemented using a message space that is smaller than the space required for
complete revelation.

Pareto optimal choice x for θ as a solution $x^*(\theta)$ to the optimization problem

$$\max_x \sum_{i=1}^{n} V_i(x, \theta_i). \qquad (4.146)$$

With appropriate regularity conditions imposed on the problem, the solution to (4.146) is a unique value of $x^*(\theta)$ that solves the first-order condition

$$\sum_{i=1}^{n} D_x V_i(x, \theta_i) = 0. \qquad (4.147)$$

Equation (4.147) has the form (4.37) in the case of $n = 2$ and $k = 1$. The mechanism (4.47) demonstrates that the objective $x^*(\theta)$ can in this case be realized using a message space of dimension 2. The following mechanism generalizes (4.47) to realize $x^*(\theta)$ for any number n of agents:

$$M = \left\{ ((m_i)_{1 \leq i \leq n}, x) \,\middle|\, m_i \in \mathbb{R}^k, x \in \mathbb{R}^k, \sum_{i=1}^{n} m_i = 0 \right\},$$

$$\text{for } 1 \leq i \leq n, \ \alpha_i(\theta_i, m) = D_x V_i(x, \theta_i) - m_i, \qquad (4.148)$$

$$\zeta\left((m_i)_{1 \leq i \leq n}, x\right) = x.$$

The message space M has dimension kn because it is the solution set in $\mathbb{R}^{k(n+1)}$ of k independent linear equations. Its dimension thus does not depend on the dimensions of the agents' parameter spaces. The dimension of the messages adjusted by agent i is k; if $\dim \Theta_i > k$ for more than one value of i, then the mechanism (4.148) demonstrates that the objective $x^*(\theta)$ is nongeneric in the sense of Theorem 16. In the special case of a real-valued objective ($k = 1$), the dimension of M is the number n of agents in the team. Any smaller dimension of message space precludes at least one agent from influencing the team choice. The message space M is thus of minimal dimension in the case of $k = 1$ for realizing a Pareto optimal choice $x^*(\theta)$ as long as each agent's parameter vector influences that choice locally.

Informational Externalities

The most general form of quasilinear utility relaxes the assumption of private values by allowing *informational externalities* in the sense that the parameter vector of one agent can directly influence the utility of another agent. Agent i's utility function now has the form

$$u_i(x, t_i, \theta) = V_i(x, \theta) - t_i, \qquad (4.149)$$

and a Pareto optimal choice $x^{**}(\theta)$ solves

$$\max_x \sum_{i=1}^{n} V_i(x, \theta).\tag{4.150}$$

With appropriate regularity conditions, a Pareto optimal choice $x^{**}(\theta)$ is the unique solution to the first-order condition

$$\sum_{i=1}^{n} D_x V_i(x, \theta) = 0.\tag{4.151}$$

This is a special case of a mapping $x^{**}: \Theta \to \mathbb{R}^k$ defined implicitly by an equation

$$\psi(x, \theta) = 0,\tag{4.152}$$

where $\psi: \mathbb{R}^k \times \Theta \to \mathbb{R}^k$. Any such mapping $\psi(x, \theta)$ can be written as a sum of n mappings so that (4.152) assumes the form of (4.151); consequently, there is really nothing special about the additive form of (4.151). Without severe restrictions on the functions $V_1, \ldots, V_n$, the solution to (4.150) will not be limited to a nowhere dense subset of $C^\infty(\Theta, \mathbb{R}^k)$ as required for nongenericity in the sense of Theorem 16.[42] Realizing the Pareto optimal choice mapping in the presence of informational externalities thus typically requires all but at most one agent to fully reveal his private information, as in a parameter transfer mechanism.

Common Value
Finally, a special case of informational externalities is defined by the assumption of a *common value*, which is that the payoff from the choice x is exactly the same to each agent. In this case,

$$V_1(x, \theta) = \cdots = V_n(x, \theta) \equiv V(x, \theta)\tag{4.153}$$

---

[42] Without such restrictions, any mapping $x^{**}: \Theta \to \mathbb{R}^k$ solves an optimization problem of the form (4.152). The private values assumption is one example of a restriction that makes the Pareto optimal mapping nongeneric in the sense of Theorem 16. Common regularity conditions in economic theory can be imposed on $v_1, \ldots, v_n$ to insure that the solution $x^{**}(\theta)$ to (4.150) is monotonic or convex/concave. Such first- and second-order properties of $x(\theta)$, however, fail to restrict it to a nowhere dense subset of $C^\infty(\Theta, \mathbb{R}^k)$, as required for nongenericity in the sense of Theorem 16.

for $1 \leq i \leq n$, where $V(x, \theta)$ is the common value function.[43] The team decision problem is then

$$\max_{x} V(x, \theta). \tag{4.154}$$

As in the general case of informational externalities, the solution $x^{***}(\theta)$ to (4.154) is nongeneric in the sense of Theorem 16 only if $V(x, \theta)$ is severely restricted.

4.8 Example: Implementation in Privacy Preserving Strategies

As discussed in Subsection 1.2.1, *Product Structure* has a particularly simple form in the case of a message process that is defined by privacy preserving strategies. Examples include the dominant, ex-post Nash, and Bayesian Nash solution concepts. This example explores the effect of this form of product structure on the potential for economizing on communication in implementing a function f. The Revelation Principle states that any objective f that can be implemented with an equilibrium of such a solution concept can also be implemented using a revelation mechanism in which honest reporting by each agent i of his information θ_i defines an equilibrium of the specified kind. This section suggests that implementation in the sense of such a solution concept typically *requires* complete revelation locally of each θ_i, given that a bound on the relative sizes of the agents' parameter spaces holds.

The following model is considered. The choice of $x \in \mathbb{R}$ affects the utility of each of n agents. Let $U_i(x, t_i, \theta_i)$ denote the utility of the ith agent given the choice x, a monetary transfer t_i from the agent, and his parameter vector θ_i. Let $f : \Theta \to \mathbb{R}$ be the objective. The message set M_i is the *strategy set* of the ith agent. Mechanisms of the form

$$\mathcal{M} = \left(\Theta, \prod_{i=1}^{n} M_i, (\mu_i)_{1 \leq i \leq n}, \zeta \right)$$

are considered. The outcome mapping ζ has the form

$$\zeta = (\eta, t_1, \ldots, t_n),$$

---

[43] The team (for instance) might be a group of employees in a firm with $V(x, \theta)$ as a measure of their collective performance (e.g., profit, sales, or return on equity).

where

$$\eta : \prod_{i=1}^{n} M_i \to \mathbb{R} \qquad (4.155)$$

selects a value of $x \in \mathbb{R}$ for each profile of messages, and

$$t_i : \prod_{i=1}^{n} M_i \to \mathbb{R} \qquad (4.156)$$

is a monetary transfer from agent i.

The mechanism $\mathcal{M}$ *implements the objective f in privacy preserving strategies* if the following properties hold:

(i) Each agent i has a strategy $\sigma_i : \Theta_i \to M_i$ that specifies his equilibrium message for each value θ_i of his information. The strategy σ_i is privacy preserving in the sense that it depends only on agent i's information θ_i.

(ii) Let $\sigma = (\sigma_1, \ldots, \sigma_n)$. Agent i's message correspondence is

$$\mu_i (\theta_i) = \sigma_i (\theta_i) \times \prod_{j \neq i} M_j$$

and the equilibrium correspondence of the mechanism $\mathcal{M}$ is

$$\mu(\theta) = \sigma(\theta).$$

(iii) Given $\theta \in \Theta$, selection of $\sigma_i(\theta_i)$ by each agent i realizes the objective f in the sense that

$$\eta \circ \sigma (\theta) = f(\theta) \qquad (4.157)$$

for all $\theta \in \Theta$.

The mechanism

$$\left(\Theta, \prod_{i=1}^{n} M_i, (\mu_i)_{1 \leq i \leq n}, \eta \right)$$

obtained by omitting the transfers from the outcome mapping ζ of $\mathcal{M}$ realizes f in the sense of (1.7) of Section 1.1. The monetary transfers $(t_1, \ldots, t_n)$ are variables that may provide additional means of influencing the incentives of the agents. The profile of strategies σ along with the outcome mapping ζ, for instance, may satisfy one of three systems inequalities (1.12), (1.13), or (1.14) as required for dominant, ex-post Nash, or Bayesian

Nash equilibrium. These inequalities are not needed in the analysis that follows, however; the key assumption here is that each agent i's strategy σ_i is privacy preserving.

From the perspective of this text, the interesting aspect of implementation in privacy preserving strategies is the elementary form of product structure that it defines. Because agent i's strategic choice $m_i = \sigma_i(\theta_i)$ is determined by his own information θ_i independently of the strategies $\sigma_{-i}(\cdot)$ of the other agents, each of the sets $\sigma_i^{-1}(m_i)$ is independent of the information of the other agents. As noted in Subsection 1.2.1, a single partition

$$\left\{ S_i^*(\theta_i) \equiv \sigma_i^{-1}(\sigma_i(\theta_i)) \right\}_{\theta_i \in \Theta_i} \tag{4.158}$$

of each space Θ_i is thus determined, independent of the value of θ_{-i}. Each set $S(\theta)$ therefore has the form

$$S(\theta) \equiv \sigma^{-1}(\sigma(\theta)) \tag{4.159}$$

$$= \prod_{i=1}^{n} S_i^*(\theta_i). \tag{4.160}$$

Nash implementation, by contrast, does not imply this restricted form of product structure, for agent i's strategy in this case may depend on both θ_i and m_{-i}.

A Rank Condition for Complete Revelation
The constraint on product structure described in (4.158)–(4.160) severely limits the possibility of implementing a function f in privacy preserving strategies using a message space smaller than required by complete revelation. To demonstrate this point, a rank condition is now derived that is sufficient to insure that agent i must fully reveal his information θ_i in any mechanism that implements f in this sense.

Consistent with the approach of this text, it is now assumed that each strategy set M_i is an open subset of $\mathbb{R}^{c_i}$ for some $c_i \leq \dim \Theta_i$, each strategy σ_i is C^∞, and

$$\operatorname{rank} D_{\theta_i} \sigma_i(\theta_i) = c_i. \tag{4.161}$$

Of interest is the possibility that $c_i < \dim \Theta_i$, which indicates less than full revelation of agent i's information.

For $\theta_i \in \Theta_i$, the regularity condition (4.161) insures that $S_i^*(\theta_i) = \sigma_i^{-1}(\sigma_i(\theta_i))$ is a submanifold of Θ_i of dimension $d_i = \dim \Theta_i - c_i$. Because σ_i is constant on $S_i^*(\theta_i)$, the mapping $\sigma(\cdot, \theta_{-i})$ is constant on $S_i^*(\theta_i)$

for all $\theta_{-i} \in \Pi_{j \neq i} \Theta_j$. The realization equality $f = \eta \circ \sigma$ therefore implies that $f(\cdot, \theta_{-i})$ is constant on $S_i^*(\theta_i)$ for all θ_{-i}.

The Frobenius Theorem implies that there exists for any $\theta_i^* \in \Theta_i$ a local coordinate system

$$u_i : O(\theta_i^*) \to (-\varepsilon, \varepsilon)^{\dim \Theta_i} \qquad (4.162)$$

on a neighborhood $O(\theta_i^*)$ of θ_i^* such that

$$S_i^*(\theta_i) \cap O(\theta_i^*) = u_i^{-1} \left\{ \left(w, u_{(i,c_i)}(\theta_i) \right) \,\middle|\, w \in (-\varepsilon, \varepsilon)^{d_i} \right\} \qquad (4.163)$$

for any $\theta_i \in O(\theta_i^*)$. In (4.163), $u_{(i,c_i)}(\theta_i)$ denotes the last c_i coordinates of $u_i(\theta_i)$. Therefore,

$$f(u_i^{-1}, \theta_{-i}) : (-\varepsilon, \varepsilon)^{\dim \Theta_i} \times \prod_{j \neq i} \Theta_j \to \mathbb{R} \qquad (4.164)$$

is independent of d_i coordinates of $(-\varepsilon, \varepsilon)^{\dim \Theta_i}$. Agent i can thus use a message space M_i of dimension $c_i < \dim \Theta_i$ only if the objective f does not depend on d_i of the variables in his information θ_i relative to some choice of coordinates for Θ_i.[44]

A rank condition on f is now derived that insures that it depends on all of the variables in agent i's information, regardless of the choice of local coordinates. This regularity condition is therefore sufficient to insure that agent i fully reveals θ_i in any mechanism that implements f in privacy preserving strategies. Because $f(\cdot, \theta_{-i})$ is constant on $S_i^*(\theta_i)$ for all $\theta_{-i} \in \prod_{j \neq i} \Theta_j$, the vector

$$D_{\theta_i} f(\theta_i, \theta_{-i}) = \left(\frac{\partial f}{\partial \theta_{i,t}} (\theta_i, \theta_{-i}) \right)_{1 \leq t \leq \dim \Theta_i} \qquad (4.165)$$

---

[44] A common example from the literature on dominant strategy implementation illustrates this point. Consider a dictatorship of agent 1. The objective in this case to maximize agent 1's valuation, i.e.,

$$f(\theta_1) \equiv \arg\max_x V_1(x, \theta_1).$$

This objective is independent of θ_j for $j \neq 1$ and hence communication from all other agents is unnecessary. The condition $D_{\theta_1} f \neq 0$ is the analogue of (4.161) in this setting; if $D_{\theta_1} f \neq 0$, then a change of coordinates on Θ_1 exists in a neighborhood of any point θ_1 relative to which f depends on only $c_1 = 1$ of agent 1's variables. The objective f can be realized with a message space of dimension 1 simply by having agent 1 communicate his preferred value of x.

must be perpendicular to the tangent plane $\mathcal{D}_i(\theta_i)$ to $S_i^*(\theta_i)$ at θ_i for all θ_{-i}. Consider the mapping

$$\frac{D_{\theta_i} f}{\| D_{\theta_i} f \|} : \Theta \to \mathbb{S}^{\dim \Theta_i - 1}, \tag{4.166}$$

where $\mathbb{S}^{\dim \Theta_i - 1}$ is the $(\dim \Theta_i - 1)$-dimensional unit sphere in $\mathbb{R}^{\dim \Theta_i}$. If

$$\text{rank } D_{\theta_{-i}} \frac{D_{\theta_i} f}{\| D_{\theta_i} f \|} (\theta^*) = \dim \Theta_i - 1 \tag{4.167}$$

for some $\theta^* \in \Theta$, then the range of the normalized vector

$$\frac{D_{\theta_i} f}{\| D_{\theta_i} f \|} (\theta_i^*, \theta_{-i}) \tag{4.168}$$

contains an open subset of $\mathbb{S}^{\dim \Theta_i - 1}$ as θ_{-i} ranges over an open neighborhood of θ_{-i}^*. The plane $\mathcal{D}_i(\theta_i^*)$, which is perpendicular to (4.168) for all θ_{-i}, can in this case contain only the zero vector and hence $d_i = \dim \mathcal{D}_i(\theta_i^*) = 0$. The dimension c_i of agent i's message space therefore equals $\dim \Theta_i$, which indicates complete revelation by agent i of his parameter vector.[45]

Condition (4.167) holding at some $\theta \in \Theta$ is sufficient to insure that agent i requires a strategy space of dimension $\dim \Theta_i$ in any mechanism that implements f in privacy preserving strategies. If

$$\sum_{j \neq i} \dim \Theta_j \geq \dim \Theta_i - 1, \tag{4.169}$$

then (4.167) is satisfied at some $\theta \in \Theta$ by every function f in an open and dense subset of $C^\infty(\Theta, \mathbb{R})$. Inequality (4.169) holds unless agent i's private information is strictly larger (as measured by dimension) than the information known privately by all other agents. Note in particular that (4.169) holds if $\dim \Theta_i = \dim \Theta_j$ is satisfied for all $1 \leq i, j \leq n$.

If (4.169) holds for each i, then a message space of dimension $\sum_{i=1}^n \dim \Theta_i$ is required to implement a generic function f in privacy preserving strategies. A parameter transfer mechanism can realize any function f using a message space of dimension $1 + \min_j \sum_{i \neq j} \dim \Theta_i$. The increase from the dimension required by a parameter transfer mechanism to that

[45] Mount and Reiter (1996, Sec. 2) generalize this discussion to the case in which the objective is a mapping $F : \prod_{i=1}^n \Theta_i \to \mathbb{R}^k$. Their Lemma 2.2 (p. 250) states necessary conditions and (stronger) sufficient conditions on the first and second derivatives of F for this mapping to depend only on c_i of the $c_i + d_i$ components of the vector $\theta_i \in \Theta_i$ after an appropriate change of coordinates in Θ_i. The above discussion is limited to the case of $k = 1$ for mathematical simplicity.

required by a revelation mechanism reflects a cost in communication attributable to the requirement of privacy preserving strategies.

An interesting aspect of this analysis is that it is driven purely by the special form of product structure in (4.158)–(4.160) that follows from privacy preserving strategies. The monetary transfers $(t_i)_{1 \leq i \leq n}$ play no role in the above argument. The standard ingredients of impossibility results for implementation such as budget balance or individual rationality are not needed, nor are inequalities of incentive compatibility such as (1.12), (1.13), or (1.14). Unlike many impossibility results in implementation theory, it is not necessary to vary the preferences over a large range;[46] the analysis here is entirely local. This emphasizes the severity of the form (4.158)–(4.160) of product structure that is implied by privacy preserving strategies.

A Special Case
The above analysis concerns the communication required to implement an arbitrary function f in privacy preserving strategies. An arbitrary function f, however, need not be implementable in this sense. It is therefore instructive to apply this analysis to a class of objectives that are implementable in dominant strategies, and therefore in privacy preserving strategies. Assuming the bound (4.169) is satisfied for each i, the principle derived above continues to hold: a generic objective in this class requires complete revelation locally in order to be implemented in dominant strategies.

Consider again a team decision problem as discussed in Section 4.7. Assume that each agent i's utility is quasilinear with a private value,

$$U_i(x, t_i, \theta_i) = V_i(x, \theta_i) - t_i. \tag{4.170}$$

Let $x^*(\theta)$ denote a C^∞ function that selects a Pareto optimal choice of $x \in \mathbb{R}$ for each $\theta \in \Theta$. A revelation mechanism equipped with the Clarke–Groves–Vickery transfers implements $x^*(\theta)$ in dominant strategies.

As shown above, the optimum $x^*(\theta)$ must be independent of $d_i > 0$ of agent i's parameters if it can be implemented in dominant strategies by a mechanism in which $\dim M_i < \dim \Theta_i$. There is no reason to expect that the Pareto optimal choice $x^*(\theta)$ would be independent of any of agent i's parameters for all possible values of θ_{-i}. Formally, condition (4.167) implies

$$\text{rank } D_{\theta_{-i}} \frac{D_{\theta_i} x^*}{\left\| D_{\theta_i} x^* \right\|} (\theta) < \dim \Theta_i - 1 \tag{4.171}$$

---

[46] One example is the line of research on dominant strategy implementation founded by Gibbard (1972) and Satterthwaite (1975).

must hold at all $\theta \in \Theta$ if a mechanism exists that implements f in dominant strategies with dim $M_i <$ dim Θ_i.

Assumptions are sometimes imposed on the private value functions $V_1, \ldots, V_n$ and on Θ to insure that $x^*(\theta)$ is monotonic or concave on Θ. Such properties of $x^*(\theta)$ would typically not limit this objective to the subset of $C^\infty(\Theta, \mathbb{R})$ for which (4.171) holds for some i and all $\theta \in \Theta$. Complete revelation is thus required generically for dominant strategy implementation even with such additional restrictions.

4.9 Genericity and the Theory of Organizations

Theorem 16 states that a generic mapping can only be realized by mechanisms that collect at least as much information from the agents as some parameter transfer mechanism. Recall that an agent's parameter vector represents all that he knows privately; its dimension could thus be quite large. The mapping F represents an objective that the agents wish to realize by exchanging information among themselves. Theorem 16 is discouraging because it suggests that the possibility of economizing on communication among members of a group for the purpose of realizing an objective F is typically limited, for in general all but at most one of the agents must report all that they know privately.

As discussed in Section 4.5, the exchange of private goods is an exceptional case in which agents can realize a Pareto optimal allocation using a set of signals (prices and allocations) that is small in comparison to their private information concerning preferences. The discussion of team decision problems in Section 4.7, however, suggests that Pareto optimality and other team objectives are typically generic in the sense of Theorem 16. It is worth emphasizing again that the profile of a mechanism bounds below the communication required to realize an objective because it concerns the equilibrium state of a message process. Additional variables may be needed to find equilibrium or to sustain it against the incentives of the agents (as illustrated in Section 4.8). The large amount of information required by Theorem 16 to realize a generic objective may thus only increase if dynamic stability or incentive compatibility is also required of the mechanism.

As a practical matter, it does not seem correct that decision making in real economic organizations such as firms requires that vast amounts of information be exchanged among the agents. The main question addressed in this final section is the following: *How is the limited communication of real organizations consistent with Theorem 16?* One response is that the mappings that are actually observed in economic settings are necessarily realized using a relatively small set of messages. Constraints on communication are a fact, and hence the objectives that are realized in practice are necessarily limited to those that can be realized in ways that respect these constraints. This challenges the field of mechanism design to develop techniques for including limits on communication as a constraint on mechanisms, in the same sense that incentive compatibility can now be addressed in Bayesian mechanism design.

It is also possible that decentralization of decision making in real economic organizations may require a trade-off in which accuracy in realizing an objective F is sacrificed in return for a reduction in communication among the agents. Formally, this suggests that it may be possible to approximate the objective F by a mapping G that can be realized using a much smaller message space than F. An answer to the question that is posed above may thus lie in the topology used in Theorem 16: while the profiles of mechanisms that can realize a generic mapping F do not change if F is perturbed in a C^∞ sense, it could also be true that perturbing F in some coarser sense may greatly expand the profiles of mechanisms that can realize the perturbed mapping. This suggests the following refinement of the above question: In what topology can a mapping F be approximated arbitrarily closely by another mapping G that can be realized by a mechanism whose profile satisfies $c_i < \dim \Theta_i$ for more than one value of i?

As mentioned in Subsection 4.4.1, I suspect that Theorem 16 holds with the weaker topology of C^2 instead of C^∞ (with the differentiability assumptions on the mechanisms also weakened to C^2). I thus conjecture that such a mapping G must approximate F in a sense that is weaker than C^2 (e.g., C^1, C^0, or an even weaker topology). Ideally, the choice of topology on objectives should mirror the costs to the agents of switching from the objective F to an approximating objective G. It is hard to imagine that derivatives of arbitrarily high orders (as in the C^∞ topology) would ever reflect genuine economic costs. The use of the C^∞ topology in the proof of Theorem 16 was a matter of mathematical expediency; a coarser topology that focuses on the values of the objective F seems far more likely to be meaningful in an economic sense.[47]

It may also be possible to expand the set of mechanisms that realize an objective F by dropping the requirement that the mechanism satisfy all of the conditions of *Message Process*. The proof of Theorem 16, however,

---

[47] Pioneering research on mechanisms with discrete message spaces and their use in approximation can be found in Hurwicz and Marschak (1985, 1988) and in Marschak (1986, 1987).

is entirely local in the sense that it concerns Taylor polynomials at an arbitrary point $\theta^* \in \Theta$. This characterization of the profiles of mechanisms that realize a generic objective requires only that the regularity assumptions of *Message Process* hold in some arbitrarily small neighborhood $O(\theta^*)$ of some point $\theta^* \in \Theta$, not throughout Θ. In order to increase the variety of profiles of mechanisms that realize a generic mapping, it is necessary to consider mechanisms that do not satisfy *Message Process* on any open subset of Θ. A more fundamental approach to the construction of mechanisms is thus needed that loosens the differentiability assumptions of this text.[48]

A more optimistic interpretation of Theorem 16 concerns parameter transfer as a positive model of organizational form. The parameter transfer mechanism is an elementary hierarchy in which the information held by all but one agent is transferred to this agent who then computes the objective. The selected agent is the "boss" of the hierarchy. A central question in the theory of organizations is "Why is hierarchy so prevalent as a form of organization?" The answer provided by Theorem 16 is that hierarchy is optimal in the sense that it collects the smallest amount of information from the agents that is sufficient to realize a generic objective.

A parameter transfer mechanism has several virtues in addition to this notion of optimality. First, it is a robust organizational form in the sense that it can realize any objective with change required only in the choice by the boss and not by the other agents as the objective changes. Wilson's critique (Wilson, 1987) of Bayesian mechanism design is that this field has focused almost entirely on designing mechanisms that perform optimally in specific instances as opposed to addressing the more practical task of designing mechanisms that perform well across a range of circumstances. Wilson's critique applies equally well to the theory of realization, which has primarily focused on designing a mechanism to realize a specific objective. In the context of the smooth model considered here, the parameter transfer mechanism responds to Wilson's critique in the sense that it can realize any

---

[48] *Hilbert's Thirteenth Problem* asks whether or not a given function f of m variables can be computed through a series of compositions of functions, each of which depends on fewer than m variables. This is related to the problem of realizing a real-valued function f. Results on the Thirteenth Problem suggest that the profiles of mechanisms that realize a function f should be closely tied to whether the mappings $\alpha_1, \ldots, \alpha_n$ that determine the agents' equilibrium messages are required to be continuously differentiable or merely continuous. See Lorentz (1976) for a discussion of Hilbert's Thirteenth Problem (in particular, his Theorems A and B).

objective while collecting the minimal amount of information from each agent that is needed to realize a generic objective.

Assuming that each parameter space Θ_i is bounded, a parameter transfer mechanism also has the virtue that it can be easily approximated by a mechanism in which each agent i selects among only a finite number of possible messages for communicating with the boss. This is accomplished simply by having each agent i round off the components of his parameter vector θ_i to an appropriate number of decimals. If each Θ_i is compact, then any continuous objective can be approximated arbitrarily closely in terms of Euclidean distance on its range by an objective that can be realized with such a discrete mechanism. All that is required is the selection of a sufficiently large number of digits for each agent to report. These discrete mechanisms also address Wilson's critique in that they can approximately realize any objective.

The third virtue is that there are no unresolved issues of dynamics related to the parameter transfer mechanisms. More precisely, there is no question of how the agents find the equilibrium state, which is simply a matter of honest reporting by all agents except the boss who then realizes the objective. This last virtue points toward a major flaw of a parameter transfer mechanism, which is that it may not be incentive compatible in the case of a given objective F. An agent may find it in his interest to misreport his parameter vector in order to influence the boss's choice, and the boss may not want to realize the objective F once he has received information from the agents. Parameter transfer seems viable as a mechanism only in situations in which the common objective of the group of agents dominates their personal interests to the extent that individual incentives become insignificant.

In summary, the genericity result of Theorem 16 suggests that economizing on communication among agents in a nontrivial way may be feasible only if the objective of the agents is "special." Echoing Hayek, specialness in this sense is one of the distinguishing features of the Walrasian correspondence that assigns allocations to agents based on their preferences. There may be no reason to believe that the objectives within firms or other nonmarket organizations are special in this sense. Theorem 16 thus implies that hierarchy (as modeled by a parameter transfer mechanism) may be informationally efficient as a mechanism in nonmarket settings. Parameter transfer has several virtues as a mechanism, including (i) its robustness to changes in the objective, (ii) the possibility of decreasing its communication through a straightforward approximation, and (iii) the absence of any concerns about discovery of equilibrium. If parameter transfer in the context of a particular problem is not especially vulnerable to incentive problems, then it may represent a good choice of a mechanism. The informational efficiency of parameter transfer in the case of a generic objective, however, has only been proven in the mathematical model of this text. Substantiating this property as an explanation for the prevalence of hierarchy requires that genericity results of this kind be proven without the strong smoothness, regularity, and Euclidean hypotheses of Theorem 16.

Bibliography

Abelson, H., "Lower Bounds on Information Transfer in Distributed Computations," *Journal of the Association for Computing Machinery* 27 (1980), 384–392.

Antonelli, G. B., *Sulla Teoria Matematica Della Economia Politica*. Pisa, 1886. Translated as Chapter 16 in *Preferences, Utility, and Demand*, edited by J. S. Chipman, L. Hurwicz, M. K. Richter, and H. F. Sonnenschein. New York: Harcourt Brace Jovanovich, 1971.

Arrow, K., and F. Hahn, *General Competitive Analysis*. New York: North-Holland, 1971.

Brown, D. J., and R. L. Matzkin, "Testable Restrictions on the Equilibrium Manifold," *Econometrica* 64 (1996), 1249–1262.

Chen, P., *On the Efficiency and Complexity of Computational and Economic Processes*, Ph.D. dissertation. Evanston: Northwestern University, 1989.

Chen, P., "A Lower Bound for the Dimension of the Message Space of the Decentralized Mechanisms Realizing a Given Goal," *Journal of Mathematical Economics* 21 (1992), 249–270.

Chiappori, P.-A., I. Ekeland, F. Kübler, and H. M. Polemarchakis, "Testable Implications of General Equilibrium Theory: A Differentiable Approach," *Journal of Mathematical Economics* 40 (2004), 105–119.

Clarke, E. H., "Multipart Pricing of Public Goods," *Public Choice* 8 (1971), 19–33.

Cournot, A. A., *Recherches sur les Principes Mathématiques de la Théorie des Richesses*. Paris: Librairie des Sciences Politiques et Sociales, M. Rivière & Cie, 1838.

Debreu, G., "Economies with a Finite Set of Equilibria," *Econometrica* 38 (1970), 387–392. Reprinted as Chapter 14 in G. Debreu, *Mathematical Economics*, no. 4 in the *Econometric Society Monograph Series*. Cambridge, UK: Cambridge University Press, 1983.

Debreu, G., "Smooth Preferences," *Econometrica* 40 (1972), 603–615. Reprinted as Chapter 15 in G. Debreu, *Mathematical Economics*, no. 4 in the *Econometric Society Monograph Series*. Cambridge, UK: Cambridge University Press, 1983.

Debreu, G., "Excess Demand Functions," *Journal of Mathematical Economics* 1 (1974), 15–23. Reprinted as Chapter 16 in G. Debreu, *Mathematical Economics*, no. 4 in the *Econometric Society Monograph Series*. Cambridge, UK: Cambridge University Press, 1983.

Gibbard, A., "Manipulation of Voting Schemes: A General Result," *Econometrica* 41 (1972), 587–601.

Golubitsky, M., and V. Guillemin, *Stable Mappings and Their Singularities*. New York: Springer-Verlag, 1973.

Groves, T., "Incentives in Teams," *Econometrica* 41 (1973), 617–631.

Hayek, F. A., "The Use of Knowledge in Society," *American Economic Review* 35 (1945), 519–530.

Hurwicz, L., "Optimality and Informational Efficiency in Resource Allocation Processes," in *Mathematical Methods in the Social Sciences*, edited by K. Arrow, S. Karlin, and P. Suppes. Palo Alto, CA: Stanford University Press, 1960.

Hurwicz, L., "On the Problem of Integrability of Demand Functions," Chapter 9 in *Preferences, Utility, and Demand*, edited by J. S. Chipman, L. Hurwicz, M. K. Richter, and H. F. Sonnenschein. New York: Harcourt Brace Jovanovich, 1971.

Hurwicz, L., "On Informationally Decentralized Systems," in *Decision and Organization, Volume in Honor of Jacob Marschak*, edited by B. McGuire and R. Radner. Amsterdam: North-Holland, 1972.

Hurwicz, L., "Outcome Functions Yielding Walrasian and Lindahl Allocations at Nash Equilibrium Points," *Review of Economic Studies* 46 (1979), 217–225.

Hurwicz, L., "On Informational Decentralization and Efficiency in Resource Allocation Mechanisms," in *Studies in Mathematical Economics*, edited by Stanley Reiter, vol. 25 in *MAA Studies in Mathematics*. Washington, DC: The Mathematical Association of America, 1986.

Hurwicz, L., and T. Marschak, "Discrete Allocation Mechanisms: Dimensional Requirements for Resource Allocation Mechanisms When Desired Outcomes Are Unbounded," *Journal of Complexity* 1 (1985), 264–303.

Hurwicz, L., and T. Marschak, "Approximating a Function by Choosing a Covering of Its Domain and k Points from Its Range," *Journal of Complexity* 4 (1988), 137–174.

Hurwicz, L., and S. Reiter, *Designing Economic Mechanisms*. Cambridge, UK: Cambridge University Press, 2006.

Hurwicz, L., S. Reiter, and D. G. Saari, "On Constructing Mechanisms with Message Spaces of Minimal Dimension for Smooth Performance Functions," mimeo., University of Minnesota, 1978.

Ingrao, B., and G. Israel, *The Invisible Hand*. Cambridge, MA: MIT Press, 1990.

Jacobson, N., *Lectures in Abstract Algebra. Vol. III: Theory of Fields and Galois Theory*. New York: Springer-Verlag, 1975.

Jordan, J. S., "The Competitive Allocation Process is Informationally Efficient Uniquely," *Journal of Economic Theory* 28 (1982), 1–18.

Jordan, J. S., "The Informational Requirements of Local Stability in Decentralized Allocation Mechanisms," in *Information, Incentives and Economic Mechanisms*, edited by T. Groves, R. Radner, and S. Reiter. Minneapolis, MN: University of Minnesota Press, 1987.

Lorentz, G. G., "The 13-th Problem of Hilbert," in *Mathematical Developments Arising from Hilbert Problems*, vol. XXVIII, edited by Felix Browder, part 2 in *Proceedings of Symposia in Pure Mathematics*. Providence, RI: American Mathematical Society, 1976.

Mantel, R., "On the Characterization of Aggregate Excess Demand," *Journal of Economic Theory* 7 (1974), 348–353.

Marschak, J., and R. Radner, *Economic Theory of Teams*. New Haven, CT: Yale University Press, 1972.

Marschak, T., "Organization Design," in *Handbook of Mathematical Economics*, vol. III, edited by K. Arrow and M. Intriligator. Amsterdam: North-Holland, 1986.

Marschak, T., "Price versus Direct Revelation: Informational Judgements for Finite Mechanisms," in *Information, Incentives, and Economic Mechanisms: Essays in Honor of Leonid Hurwicz*, edited by T. Groves, R. Radner, and S. Reiter. Minneapolis, MN: University of Minnesota Press, 1987.

Mas-Colell, A., "On the Equilibrium Price Set of an Exchange Economy," *Journal of Mathematical Economics* 4 (1977), 117–126.

Maskin, E., "Nash Equilibrium and Welfare Optimality," *Review of Economic Studies* 66 (1999), 23–38.

Myerson, R., *Game Theory: Analysis of Conflict*. Cambridge, MA: Harvard University Press, 1991.

Mount, K., and S. Reiter, "The Informational Size of Message Spaces," *Journal of Economic Theory* 8 (1974), 161–192.

Mount, K., and S. Reiter, "On the Existence of a Locally Stable Dynamic Process with a Statically Minimal Message Space," in *Information, Incentives and Economic Mechanisms*, edited by T. Groves, R. Radner, and S. Reiter. Minneapolis, MN: University of Minnesota Press, 1987.

Mount, K., and S. Reiter, "A Lower Bound on Computational Complexity Given by Revelation Mechanisms," *Economic Theory* 7 (1996), 237–266.

Osana, H., "On the Informational Size of Message Spaces for Resource Allocation Processes," *Journal of Economic Theory* 17 (1978), 66–78.

Reichelstein, S., *Information and Incentives in Economic Organizations*, Ph.D. dissertation. Evanston: Northwestern University, 1984.

Reichelstein, S., and S. Reiter, "Game Forms with Minimal Strategy Spaces," *Econometrica* 56 (1988), 661–692.

Reiter, S., "Information, Incentive and Performance in the (New)[2] Welfare Economics," *American Economic Review* 1 (1977), 226–234. Reprinted as Chapter 5 in *Studies in Mathematical Economics*, edited by Stanley Reiter, vol. 25 in *MAA Studies in Mathematics*. Washington, DC: The Mathematical Association of America, 1986.

Saari, D. G., "A Method for Constructing Message Systems for Smooth Performance Functions," *Journal of Economic Theory* 33 (1984), 249–274.

Saari, D. G., "The Representation Problem and the Efficiency of the Price Mechanism," *Journal of Mathematical Economics* 14 (1985), 135–167.

Saari, D. G., "On the Types of Information and on Mechanism Design," *Journal of Computational and Applied Mathematics* 22 (1988), 231–242.

Saari, D. G., "On the Design of Complex Organizations and Distributive Algorithms," *Complexity Theory* 6 (1990), 102–118.

Saari, D. G., "Sufficient Statistics, Utility Theory and Mechanism Design," in *The Economics of Informational Decentralization: Complexity, Efficiency, and Stability*, edited by J. Ledyard. Boston: Kluwer Academic Publishers, 1995.

Saari, D. G., and S. R. Williams, "On the Local Convergence of Economic Mechanisms," *Journal of Economic Theory* 40 (1986), 152–167.

Samuelson, P. A., "The Problem of Integrability in Utility Theory," *Economica* 17 (1950), 355–385.

Sanghavi, S., *Decentralized Network Algorithms*, Ph.D. dissertation. Urbana-Champaign: University of Illinois at Urbana-Champaign, 2006.

Sanghavi, S., and B. Hajek, "A New Mechanism for the Free Rider Problem, mimeo., University of Illinois, in press.

Satterthwaite, M. A., "Strategy Proofness and Arrow's Conditions: Existence and Correspondence Theorems for Voting Procedures and Social Welfare Functions," *Journal of Economic Theory* 10 (1975), 187–217.

Schmeidler, D., "Walrasian Analysis via Strategic Outcome Functions," *Econometrica* 48 (1980), 1585–1593.

Sonnenschein, H., "Market Excess Demand Functions," *Econometrica* 40 (1972), 549–563.

Sonnenschein, H., "Do Walras Identity and Continuity Characterize the Class of Community Excess Demand Functions?" *Journal of Economic Theory* 6 (1973), 345–354.

Spivak, M., *Calculus on Manifolds*, New York: W. A. Benjamin, 1965.

Spivak, M., *A Comprehensive Introduction to Differential Geometry*, vol. I. Berkeley, CA: Publish or Perish, 1979.

Vickrey, W., "Counterspeculation, Auctions, and Competitive Sealed Tenders," *Journal of Finance* 16 (1961), 8–37.

Walker, M., "On the Informational Size of Message Spaces," *Journal of Economic Theory* 15 (1977), 366–375.

Warner, F., *Foundations of Differentiable Manifolds and Lie Groups*, Glenview, IL: Scott, Foresman and Company, 1971.

Williams, S. R., "Letter to Leonid Hurwicz," May 19, 1981.

Williams, S. R., *A Geometric Study of Smooth Decentralized Economic Mechanisms*, Ph.D. dissertation. Evanston: Northwestern University, 1982a.

Williams, S. R., "Letter to Leonid Hurwicz," February 27, 1982b.

Williams, S. R., "Letter to Leonid Hurwicz," April 30, 1982c.

Williams, S. R., "Implementing a Generic Smooth Function," *Journal of Mathematical Economics* 13 (1984), 273–288.

Williams, S. R., "Necessary and Sufficient Conditions for the Existence of a Locally Stable Message Process," *Journal of Economic Theory* 35 (1985), 127–154.

Williams, S. R., "Realization and Nash Implementation: Two Aspects of Mechanism Design," *Econometrica* 54 (1986), 139–151.

Wilson, R., "Game-Theoretic Analysis of Trading Processes," in *Advances in Economic Theory, Fifth World Congress*, edited by T. Bewley. Cambridge, UK: Cambridge University Press, 1987.

Wilson, R., "Design of Efficient Trading Procedures," in *The Double Auction Market: Institutions, Theories, and Evidence*, edited by D. Friedman and J. Rust, *Proceedings Vol. XIV* of the *Sante Fe Institute Studies in the Sciences of Complexity*. Reading, MA: Addison-Wesley, 1993.

Index

For EU product safety concerns, contact us at Calle de José Abascal, 56–1°,
28003 Madrid, Spain or eugpsr@cambridge.org.